"Information through Innovation"

Contributors

The Publisher would like to express great appreciation to those individuals who contributed to the overall development of the STAR Series.

Joseph Dennin
Fairfield University

Edward Harms
Interactive Business Systems, Inc.

Mary Z. Last
Grand Valley State University

H. Albert Napier
Rice University

Rod B. Southworth
Laramie County Community College

Patrice Gapen
Laramie County Community College

Philip J. Judd
Napier & Judd, Inc.

Patricia McMahon
Moraine Valley Community College

Philip J. Pratt
Grand Valley State University

Kathleen M. Stewart
Moraine Valley Community College

Star FoxPro 2.5

A volume in the boyd & fraser STAR Series

David B. Chew
David Chew Consulting

boyd & fraser publishing company

Credits:

Acquisitions Editor: Anne E. Hamilton
Production Coordinator: Patty Stephan
Manufacturing Coordinator: Tracy Megison
Composition: Gex, Inc.

©1995 by boyd & fraser publishing company
One Corporate Place • Ferncroft Village
Danvers, Massachusetts 01923

International Thomson Publishing
boyd & fraser publishing company is an ITP company.
The ITP trademark is used under license.

All rights reserved. No part of this publication may be reproduced or used in any form or by any means—graphic, electronic, or mechanical, including photocopying, recording, taping or information storage and retrieval systems—without written permission from the publisher.

Names of all products mentioned herein are used for identification purposes only and may be trademarks and/or registered trademarks of their respective owners. boyd & fraser publishing company disclaims any affiliation, association, or connection with, or sponsorship or endorsement by such owners.

Manufactured in the United States of America.

I S B N : 0 - 87709 - 020 - 3

1 2 3 4 5 6 7 8 9 10 BN 8 7 6 5 4

Brief Table of Contents

TOPIC 1 *Using FoxPro* 5
TOPIC 2 *Creating a Database File* 11
TOPIC 3 *Loading a Database* 17
TOPIC 4 *Backing Up Your Database* 27
TOPIC 5 *Querying a Database* 31
TOPIC 6 *Using Conditions* 39
TOPIC 7 *Calculating Statistics* 53
Checkpoint 1 59
TOPIC 8 *Locating a Record* 65
TOPIC 9 *Using the Browse Window* 69
TOPIC 10 *Using Conditions to Change Records* 73
TOPIC 11 *Deleting Records* 79
TOPIC 12 *Creating and Using a Custom Screen* 83
TOPIC 13 *Sorting a Database File* 97
TOPIC 14 *Creating and Using Indexes* 105
Checkpoint 2 115
TOPIC 15 *Creating a Report Layout* 119
TOPIC 16 *Printing a Report* 133
TOPIC 17 *Including Subtotals* 139
TOPIC 18 *Modifying the Structure* 145
TOPIC 19 *Using Multiple Database Files* 155
TOPIC 20 *Creating Relational Queries* 161
TOPIC 21 *Using Relational Queries* 165
Checkpoint 3 173

Contents

Editor's Foreword xi

Introduction to Databases 1

TOPIC 1 *Using FoxPro* 5

    Loading FoxPro 5
    Selecting an Option 6
    Moving from the Menu System to the Command Window 6
    Escaping from an Operation 7
    Exiting FoxPro 7
    Getting Help 7
    Tutorial 8 • Exercises 10

TOPIC 2 *Creating a Database File* 11

    Creating a Database File 11
    Tutorial 13 • Exercises 16

TOPIC 3 *Loading a Database* 17

    Opening a Database File 17
    Adding Records to a Database File 17
    Changing Records in a Database File 19
    Deleting Records from a Database File 19
    Listing Records in a Database File 20
    Tutorial 20 • Exercises 25

TOPIC 4 *Backing Up Your Database* 27

    Making a Backup Copy 27
    Restoring a Database File from a Backup Copy 27
    Tutorial 27 • Exercises 29

TOPIC 5 *Querying a Database* 31

    Creating a Query 31
    Applying a Query 32
    Printing the Results 33
    Displaying All Fields 33
    Displaying Only Certain Fields 33
    Returning to the Command Window 34
    Tutorial 34 • Exercises 38

TOPIC 6   *Using Conditions*   39

    Using a Condition   39
    Using Operators   39
    Entering an Example   40
    Combining Conditions with AND   41
    Combining Conditions with OR   41
    Tutorial   41   •   Exercises   52

TOPIC 7   *Calculating Statistics*   53

    Counting Records   53
    Calculating a Sum   53
    Calculating an Average   53
    Tutorial   53   •   Exercises   57

Checkpoint 1   59

    What You Should Know   59
    Review Questions   60
    Checkpoint Exercises   61

TOPIC 8   *Locating a Record*   65

    Locating a Record That Satisfies a Condition   65
    Finding the Next Record That Satisfies a Condition   66
    Tutorial   66   •   Exercises   68

TOPIC 9   *Using the Browse Window*   69

    Updating Records with the Browse Window   69
    Adding Records with the Browse Window   70
    Tutorial   70   •   Exercises   71

TOPIC 10   *Using Conditions to Change Records*   73

    Using the Record, Replace Command   73
    Tutorial   73   •   Exercises   78

TOPIC 11   *Deleting Records*   79

    Using Conditions to Mark Records for Deletion   80
    Using Conditions to Unmark Records   80
    Tutorial   80   •   Exercises   82

TOPIC 12   *Creating and Using a Custom Screen*   83

    Creating an Initial Screen   84
    Adding Blank Lines   84
    Changing the Prompts   84
    Repositioning Fields and Prompts   84

　　　　　　　　Adding Boxes　　84
　　　　　　　　Saving a Screen　　84
　　　　　　　　Generating Screen Code and Using a Screen　　84
　　　　　　　　Modifying a Screen　　85
　　　　　　　　Tutorial　　85　•　Exercises　　96

TOPIC 13　　*Sorting a Database File*　　97
　　　　　　　　Sorting a Database File on a Single Field　　97
　　　　　　　　Using a Sorted File　　98
　　　　　　　　Sorting on More Than One Field　　98
　　　　　　　　Removing Files　　98
　　　　　　　　Tutorial　　99　•　Exercises　　104

TOPIC 14　　*Creating and Using Indexes*　　105
　　　　　　　　Creating an Index on a Single Field　　106
　　　　　　　　Creating an Index on More Than One Field　　106
　　　　　　　　Using an Index to Order Records　　106
　　　　　　　　Using an Index to Find a Record　　106
　　　　　　　　Removing Unwanted Indexes　　106
　　　　　　　　Tutorial　　107　•　Exercises　　114

Checkpoint 2　　115
　　　　　　　　What You Should Know　　115
　　　　　　　　Review Questions　　116
　　　　　　　　Checkpoint Exercises　　116

TOPIC 15　　*Creating a Report Layout*　　119
　　　　　　　　Beginning the Report Creation Process　　121
　　　　　　　　Altering the Report Layout　　122
　　　　　　　　Adding or Deleting Lines in a Band　　122
　　　　　　　　Selecting Fields and Text Objects　　122
　　　　　　　　Removing Fields from a Report　　122
　　　　　　　　Moving Fields in a Report　　123
　　　　　　　　Resizing Fields in a Report　　123
　　　　　　　　Adding Fields　　123
　　　　　　　　Finishing the Report Layout Process　　123
　　　　　　　　Modifying a Report Layout　　123
　　　　　　　　Tutorial　　123　•　Exercises　　132

TOPIC 16　　*Printing a Report*　　133
　　　　　　　　Printing a Report　　133
　　　　　　　　Selecting Records for a Report　　133
　　　　　　　　Tutorial　　133　•　Exercises　　137

TOPIC 17   *Including Subtotals*   **139**
     Grouping   **139**
     Printing a Report with Subtotals   **140**
     Tutorial   **140**   •   Exercises   **144**

TOPIC 18   *Modifying the Structure*   **147**
     Changing Field Characteristics   **147**
     Adding a New Field   **147**
     Deleting a Field   **147**
     Tutorial   **147**   •   Exercises   **153**

TOPIC 19   *Using Multiple Database Files*   **155**
     Preparing for Relational Query Creation   **157**
     Tutorial   **157**   •   Exercises   **159**

TOPIC 20   *Creating Relational Queries*   **161**
     Beginning the Relational Query Process   **161**
     Relating the Database Files   **161**
     Selecting Fields   **161**
     Finishing the Relational Query Creation Process   **161**
     Tutorial   **161**   •   Exercises   **164**

TOPIC 21   *Using Relational Queries*   **165**
     Using a Relational Query   **165**
     Sorting a Relational Query   **165**
     Tutorial   **166**   •   Exercises   **172**

             Checkpoint 3   **173**
     What You Should Know   **173**
     Review Questions   **174**
     Checkpoint Exercises   **174**

Comprehensive Exercise 1   **177**

Comprehensive Exercise 2   **182**

Index   **187**

Editor's Foreword

This book is one of many in the boyd & fraser *Software Training and Reference (STAR) Series*. The manuals in this Series are intended to provide an exceptionally innovative approach to learning popular application software programs, while at the same time providing a source for future reference—so that skills learned can be applied to constantly changing activities.

The overall development of the STAR Series is based on the following principles:

▶ In order for any application software manual to be effective, it must be organized with the outlook or orientation of a novice user in mind. A novice intuitively approaches a program from the perspective of what he or she would like "to do" or accomplish, rather than from the command perspective of experienced users. *Thus the STAR Series utilizes a selection of topics oriented toward the novice user.*

▶ Various application software programs within the same general category (e.g., word processing, spreadsheet, database) have some underlying concepts in common. If users understand these common concepts, they will more likely take greater advantage of the associated program features. In addition, they will have less difficulty implementing the concepts within some different future program environment. Although the "how to" of a particular program feature may change or evolve, the "why" and "when" are less likely to do so. That is, although particular application software skills are often not transferrable between programs, the underlying concepts are. *Thus each STAR Series topic begins with a conceptual discussion.*

▶ There is no substitute for "learning by doing." Complete understanding of the concepts-skill link can only really be achieved through hands-on activity. *Thus each STAR Series topic centers around a hands-on tutorial application, highlighting the skill(s) necessary to implement the program feature.*

▶ Completion of a particular example alone, however, is insufficient for understanding the various nuances of a skill. *Thus each STAR Series manual provides relatively extensive exercises and problems, as well as reference material applicable to generalized situations.*

▶ In most other tutorial-based software training manuals, the actual keystroke activities required to accomplish a tutorial are all too often lost in the surrounding explanatory material. Many users of these manuals become confused and frustrated. *Thus the STAR Series provides clear, easily distinguishable tutorial steps and directions.*

Each manual within the STAR Series is organized in the same consistent format. The selection of end-user-oriented topics focuses on those most fundamental to the effective use of the program. In addition, each manual within the same general application software category is organized as similarly as possible, while still allowing for individual program variations. Each STAR Series topic contains the following sections:

1. The **concepts section** defines the particular program feature and presents its usefulness and applicability from a conceptual standpoint.
2. The **tutorial section** is a complete keystroke-by-keystroke presentation of the feature. Each action step is easily identified, and numerous screen images provide both useful "status checks" and reassuring positive reinforcement.
3. The **procedure summary section** not only provides a useful review of the required implementation procedures or skills, but it also serves as a general keystroke reference for applying those skills to future activities.
4. The **exercise section** encourages further hands-on skill development.

Throughout the topic presentation are numerous **tips** that include short items of interest, alternative methods for feature implementation, reference to associated topics, and advice on how to avoid common mistakes or overcome common difficulties.

Each STAR Series manual is divided into three or more parts, each of which concludes with a **checkpoint**. The checkpoints contain numerous "What You Should Know" items designed to emphasize what can be accomplished within the particular program environment. The checkpoints also contain review questions and problems of intermediate difficulty, focusing on material covered up to that checkpoint. Each manual concludes with a **comprehensive problem** that integrates many of the program features within a single application.

DOS Coverage

To keep the overall length (and price) of each STAR Series manual down to a reasonable level, and to avoid possibly unnecessary repetition of fundamental DOS concepts and skills, DOS coverage for the Series is provided separately in single stand-alone texts. Inexpensive sixty-four page booklets published by boyd & fraser, by Rod B. Southworth, provide this coverage.

Instructor's Materials

A comprehensive *Instructor's Manual* is available for use in conjunction with each STAR Series offering. These contain topic overviews, key terms, lecture notes, software suggestions, solutions to all exercises and problems, answers to checkpoint review questions, additional comprehensive exercises and solutions, and over 250 test questions. Also available is an *Instructor's Resource Disk* that contains tutorial, exercise, and problem files in various stages of completion.

Series Philosophy — Diversity and Currency

boyd & fraser intends to extend the STAR Series to include coverage of all popular application software programs. In addition, we are committed to providing timely coverage of all program updates and revisions. It is hoped that the consistent STAR Series organization and format will provide a flexible approach to either learning multiple application programs or updating to newer program versions. Contact your local South-Western/boyd & fraser Representative for information on current and future STAR Series offerings.

Introduction to Databases

Creating, storing, sorting, and retrieving data are important tasks faced by individuals living in a complex society. In our personal lives, most of us maintain a variety of records such as the names, addresses, and telephone numbers of friends and business associates; records of investments; and records of expenses for income tax purposes. Not only must these types of records be maintained, but the records must be arranged so that the data within each record can be easily accessed when required. In the business world, maintaining information that can be quickly and easily accessed is crucial to success. Employee personnel records must be maintained; inventory records must be kept; and payroll information and other types of data must be accumulated and periodically updated.

We use the term **database** to describe a collection of data organized in a manner that allows access, retrieval, and use of that data. The basic idea of a database is quite simple. It is a structure that can hold data concerning many different types of objects (technically called **entities**) as well as the relationships among these objects. For example, a database for a company might hold data on such objects as sales reps and customers. In addition, the database would include the relationship between sales reps and customers. For example, using the data in the database, we must be able to determine which sales rep represents a particular customer as well as which customers are represented by a given sales rep.

Figure 1 gives a sample of such a database. Note that it consists of two tables: SLSREP and CUSTOMER. The columns in the SLSREP table include the sales rep number, name, address, total commission, and commission rate. Thus the name of sales rep 3 is Mary Jones. She lives at 123 Main St. in Grant, Michigan. Her total commission is $2150.00, and her commission rate is 5 percent.

The first five columns in the CUSTOMER table include the customer number, name, address, current balance, and credit limit. Thus the name of customer 622 is Dan Martin. He lives at 419 Chip St. in Grant, Michigan. His current balance is $575.50, which happens to exceed his $500 credit limit.

Figure 1
Sales Rep and Customer Tables

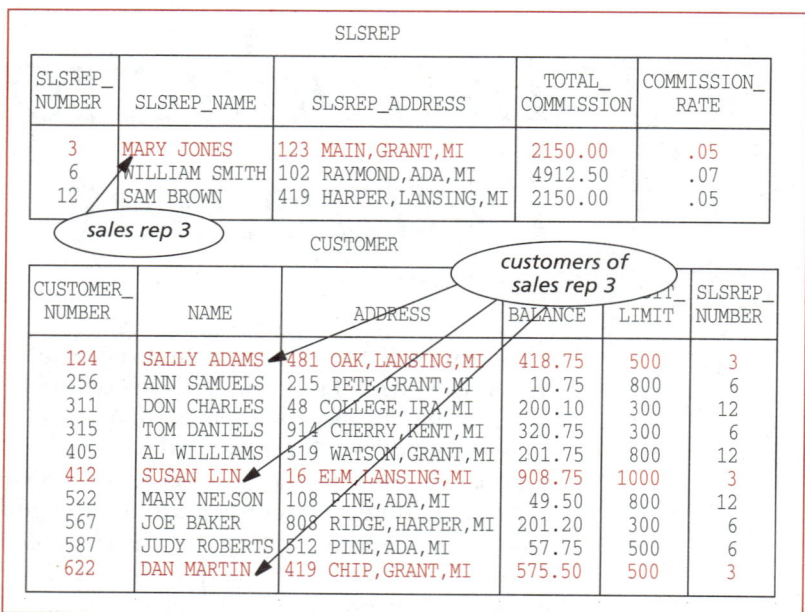

The last column in the CUSTOMER table serves a very special purpose. It relates customers and sales reps. Using this column, we can see that Dan Martin's sales rep is sales rep 3 (Mary Jones). Likewise, we can see that Mary Jones represents customers 124 (Sally Adams), 412 (Susan Lin), and 622 (Dan Martin). We do this by first looking up Mary's number in the SLSREP table and then looking for all the rows in the CUSTOMER table that contain this number in the column labeled SLSREP_NUMBER.

In a very real sense, the tables shown in Figure 1 form a database even if they were simply kept on paper. To obtain maximum benefit and flexibility from this database, however, the database should be kept on a computer. Then, all we would need is a tool to help users access this database. The term "database management system" describes such a tool. A **database management system**, or **DBMS**, is a software product with which users can easily create a database; make additions, deletions, and changes to data in the database; sort the data in the database; and retrieve data from the database in a variety of ways.

One increasingly popular DBMS available for personal computers is FoxPro 2.5. FoxPro 2.5 was developed by Fox Software/Microsoft as a powerful DBMS, yet its commands allow users to easily create and manage the databases they need for either personal or business use. FoxPro 2.5 is one of a general category of database management systems called **relational**. In simplest terms, this means that we can visualize the data in the database exactly as we saw earlier, that is, as a collection of tables, each consisting of a series of rows and columns.

Note: From this point on, FoxPro 2.5 is referred to simply as FoxPro.

Before we proceed, you should be aware of the following information concerning working with FoxPro:

1. In general, filenames can contain a three-character extension (the characters following the period in the name of the file). FoxPro has its own extensions that it adds to filenames. This is nothing for you to worry about. You just indicate the regular part of the name, and FoxPro does the rest automatically. On some screens you will see these extensions, but you do not need to do anything with them.

2. The NUMLOCK key on your keyboard switches your keyboard in and out of NumLock mode. In NumLock mode, you can use the numeric keypad on your keyboard to enter numbers. If you are not in NumLock mode, you use the keypad for cursor movement. (If your keyboard does not have separate cursor movement keys, you do not want to be in NumLock mode. If you have separate cursor movement keys, you might very well decide to be in NumLock mode. It's up to you.) If you are in NumLock mode, the letters "Num" appear on some screens. The screens shown in the text include these letters. If you are not in NumLock mode, your screens do not include these letters. This is not a problem. Just be aware of this slight difference between what appears on your screen and what is shown in the text.

3. Most relational database management systems use the terms table, row, and column. FoxPro, however, uses the terms database file, record, and field. As you read through the FoxPro material, be aware of this difference. The correspondence between the two sets of terms is as follows:

General Term	FoxPro Term
table	database file
row	record
column	field

We use the employee records shown in Figure 2 in our sample database. Each record contains an employee number, the employee's name, the data hired, a department name, the employee's pay rate, and an entry indicating whether or not the employee is a member of the union. The rows in this table are the records. The columns are the fields. The whole table is a database file.

Figure 2
Employee Table

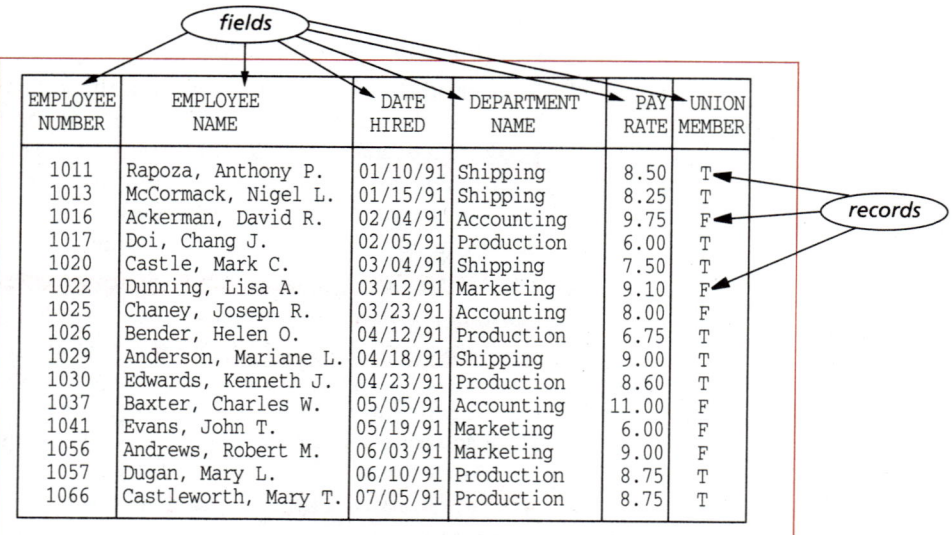

TOPIC 1

Using FoxPro

CONCEPTS To use FoxPro, you must first load the computer's operating system. Then you can load FoxPro into the computer's main memory.

Loading FoxPro

Once you have loaded FoxPro, your screen should look like the one shown in Figure 1.1. FoxPro uses a windows metaphor to organize the way in which you work with FoxPro. Each window is a separate work area that allows you to perform certain tasks within the program. These windows can be opened, closed, moved, resized, and scrolled.

Figure 1.1
The Logon Screen

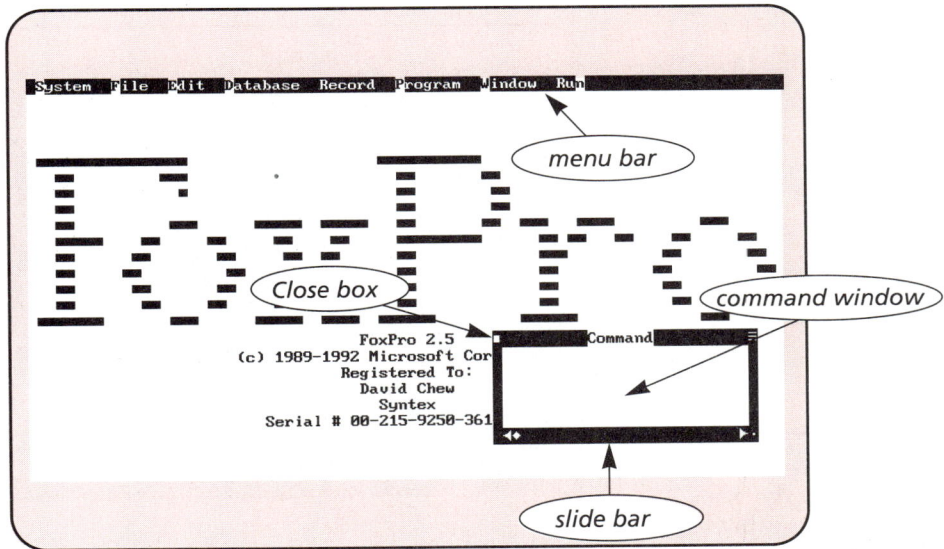

The first window that appears when you are loading FoxPro is the Command window. The **Command window** allows you to access system prompt commands. Commands typed in this area are ones that are commonly used in all xBase language programs such as FoxPro. (xBase is a termed used to describe a command language derived from the dBASE database program.) In other database programs, these commands may be referred to as dot prompt commands. The line at the top of the screen is called the **menu bar**. It offers you the option of choosing commands called **menu options** rather than typing in system prompt commands. This **menu system** is the primary interface used in this book. Control of the FoxPro program automatically starts with the Command window and defaults back to the Command window on completion of each task.

All of this detail may seem confusing at first. Once you master a few simple rules, however, you will be able to work your way through the various steps without much difficulty.

Selecting an Option

To select an option from a menu, you first press the ALT or F10 key. You are now in the menu system (Figure 1.2), where you indicate the option you want to select by picking it from a menu. (Don't worry about the meaning of the specific choices for now.) The highlighted menu choice on the menu bar is called the **menu pad**. The menu pad is currently on the System menu. Pressing the DOWN ARROW or the ENTER key causes the menu popup to appear. The **menu popup** lists the choice of menu options. Notice that the first choice, "About FoxPro...," is currently highlighted. When you repeatedly press the DOWN ARROW, the highlight moves down through some of the other choices. Depending on what actions you have taken before you pressed ALT, some of these options may not be currently available to you. The highlight automatically skips over such options.

> **TIP:** Instead of using the arrow keys, you can press the key that corresponds with the highlighted character of each menu option. Both methods are used in the exercises.

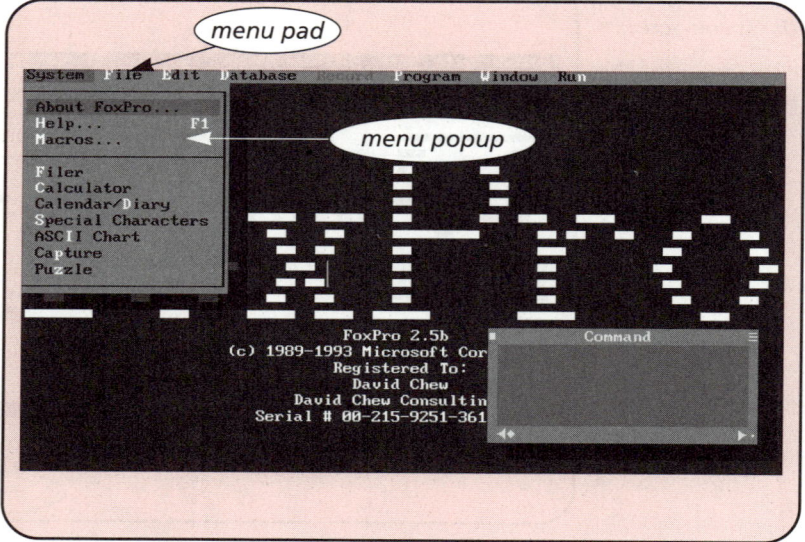

Figure 1.2
Menu System

> **TIP:** You can access all the FoxPro menu options with a mouse. The mouse pointer appears as a small box (orange on a color screen). Point and click the left mouse button once for each menu item to call the respective menu popup. Point and click a menu option to select it. Click on the Close box once (Figure 1.1) to automatically close the window. Hold down the mouse button on the slide bar (Figure 1.1) to scroll any hidden information in the window.

Pressing the RIGHT ARROW moves the menu pad and menu popup to the next item on the menu bar, in this case the File menu. Pressing the LEFT ARROW key moves you to the previous menu pad and menu popup.

The final step in the process is to actually make the selection. To do so, first make sure that the option you want to select is highlighted by using the appropriate arrow keys and then press ENTER.

Moving from the Menu System to the Command Window

FoxPro begins with the system prompt in the Command window. When a task is completed, control of FoxPro returns to the Command window. If you want to return to the Command window without completing a task or while in the menu system, press CONTROL-F2 or select the Window, Command option from the menu system. FoxPro allows you the choice of using either system prompt or menu commands.

Escaping from an Operation

Sometimes you might find that you unintentionally chose the wrong option. In other cases, you might not want to proceed with some action you have started, but you are not sure how to get out. In such situations, simply press the ESCAPE key. Sometimes this immediately returns you to the Command window. Other times, you may first be asked whether or not you really want to escape from the task on which you are working. In still others, you may need to press ESCAPE more than once to return to the Command window.

Exiting FoxPro

You can exit FoxPro at any time by selecting the Quit command of the File menu or by typing "QUIT" and pressing ENTER at the system prompt. The message "FoxPro 2.5 - Normal shutdown" appears, and you return to the DOS prompt.

Getting Help

FoxPro has an extensive Help facility. You can get help on a variety of topics while you are at the computer by simply pressing F1. When you do, you see a screen similar to Figure 1.3.

Figure 1.3
Help Facility

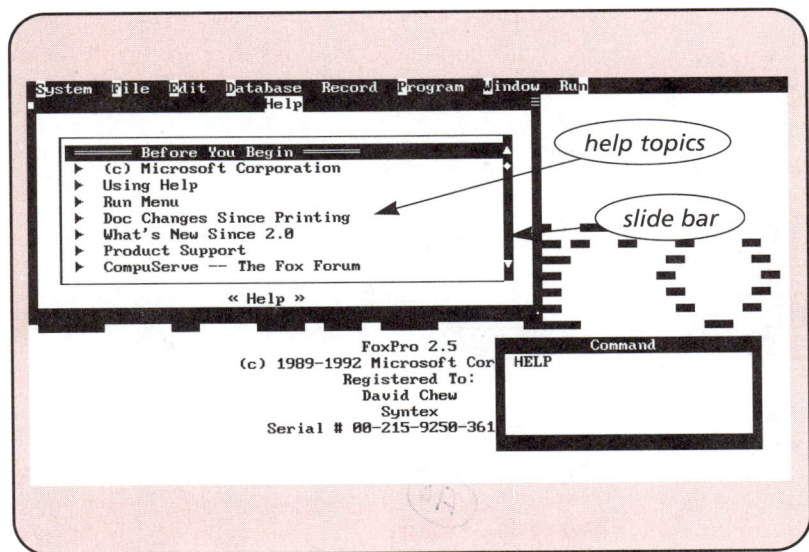

To select a help topic, scroll through the list of topics with the UP or DOWN ARROW keys, highlight the one you want, and press ENTER. A list of functions—called **push buttons**—enclosed in < and > symbols appears along the left side of the Help window. The function enclosed in << and >> symbols is called the **default push button**. Pressing ENTER automatically executes this function. You select the other push buttons by pressing the TAB key to highlight the desired button and pressing ENTER. Note that the See Also box is a push button used to select related topics. You can also execute a menu system command such as ALT, File, Print to get a printed copy of the information. When you have finished looking, press ESCAPE.

Topic 1: Using FoxPro

When you request help from within a particular task, you get information that relates to that task. If, for example, you have highlighted a particular menu option, the information will concern that menu option. However, you can use the table of contents to obtain help on any topic.

TUTORIAL In this tutorial, you become familiar with the basic way to use FoxPro. You begin by starting FoxPro. (The way in which you do so depends on your particular computer. Check with your instructor to make sure the following steps are appropriate in your specific situation.)

1 **Load FoxPro.** Place your data disk in drive A.

Type	a:	in either upper- or lowercase.
Press	← ENTER	Makes drive A the default drive.

The next command creates the required path to the directory containing FoxPro.

Type	cd c:\foxpro25	Creates required path to directory containing FoxPro.

This command assumes that FoxPro is located in a directory called "foxpro25" on drive C.

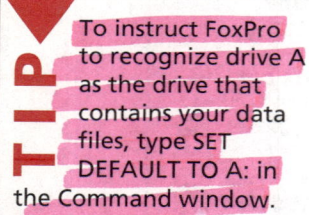

TIP To instruct FoxPro to recognize drive A as the drive that contains your data files, type SET DEFAULT TO A: in the Command window.

Press	← ENTER	Makes directory containing FoxPro the default directory.
Type	fox	in either upper- or lowercase.
Press	← ENTER	

FoxPro is now loaded into main memory, and you will see the FoxPro banner on the screen and the Command window. ◄

2 **Select the File, Open option from the File menu.**

Press	ALT	Moves to menu system.
Press	F	Moves to File menu.
Press	O	Selects Open command.

3 **Move to the Command window from the menu system.**

Press	ALT	Selects menu system.
Press	CTRL - F2	Returns to Command window.

8

FoxPro

4 **Escape** from the operation you have begun.

| Press | ESC | Returns to system prompt in Command window. |

5 **Exit** FoxPro.   *Press each key one @ a time* (F10)

| Press | ALT , F , Q | Selects File, Quit. |

6 **Restart** FoxPro.

| Type | fox | in either upper- or lowercase. |
| Press | ↵ ENTER | |

7 **Get help** on the File, Open menu option.

Press	ALT	Selects menu system.
Press	→	Moves menu pad to File.
Press	↓ twice	File menu popup appears; highlights Open.
Press	↵ ENTER	Selects File, Open menu option.
Press	F1	Gets help information.
Press	ESC	Removes Help window.
Press	ESC	Returns to Command window.

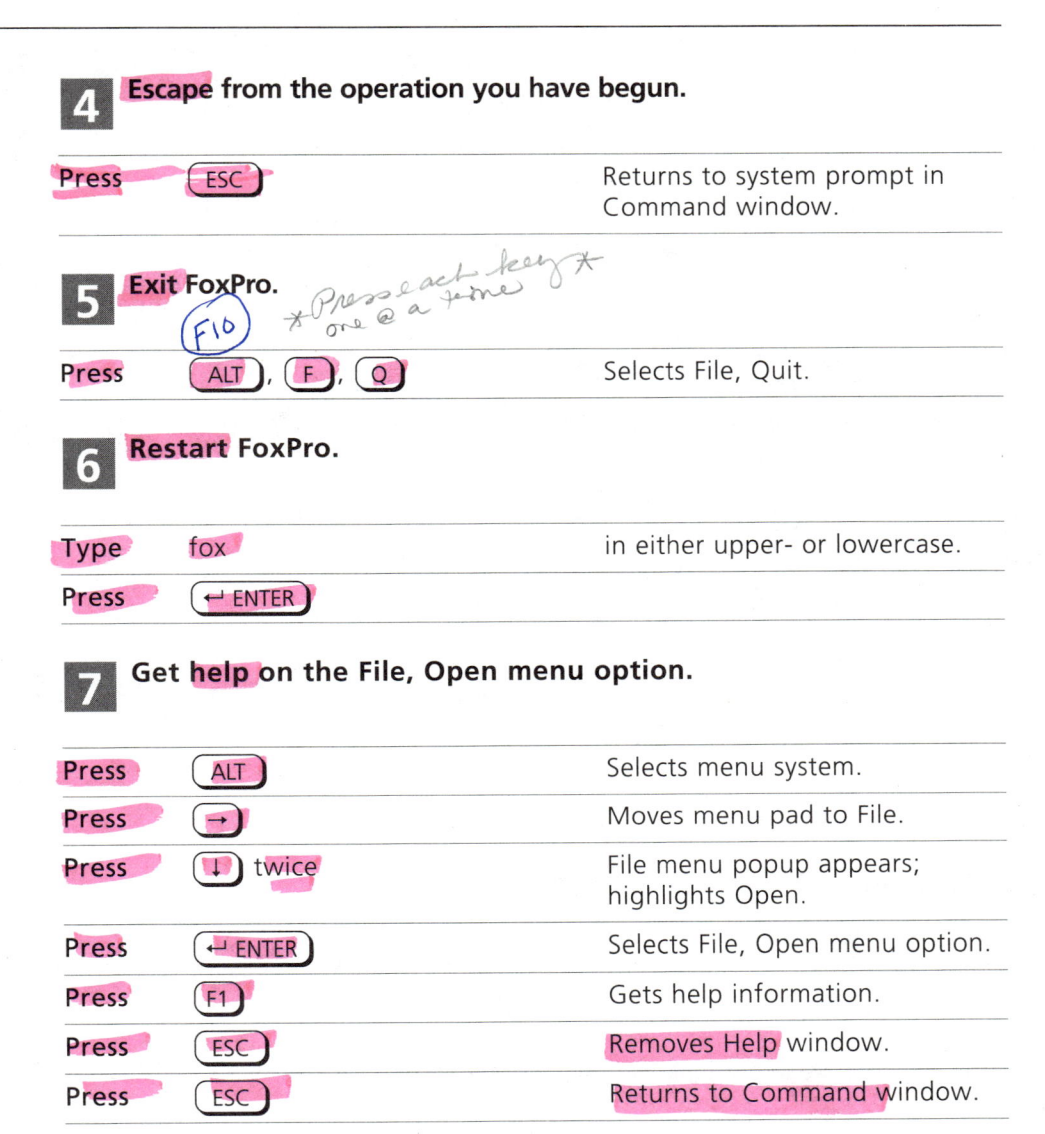

PROCEDURE SUMMARY

LOADING FOXPRO

Be sure the DOS prompt displays the directory containing the FoxPro program.

| At the DOS prompt, type | FOX |
| Enter the input. | ↵ ENTER |

Topic 1: Using FoxPro   **9**

SELECTING AN OPTION

Access the menu system.	`ALT`
Move to the desired menu.	`←` or `→`
Move the highlight to the desired option.	`↑` or `↓`
Make the selection.	`↵ ENTER`

MOVING FROM THE MENU SYSTEM TO THE COMMAND WINDOW

| Access the menu system. | `ALT` or `F10` |
| Return to the Command window. | `CTRL`-`F2` |

ESCAPING FROM AN OPERATION

| Abandon the operation. | `ESC` |

EXITING FOXPRO

Activate the menu.	`ALT`
Select File.	`F`
Select Exit.	`Q`

GETTING HELP

| Get Help. | `F1` |
| Once you have viewed the information, leave Help. | `ESC` |

EXERCISES

1. Load FoxPro.
2. Select the Run, New Query menu command.
3. Escape from the operation you have begun.
4. Exit FoxPro.
5. Restart FoxPro.
6. Move to the menu system.
7. Move back to the Command window.
8. Get help on the Run, New Query menu command.

TOPIC 2

Creating a Database File

CONCEPTS Before you can use a database file, you must create it. To do so, you must describe the structure of the file to FoxPro; that is, you must describe the fields that make up the database and indicate the characteristics of these fields.

Creating a Database File

You must assign the database file a name. The rules for database filenames are as follows:

1. The name can be up to eight characters long.
2. The first character must be a letter of the alphabet.
3. The remaining characters can be letters, numbers, or the underscore (_).
4. No blank spaces are allowed.

You use the **Structure dialog box** (Figure 2.1) to describe the fields in your database file. On this screen, you enter the information on all the fields

Figure 2.1
Structure Dialog Box

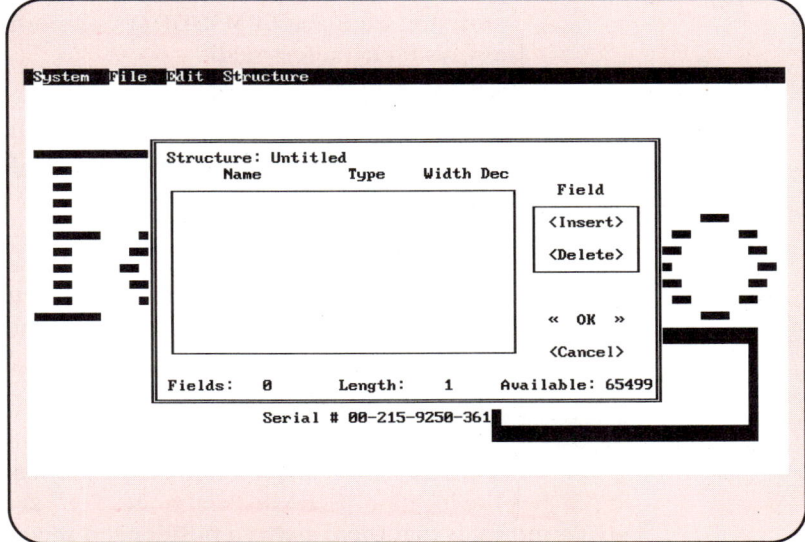

in the database file. The status line appears as a prompt when the cursor is placed on an entry item. Labels in the Structure dialog box are:

Structure	Displays the name of the database file. Since it has not yet been given, Untitled is displayed.
Fields	Displays the number of fields created in the file.
Length	Displays the total number of characters used in the database plus 1 character in the beginning.
Available	Displays the total number of available memory in bytes.

To define the structure of the database file, you must specify the following information for each field:

1. **Field Name.** Each field in a database file must be given a unique name. The name should describe the field's contents. The first character of the name must be alphabetic. The remaining characters can be letters of the alphabet, numerical digits, or the underscore (_). No blank spaces are allowed within the field name.

2. **Field Type.** For each field, you must indicate the field type, that is, the type of data that the field will contain. The available field types are:

    - **CHARACTER fields** — store any printable character that can be entered from the keyboard. This includes letters of the alphabet, numbers, special characters, and blanks. A maximum of 254 characters may be included in a CHARACTER field.

    - **DATE fields** — store dates. Unless otherwise specified, dates are stored in the form of MM/DD/YY (month/day/year). The DATE field is always 8 characters wide.

    - **NUMERIC fields** — store integer numbers or decimal numbers. Integer numbers are numbers that do not contain a decimal point. NUMERIC fields may contain a plus (+) or minus (−) sign. Accuracy is to 15 digits. A field must be defined as NUMERIC if it is to be used in an arithmetic calculation.

    - **LOGICAL fields** — consist of a single value representing a true or false condition. The entry must be T (True), F (False), Y (Yes), or N (No). The LOGICAL field is always 1 character wide.

    - **MEMO fields** — store large blocks of text such as words or sentences. MEMO fields may be up to 4000 characters long.

3. **Field Width.** For each field, you must type its width, that is, the maximum number of characters that the field will contain. (The decimal position specifies the location of the decimal point. For example, a decimal position of 2 indicates that there are two positions to the right of the decimal point.)

4. **Decimal Places.** For NUMERIC fields only, you must enter the number of decimal places, that is, the number of positions to the right of the decimal point.

5. **Index.** You must indicate whether or not FoxPro is to maintain an index for the field. (You will learn about indexes in Topic 14. For now, just make the entries as indicated in the text for indexes.)

You should know two special things about entering this information:

1. Pressing SHIFT-TAB after entering the field name allows you to specify whether to use an index. Pressing the SPACEBAR displays the choices of indexes.
2. When you enter the field type, all you need to do is press the SPACEBAR, type the first letter of the field type you want displayed, and press ENTER.

If you discover that you have made a mistake in creating your database file after you have returned to the Command window, you can correct the structure of your database in two ways. If you have not added any records to the file, you can start over by selecting the System, Filer command and deleting your database file. Once you have erased the file, you can begin the process from scratch. If you do not discover the mistake until after you have added all the data, you must modify the structure of your database. (See details in Topic 18.)

TUTORIAL In this tutorial, you first create the EMPLOYEE database file by describing the fields within it to FoxPro. Figure 2.2 gives the field names that are used in this database file as well as the characteristics of the fields.

Figure 2.2
Field Names and Characterics of EMPLOYEE File

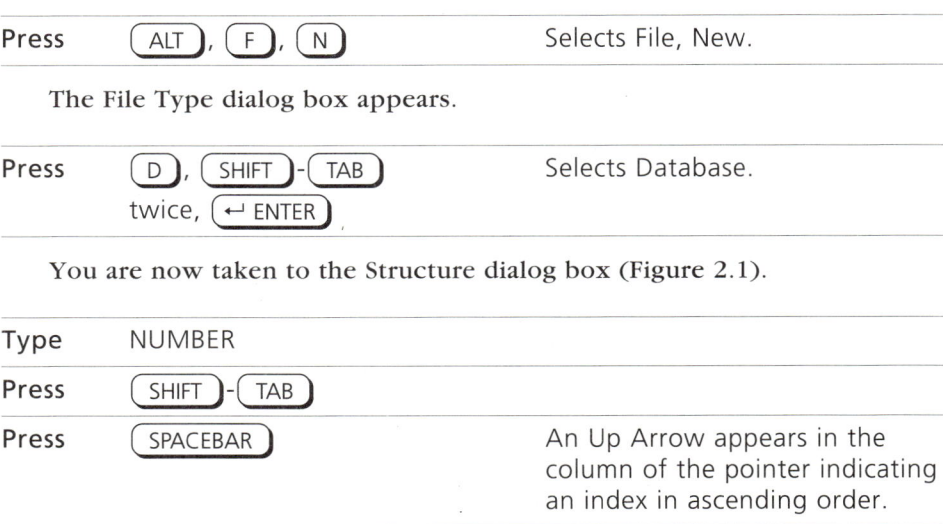

FIELD DESCRIPTION	FIELD NAME	FIELD TYPE	WIDTH	DECIMAL POSITIONS
EMPLOYEE NUMBER	NUMBER	CHARACTER	4	
EMPLOYEE NAME	NAME	CHARACTER	20	
DATE HIRED	DATE	DATE	8	
DEPARTMENT NAME	DEPARTMENT	CHARACTER	10	
PAY RATE	PAY_RATE	NUMERIC	5	2
UNION MEMBER	UNION	LOGICAL	1	

decimal positions only necessary for numeric fields

1 Create the EMPLOYEE database file.

Press	ALT , F , N	Selects File, New.

The File Type dialog box appears.

Press	D , SHIFT - TAB twice, ↵ ENTER	Selects Database.

You are now taken to the Structure dialog box (Figure 2.1).

Type	NUMBER	
Press	SHIFT - TAB	
Press	SPACEBAR	An Up Arrow appears in the column of the pointer indicating an index in ascending order.

Topic 2: Creating a DatabaseFile   **13**

Press	TAB twice	
	The correct field type is already displayed.	
Type	4	
Press	ENTER	Selects field width of 4; completes field entry.

Proceed to enter the second field. There is no index on the following fields.

Type	NAME	
Press	TAB twice	
Type	20	
Press	ENTER	Selects field width of 20; completes field entry.

Make the remaining entries as shown in Figure 2.3. To specify DATE as a field type, press the SPACEBAR and then press D, the first letter of the field type. "Date" is highlighted in the menu popup. Press ENTER to accept the selection. FoxPro then automatically specifies the width as 8. (The slashes in a date count as positions in the field.) To specify NUMERIC as a field type, press the SPACEBAR and then Press N. "Numeric" is highlighted. Press ENTER to accept the selection. Enter 5 as the width and 2 as the decimal places, pressing ENTER after each entry. To specify LOGICAL as a field type, press the SPACEBAR and then press L. "Logical" is highlighted. Select it by pressing ENTER. FoxPro automatically specifies the width as 1. ◄

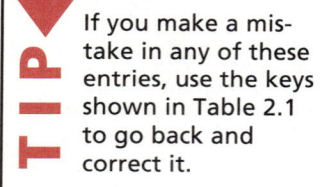

If you make a mistake in any of these entries, use the keys shown in Table 2.1 to go back and correct it.

Figure 2.3
Remaining Entries

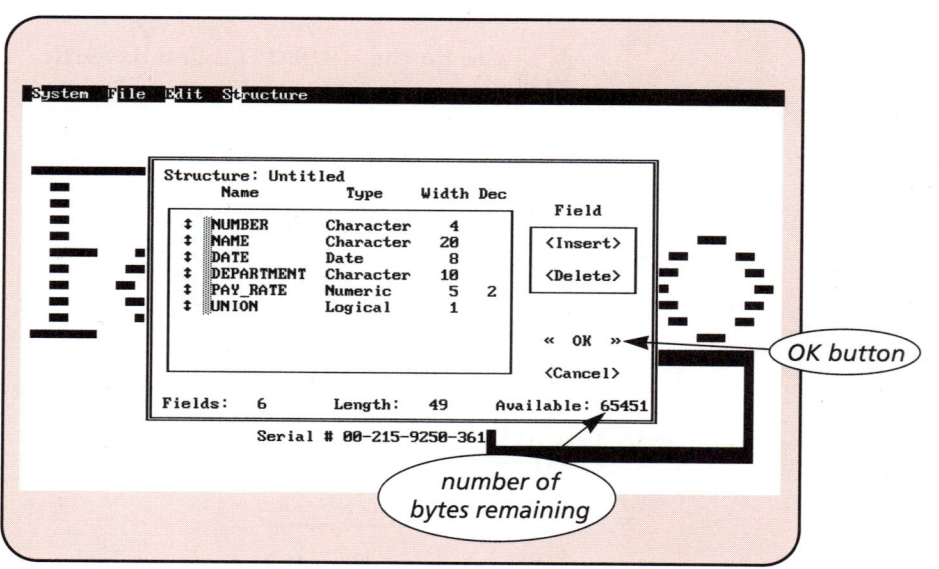

Table 2.1
Special Keys Used When Designing a Database

KEY	PURPOSE
↑	Moves highlight up one row.
↓	Moves highlight down one row.
→	Moves cursor one position to the right.
←	Moves cursor one position to the left.
TAB	Moves cursor one column to the right.
SHIFT-TAB	Moves cursor to previous choice of entry.
← BACKSPACE	Moves cursor one position to the left and erases character that was in that position.
↵ ENTER	Completes current entry and moves cursor or highlight to the next column. If you are in the last column in a row, moves to the first column in the next row. If you are on the field type column, pressing ENTER calls the menu popup of field type choices.
CTRL-I	Inserts a blank row at current cursor position.
CTRL-D	Deletes row at current cursor position.

The database fields are defined when all the entries are complete. You now indicate to FoxPro that you are done.

Press	TAB	to highlight OK button.
Press	↵ ENTER	Selects OK button.

A new dialog box appears requesting a name for the database.

Press	TAB three times	Highlights drive letter.
Press	↵ ENTER	Drive letter choices appear.
Press	↑ or ↓ as needed	
Press	↵ ENTER	Selects drive letter.
Type	EMPLOYEE	
Press	SHIFT-TAB twice	
Press	↵ ENTER	Selects SAVE button.

A dialog box appears asking whether or not you want to input data.

Topic 2: Creating a DatabaseFile **15**

Press	→	Selects NO button.
Press	↵ ENTER	Returns to Command window.

When you have finished the process, feel free to leave FoxPro. To do so, select the File, Exit menu command. When you are ready to resume your work, start FoxPro in precisely the same manner that you did earlier.

PROCEDURE SUMMARY

CREATING A DATABASE FILE

Call the menu bar.	ALT
Call the File menu popup.	F
Select New.	N
Define the structure of the database by specifying the fields.	(your input)
Select OK.	TAB as needed, ↵ ENTER
Enter the database filename.	(your input) SHIFT-TAB, SHIFT-TAB, ↵ ENTER
Select whether to input data now.	(arrow keys) ↵ ENTER

EXERCISES

A database file is to be designed and created to store a list of personal checks and related information. The field characteristics are illustrated in the following table:

FIELD DESCRIPTION	FIELD NAME	FIELD TYPE	WIDTH	DECIMAL POSITIONS
CHECK NUMBER	CHECKNUM	CHARACTER	4	
DATE	DATE	DATE	8	
PAYEE	PAYEE	CHARACTER	18	
CHECK AMOUNT	AMOUNT	NUMERIC	6	2
EXPENSE	EXPENSE	CHARACTER	14	
TAX DEDUCTIBLE	TAXED	LOGICAL	11	

Perform the following tasks:

1. Insert your data disk into drive A and then load FoxPro.
2. Create the database file and name it CHECK.
3. Enter the six fields in the preceding table.

FoxPro

TOPIC 3

Loading a Database

CONCEPTS Once you have created your database file, you are ready to add records to it. To add records, the database file must be active.

Opening a Database File

To use a database file in FoxPro, it must be open. You open database files using the File, Open menu option. When you select this option, a **dialog box** appears. This box provides scroll lists and push button options to help you select the desired database file. A scroll list contains the available files. You use the highlight to select the file you want to open. You can view additional files in the scroll list by pressing the UP or DOWN ARROW. The **slide bar** on the right of the scroll list indicates where your pointer is in relation to the entire list. ◀ 🖱

Adding Records to a Database File

Once you have created and activated the database file, you are ready to add records to it. With the database file open, select the Record, Append command to add the records. The Append window appears (Figure 3.1). Table 3.1 describes the use of various keys you can use during the data entry process.

TIP It is a common mistake to forget to open a database file. If you find you cannot take a particular action, verify that you opened your database file. It is open if its name appears dimmed in the File Open dialog box.

TIP Objects in a dialog box can also be selected using a mouse device. Placing the mouse pointer and holding the left mouse button on either the UP or DOWN ARROW in the slide bar causes the list to move vertically. Pointing and then clicking a push button once selects the function.

Figure 3.1
Append Window

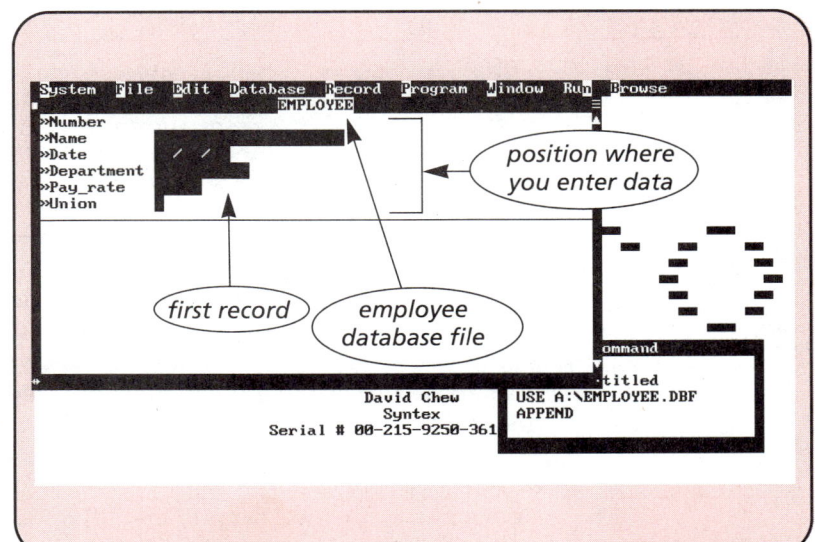

Topic 3: Loading a Database   17

Table 3.1
Special Keys Used When Entering Data

KEY	PURPOSE
↑	Moves cursor up one row.
↓	Moves cursor down one row.
→	Moves cursor one position to right.
←	Moves cursor one position to left.
TAB	Moves to next field.
SHIFT - TAB	Moves to previous field.
PAGE DOWN	Moves to next record if you are on Change window. Moves down one screenful if you are on Browse screen.
PAGE UP	Moves to previous record if you are on Change window. Moves up one screenful if you are on Browse window.
HOME	Moves to beginning of field if you are on Change window. Moves to first field in record if you are on Browse window.
END	Moves to end of field if you are on Change window. Moves to last field in record if you are on Browse window.
← BACKSPACE	Moves cursor one position to left and erases character that was in that position.
DELETE	Deletes character at current cursor position.
↵ ENTER	Completes current entry and moves cursor to next field.
CTRL - Y	Deletes all characters to right of cursor.
ESC	Leaves current record without saving changes.
INSERT	Switches between Insert mode and Replace mode. If in Insert mode, "Ins" displays on status line.

You enter the data one field at a time. The cursor automatically moves to the next line if the entered data occupies the entire field width. If the data does not fill the field, you must press ENTER after you have entered the data for that field. When you have finished entering the data for one record, FoxPro automatically saves the record. Thus there is no need for a special "Save" step as you often encounter in using word processors or spreadsheet programs.

When you enter data, keep in mind the following points concerning two special types of fields:

1. A DATE field contains slashes. When typing a date, type a two-digit month, a two-digit day, and a two-digit year. FoxPro correctly positions the date around the slashes so you do not need to type them.

2. A LOGICAL field (like UNION) contains a question. When entering a value for a LOGICAL field, you should restrict yourself to entering just T (for true) or F (for false) even though FoxPro allows you to enter Y (for yes) or N (for no). It is confusing to use T or F some of the time and Y or N at other times. Further, FoxPro displays this data as T or F. If you enter Y, it displays as a T; if you enter N, it displays as an F. Thus it makes sense to use T or F only.

When you entered the Append mode, you may have noticed that an additional item appeared on the menu bar. The Browse menu popup allows you to change the view of the database to tabular format known as the **browse view**. Once you have some records in your database file, you can select a browse view of your data rather than the defaulted **change view** by selecting the Browse, Browse menu command. (We'll look at the browse view features in Topic 9.) Select the Browse, Change menu option to return to change view.

Changing Records in a Database File

Not only do you need to be able to add new records, you must also be able to make changes to existing records. To change existing records, the database file must be open. When it is open, you can use the Record, Change menu option. Your records appear in a window with each record separated by a line (change view).

To correct a particular record, it must be on the screen. If it is not, you can use PAGE UP or PAGE DOWN to bring the desired record to the screen. Pressing PAGE UP moves you to the previous record, and pressing PAGE DOWN moves you to the next record. Press PAGE UP or PAGE DOWN enough times to bring the record you want to the screen so that you can make the necessary corrections.

As mentioned in the previous section, the view can be changed to a browse view by selecting the Browse, Browse menu option.

Deleting Records from a Database File

You will occasionally find that you have records in your database file that should no longer be there. In some cases, they are simply mistakes; you typed the wrong record. In others, the records belonged there at one time, but they do not belong in the file any longer. If, for example, an employee is no longer with the company, his or her record should no longer be in the EMPLOYEE file. In such cases, you need to be able to delete (remove) these records. You can delete a record by using the Change window, bringing the cursor within the record, and pressing CONTROL-T.

When you delete a record, FoxPro does not actually remove the record from the database file. Instead, it merely marks the record as being "deleted." You should see a diamond or diamonds, depending on the view, along the left side of the record. This indicates that the record has been so marked. Such a record can be unmarked by pressing CONTROL-T a second time. To permanently remove these marked records, you use the Database, Pack menu option. When the records are permanently removed, you can no longer unmark them.

Topic 3: Loading a Database   **19**

Listing Records in a Database File

After you have created your database file and added the necessary data to it, you need to be able to list the records and fields in the file. For example, after you have added the records to the EMPLOYEE file, you would like to list the records in it in order to make sure you have entered them correctly. Typing LIST TO PRINT in the Command window allows you to obtain a list of your records.

TUTORIAL In this tutorial, you load the EMPLOYEE database file and add data to it.

1 Open the EMPLOYEE database file.

Press	ALT , F , O	Selects File, Open.

A File dialog box appears. If the file name is grayed, the file is already open. Press ESCAPE and proceed to add the first record.

Press	↑ or ↓ as needed	Moves to EMPLOYEE.
Press	↵ ENTER	Opens EMPLOYEE file.

Enter the first of the records shown in Figure 3.2. Experiment with making corrections.

Figure 3.2
Records

EMPLOYEE NUMBER	EMPLOYEE NAME	DATE HIRED	DEPARTMENT NAME	PAY RATE	UNION MEMBER
1011	Rapoza, Anthony P.	01/10/93	Shipping	8.50	T
1013	McCormack, Nigel L.	01/15/93	Shipping	8.25	T
1016	Fong, Ronald	02/04/93	Accounting	9.75	F
1017	Ackerman, Mary R.	02/05/93	Production	6.00	T
1020	Castle, Mark C.	03/04/93	Shipping	7.50	T
1022	Dunning, Greta L.	03/12/93	Marketing	9.10	F
1025	Chaney, Joseph R.	03/23/93	Accounting	8.00	F
1026	Bender, Ginger O.	04/12/93	Production	6.75	T
1029	Anderson, Carole L.	04/18/93	Shipping	9.00	T
1030	Edwards, Kenneth J.	04/23/93	Production	8.60	T
1037	Baxter, Charles W.	05/05/93	Accounting	11.00	F
1041	Evans, John T.	05/19/93	Marketing	6.00	F
1056	Andrews, Robert M.	06/03/93	Marketing	9.00	F
1057	Hall, Sandy H.	06/10/93	Production	8.75	T
1066	Castleworth, Mary T.	07/05/93	Production	8.75	T

Press	ALT , R , A	Selects Record, Append; moves to Change window.

Type	1011	
Type	Rappozi, Athony P.	(an intentional mistake)
Press	⏎ ENTER	
Type	011093	
Type	Shipping	
Press	⏎ ENTER	
Type	8.50	

You now correct the mistake you made when you entered the name.

Press	↑ repeatedly	until you have moved back to NAME.
Type	Rapoza, Anthony P.	

Instead of typing the entire correct name, you could use the keys shown in Table 3.1 to make the corrections. Feel free to experiment with these keys at this point.

Press	⏎ ENTER repeatedly	until you have moved back to UNION.
Type	T	

2 **Make the entries for Record 2 (including some mistakes).** We will use these mistakes later to illustrate the process of correcting errors in existing records.

Type	1013	
Type	McCrmaack, Nigel L.	(an intentional mistake)
Press	⏎ ENTER	
Type	011593	
Type	Shiping	(an intentional mistake)
Press	⏎ ENTER	
Type	8.75	
Type	F	

Topic 3: Loading a Database

3 **Add an extra record.** Use your own name as the employee name. Make up whatever data you want for the rest of the fields. Exit FoxPro when you are done. Add the data as you did in the previous task and move on to the next record.

Press	ALT , F , Q	Selects ~~File, Quit; exits F~~oxPro.

4 **Restart FoxPro and add the remaining records shown in Figure 3.2.**

Start	FoxPro	as you did before.
Open	EMPLOYEE	as you did before.
Press	ALT , R , A	Selects Record, Append.

Now add the rest of the records shown in Figure 3.2 as you did before. If you make any mistakes in entering a particular record and discover them while you are still working on the record, you can correct them using the same techniques you used to correct Anthony Rapoza's name. If you don't discover them in time, don't worry. The next task shows how to change existing records.

Press	ALT , F , Q	Selects File, Quit; exits FoxPro.

You do not need to add all the records in one sitting.

5 **Correct the second record.**

Open	EMPLOYEE	
Press	ALT , R , E	Selects Record, Change.

Record 1 is currently on the screen, and you want to correct record 2.

Press	PAGE DOWN	Moves to record 2.
Type	McCormack, Nigel L.	as new name.
Type	Shipping	as new department.
Type	8.25	as new pay rate.
Type	T	as new value for UNION.

22   *FoxPro*

> **TIP** While in Change mode, if you make corrections to the last field in the last record in the file, you need to press CTRL-N to add more records.

> **TIP** If you inadvertently mark the wrong record, you can unmark it by pressing CTRL-T a second time.

| Press | ALT , F , Q | Selects File, Quit; exits FoxPro. |

Making corrections to the last field of the last record is a different situation. ◀

6 **Mark the third record (the extra one you added) for deletion.**

| Open | EMPLOYEE | |
| Press | ALT , R , E | Selects Record, Change. |

Record 1 is currently on the screen, and you want to delete record 3.

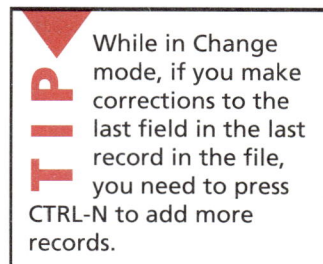

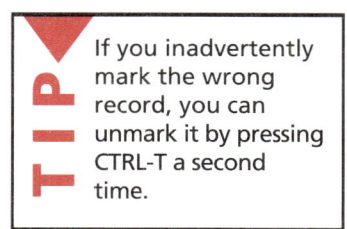

Press	PAGE DOWN twice	Moves to record 3.
Press	CTRL - T	Marks record for deletion. ◀
Press	ALT , F , Q	Selects File, Quit; exits FoxPro.

7 **Remove any marked records.**

Open	EMPLOYEE	
Press	ALT , D , P	Selects Database, Pack.
Press	↵ ENTER	Selects YES button.

The marked records are now permanently removed.

| Press | ALT , F , Q | Selects File, Quit; exits FoxPro. |

8 **List all the records in the EMPLOYEE database file.** From the Command window, you can list the records that you have entered.

| Type | LIST |
| Press | ↵ ENTER |

The records are displayed in the Logon screen. The command can be typed in upper- or lowercase letters. If you want to print the records on a printer, you can also use this command by adding the phrase "TO PRINT."

| Type | LIST TO PRINT |
| Press | ↵ ENTER |

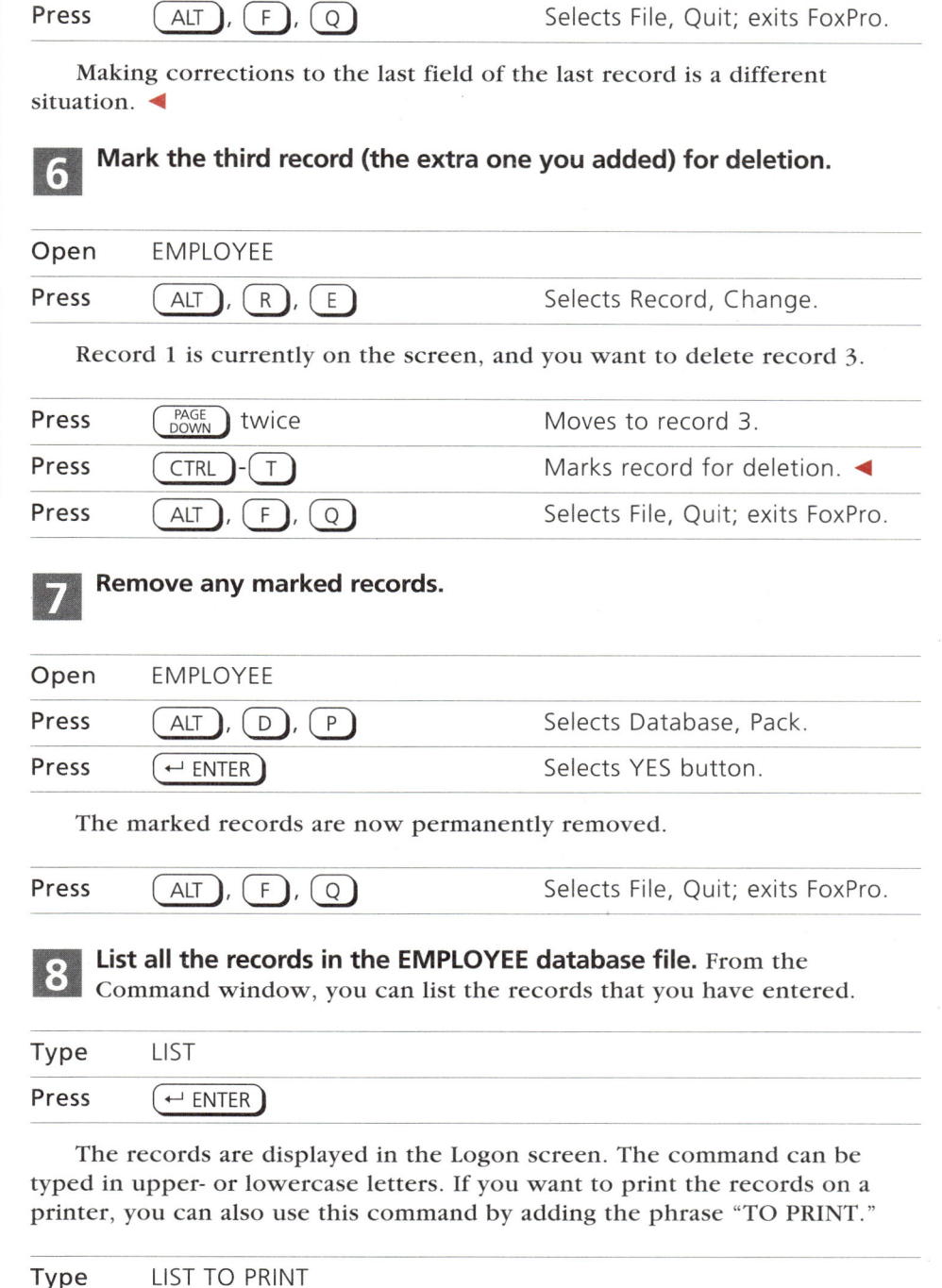

Topic 3: Loading a Database

PROCEDURE SUMMARY

OPENING A DATABASE FILE

Select File, Open.	[ALT], [F], [O]
Highlight file choice.	[↑] or [↓] (as needed), [TAB] (as needed)
Select the OK button.	[← ENTER]

ADDING RECORDS TO A DATABASE FILE

Make sure the database file is open.	
Select Record, Append.	[ALT], [R], [A]
Select either File, Close or File, Quit.	[ALT], [F], [C] or [ALT], [F], [Q]

CHANGING RECORDS IN A DATABASE FILE

Make sure the database file is open.	
Select Record, Change.	[ALT], [R], [E]
Bring the record you want to correct to the screen.	[PAGE UP] or [PAGE DOWN]
Make the necessary changes.	(your input)
If other records are to be changed, change them in the same way.	
Select either File, Close or File, Quit to complete editing the record.	[ALT], [F], [C] or [ALT], [F], [Q]

DELETING RECORDS FROM A DATABASE FILE

To mark records for deletion:

Make sure the database file is open.	
Select Record, Change.	[ALT], [R], [E]
Bring the record you want to mark for deletion to the screen.	[PAGE UP] or [PAGE DOWN]
Mark the record for deletion.	[CTRL]-[T]
If other records are to be marked, mark them in the same way.	
If you have marked any record that should not be marked, bring the record to the screen and unmark it.	[CTRL]-[T]

FoxPro

	Select either File, Close or File, Quit to close the Change window.	ALT , F , C or ALT , F , Q
	To permanently remove marked records:	
	Make sure the database file is open.	
	Select Database, Pack.	ALT , D , P
	Confirm the selection.	Y
LISTING RECORDS IN A DATABASE FILE	Make sure the database file is open.	
	Type LIST.	LIST ENTER
	To print a copy of the report:	
	Type LIST TO PRINT in the Command window.	LIST TO PRINT ENTER

EXERCISES

1. Add the following data to the CHECK database file. When you enter the third check (check 111), enter the name of the payee as Etteson Company and enter the check amount as 25.55. After you have entered this check, enter a check that does not belong in the database. You may make up any data you want for this check. (We will use this later to illustrate the process of deleting records.) Then enter the remaining checks. Remember that you do not need to enter all the checks at once.

CHECKNUM	DATE	PAYEE	AMOUNT	EXPENSE	TAXDED
109	01/19/91	Oak Apartments	750.00	Household	T
102	01/05/91	Sav-Mor Groceries	85.00	Food	F
111	01/19/91	Edison Company	55.25	Household	F
106	01/12/91	Performing Arts	25.00	Charity	T
105	01/12/91	Union Oil	22.75	Automobile	T
101	01/05/91	American Express	45.30	Entertainment	T
107	01/19/91	Sav-Mor Groceries	64.95	Food	F
108	01/19/91	Amber Inn	22.45	Entertainment	T
104	01/12/91	Brady's Shoes	69.50	Personal	F
110	01/19/91	Standard Oil	33.16	Automobile	T
103	01/05/91	Pacific Telephone	23.72	Household	F

Topic 3: Loading a Database

2. Correct the data for check 111 by changing the name of the payee to Edison Company and the check amount to 55.25.

3. Delete the extra check that does not belong in the database file (the one you added in the exercises for the last topic). Permanently remove this check from the file.

4. Display the data in the CHECK database file.

TOPIC 4

Backing Up Your Database

CONCEPTS A database file can be damaged. A power failure or a general computer failure, for example, that occurs while you are updating a database can destroy the database. As a safeguard, you should periodically make a copy of your database file. This copy is called a **backup copy**, and the database file itself is called the **live copy**.

Making a Backup Copy [28]

You can make backup copies using the Filer program located within FoxPro. You use Filer to copy the live version of the database file over a backup version. The extension for a database file is .DBF.

Restoring a Database File from a Backup Copy [29]

If you discover a problem with a database file, you can use Filer to copy the backup versions over the live ones. This effectively returns the database file to the state it was in when you made the last backup.

TUTORIAL In this tutorial, you make a backup copy of the EMPLOYEE database file. You then use the backup copy to recover the data in the file.

> **TIP** Although you do not need to exit FoxPro to copy a file, you may want to make sure that the live database file is closed. This can be done by typing CLOSE DATABASES at the Command window.

1 **Make a backup copy of the EMPLOYEE database file.** Call the backup copy EMPBACK.DBF. Assume that the database file is on the diskette in drive A and that the backup copy is to be placed on this same diskette. ◀

Press	[ALT], [S], [F]	Selects System, Filer.
Press	[TAB], [↵ ENTER]	Selects Drive popup list.
Press	[↑] as needed, [↵ ENTER]	Selects drive letter A.
Press	[↑] or [↓] as needed	Highlights EMPLOYEE.DBF.
Press	[SPACEBAR], [CTRL]-[C]	Tags file; opens Copy dialog box.
Press	[TAB] as needed	Moves to "Copy tagged files as" entry.

Topic 4: Backing Up Your Database

> **TIP:** You may want to place the backup copy on a separate disk or diskette. If you do, replace the A that precedes the name of the backup file with the appropriate drive designation.

Type	EMPBACK.DBF	
Press	`TAB` as needed	Moves to COPY button.
Press	`↵ ENTER`	Selects COPY button.
Press	`ESC`	Closes Filer; returns to Command window.

You are returned to the Filer screen. The choice of the name EMPBACK.DBF was purely arbitrary. You can choose whatever name you want, but make sure you can easily recognize it. ◀

2 **Restore the EMPLOYEE database file.** You discovered a problem in the EMPLOYEE database file. Recover the file by copying the backup version over the live version.

Press	`ALT`, `S`, `F`	Selects System, Filer.
Press	`TAB`, `↵ ENTER`	Selects Drive popup list.
Press	`↑` as needed, `↵ ENTER`	Selects drive letter A.
Press	`↑` or `↓` as needed	Highlights EMPLOYEE.DBF.
Press	`SPACEBAR`, `CTRL`-`C`	Tags file; opens Copy dialog box.
Press	`TAB` as needed	Moves to "Copy tagged files as" entry.
Type	EMPBACK.DBF	
Press	`R`	Selects "Replace existing file" checkbox.
Press	`TAB` as needed	Moves to COPY button.
Press	`↵ ENTER`	Selects COPY button.
Press	`ESC`	Closes Filer; returns to Command window.

PROCEDURE SUMMARY

MAKING A BACKUP COPY

Open Filer.	`ALT`, `S`, `F`
Select the Drive popup list.	`TAB`, `↵ ENTER`
Select the drive letter.	`↑` or `↓` (as needed), `↵ ENTER`

FoxPro

Highlight and tag the live database file.	↑ or ↓ (as needed), SPACEBAR
Open the Copy dialog box.	CTRL-C
Move to the "Copy tagged files as" entry.	TAB (as needed)
Type the backup filename.	(your input)
Select the "Replace existing file" checkbox.	R
Select the COPY button.	TAB (as needed), ↵ ENTER
Close Filer.	ESC

RESTORING A DATABASE FILE FROM A BACKUP COPY

Open Filer.	ALT, S, F
Select the Drive popup list.	TAB, ↵ ENTER
Select the drive letter.	↑ or ↓ (as needed), ↵ ENTER
Highlight and tag the backup file.	↑ or ↓ (as needed), SPACEBAR
Open the Copy dialog box.	CTRL-C
Move to the "Copy tagged files as" entry.	TAB (as needed)
Type the live database filename.	(your input)
Select the "Replace existing file checkbox."	R
Select the COPY button.	TAB (as needed), ↵ ENTER

EXERCISES

1. Make a backup copy of the CHECK database file. Call it CHECKBCK.DBF.
2. Use this backup copy to restore the data in the CHECK database file.

Topic 4: Backing Up Your Database

TOPIC 5

Querying a Database

CONCEPTS One of the major benefits of a database management system like FoxPro is the ease with which you can retrieve specific data in a database. This is often called *querying* a database. (Generally, to query means to ask for information; specifically, you are asking FoxPro for information.) You access data in a file by using what FoxPro terms **queries**. When creating queries, you specify the conditions that the data you want must satisfy. For example, you might specify that the pay rate of certain employees must be $6.00. You can also specify the fields that you want included. You might choose, for example, to only include the name, department, and pay rate. FoxPro commonly refers to the query feature as **Relational Query By Example (RQBE)**.

Creating a Query

To create a query, you use the RQBE window (Figure 5.1). Near the top left of this screen is a **File list**. It lists the name of the open database files. The available fields for the current file are listed in the **Output Fields list**. This list specifies the fields that are included, that is, the fields that are displayed when you see the results of the query. The bottom portion of the screen defines the conditions for your queries, that is, the requirements that must be satisfied in order for a record to be displayed.

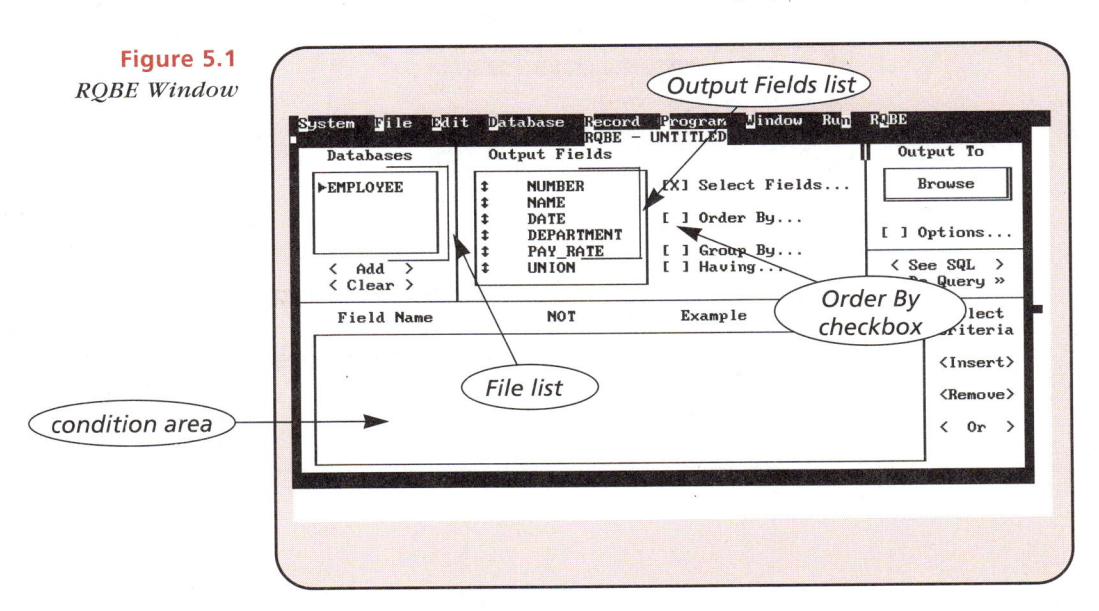

Figure 5.1
RQBE Window

Topic 5: Querying a Database

31

> **TIP:** If your computer is equipped with a mouse and mouse driver software, any movement using the TAB key or the arrow keys can be substituted with single clicks of the left mouse button within the desired area. Commands using menu item selections, buttons, and checkboxes can also be substituted with a single mouse click of the left mouse button.

Initially all fields are included in the Output Fields list, so all fields in the File list will have these down arrows. This need not always be the case, however. You can select fewer fields to display in your queried output by choosing the Select Fields checkbox. Some fields may be numbered in the Output Fields list. This indicates the sort order priority when the output is finally displayed. The sort order is changed by choosing the **Order By checkbox**.

There are two important types of movements within the RQBE window. The first type of movement is within a list. If the list items extend beyond what can be displayed, pressing the UP or DOWN ARROW keys allows you to see the hidden items. Pressing the ENTER key when the cursor is on a **button**, which is enclosed in < and > symbols, or a **checkbox**, which contains [ ] symbols, selects the command and pops up another selection box. If the highlight is located in the conditions list, pressing the LEFT or RIGHT ARROWS advances to the next item for the condition. Depending on the condition item, pressing ENTER either toggles on or off a condition item or displays a list of choices.

The second type of movement is from one list or command to another. Pressing the TAB key takes you to the next list or command. Pressing SHIFT-TAB (holding the SHIFT key down while you press the TAB key) moves you to the previous list or command.

Applying a Query

When you have finished designing a query, you would like to see the results. This is called *applying* a query. All you need to do is tab to the Do Query button and press ENTER. This takes you to the Browse window where the results of your query are displayed (see Figure 5.2). At the Browse window, only the records that satisfy your conditions are displayed and only the fields that you selected are included.

Figure 5.2
Browse Window

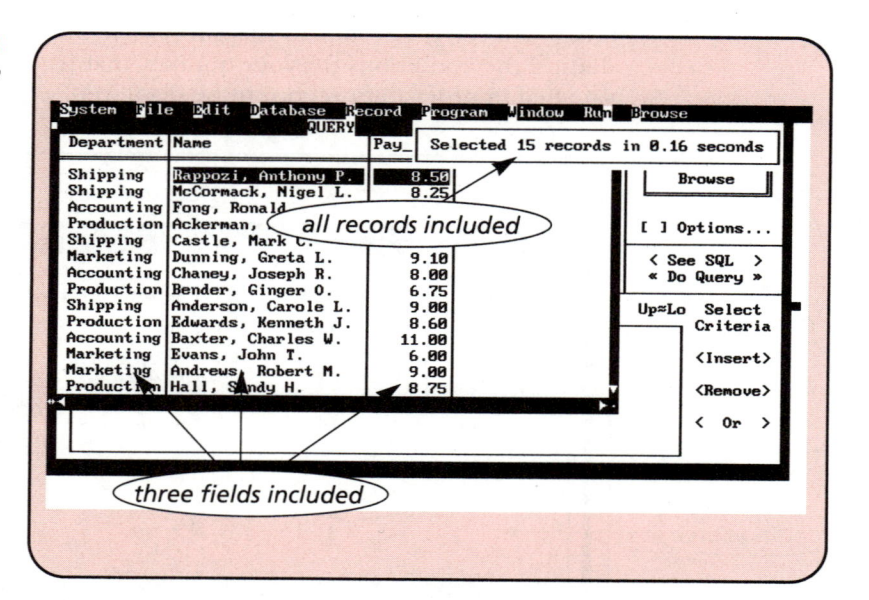

Performing this query actually opens another **work area**. A work area is a space in memory where FoxPro places an individual database file. FoxPro can maintain up to 25 different work areas. Multiple open work areas are especially useful when performing relational operations (Topic 19). If you want to continue working with the EMPLOYEE database, you need to return to the previous work area. This is done with the Window, View command. This command opens a window that allows you to move between work areas (Figure 5.3). You can return to the previous work area by highlighting the desired work area and pressing the SPACEBAR.

Figure 5.3
View Window

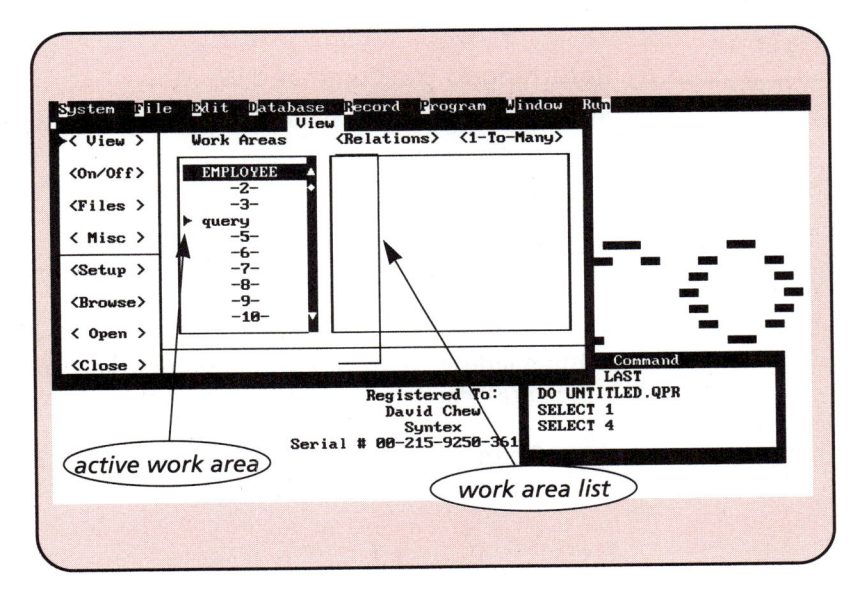

Printing the Results

Having applied the query, you can see the results in the Browse window. If you want the results printed, close the Browse window and change the Output To box to Report/Label. Select the Options checkbox and select Report and Quick Report. Uncheck the Preview Report/Label checkbox, and select To Printer for the output destination. The results are then printed using Quick Report.

Displaying All Fields

Displaying all the fields and all the records produces a list of all the records in the database file. Such a list gives you complete details about your database file. Every piece of information about every employee, for example, in the EMPLOYEE database file would appear on such a list.

Displaying Only Certain Fields

Sometimes you may not be interested in all the fields in your database file, but only in certain ones. Fortunately you can specify only those fields that you want included. This can greatly simplify the list. Suppose, for example, you were only interested in the name, department, and pay rate for the employees in the EMPLOYEE file. A list that only included these fields would

Topic 5: Querying a Database 33

> **TIP**
>
> If you make a mistake, just start over by selecting the REMOVE ALL button. Another technique for selecting fields is to choose all the fields using the ALL button and selectively remove the fields using by highlighting them under the Selected Output list and pressing ENTER.

be much simpler to use than one that included all fields. This is especially true for database files that contain large numbers of fields.

The Output Fields list (the list of fields near the top left of the RQBE window) indicates which fields are part of the view, that is, which fields you see when you apply the query. Initially the Output Fields list contains all fields. Adding or removing fields is done through the Select Fields checkbox.

After choosing the Select Fields checkbox, you move the highlight under the field name in the Selected Output list that you want to remove and press ENTER. If you want to reorder the fields, select the REMOVE ALL button. Highlight and press ENTER for each field in the Database Fields list in the order you want the fields to appear. ◄

Returning to the Command Window

You have two choices when you return from the RQBE window to the Command window. You can save your work or abandon it. That is, you can choose whether or not you want to save the query that you have created. Later, you will see special situations where you will want to save a query. For now, however, do not save any queries.

TUTORIAL

In this tutorial, you first learn how to move around on the RQBE window. Then you display all the fields and all the records in the EMPLOYEE database file. Next you restrict the fields to be displayed.

1 Open the EMPLOYEE database file and move to the RQBE window.

Press	ALT, F, N, Q, TAB twice, ↵ ENTER	Selects File, New, Query.
Highlight	EMPLOYEE.DBF	
Press	↵ ENTER	

You should now see the RQBE window (Figure 5.1).

2 Display all the records in the EMPLOYEE database file in a Browse window. To display all records, do not enter any conditions to restrict the records to be displayed. Verify that the word "Browse" appears in the Output To box. If it does not appear, press TAB until the highlight is moved within the Output To box. Press ENTER and select Browse from the popup list.

Press	Q	Selects DO QUERY button; performs query.

A Browse window appears with all the records.

Press	ESC	Closes Browse window.

You are now returned directly to the RQBE window.

3 Print the records using the Quick Report feature.

Press	TAB	until highlight is within Output To box; highlights the word "Browse."
Press	← ENTER	Displays popup list.
Press	↑ or ↓ as needed	Selects and highlights Report/Label.
Press	← ENTER	Places Report/Label in Output To box.
Press	TAB	Highlights Options checkbox.
Press	← ENTER	RQBE Display Options dialog box appears.
Press	R, Q, ← ENTER	Selects Report and column formatted Quick Report.
Press	P, T	Removes screen preview option; selects printer as destination.
Press	TAB	until OK button is highlighted.
Press	← ENTER	Returns to RQBE window.
Press	Q	Selects DO QUERY button; performs query.

A warning box may appear asking whether or not you want to overwrite the query. If this appears, press Y to select the YES button. The report begins printing on the printer.

4 Display the name, department, and pay rate for all employees.

Press	F	Displays Select Fields option box.
Press	L	Removes all fields from Selected Output list.
Press	TAB	until highlight is within Database Fields list.
Press	↑ or ↓ as needed	to highlight NAME field.
Press	← ENTER	Adds NAME field to Selected Output list.

Topic 5: Querying a Database　　　　　　　　　　　　　　　　　　　**35**

Press	↑ or ↓ as needed	to highlight DEPARTMENT field.
Press	← ENTER	Adds DEPARTMENT field to Selected Output list.
Press	↑ or ↓ as needed	to highlight PAY_RATE field.
Press	← ENTER	Adds PAY_RATE field to Selected Output list.
Press	TAB as needed	until OK button is highlighted.
Press	← ENTER	Returns to RQBE window.
Press	Q	Selects DO QUERY button; performs query.

The output is produced on the printer since this was selected previously. The results include only the desired fields.

5 **Display department, name, and pay rate for all employees.** This is the same as the previous task, except that the fields are in a different order.

Press	F	Displays Select Fields option box.
Press	L	Removes all fields from Selected Output list.
Press	TAB	until highlight is within Database Fields list.
Press	↑ or ↓ as needed	to highlight DEPARTMENT field.
Press	← ENTER	Adds DEPARTMENT field to Selected Output list.
Press	↑ or ↓ as needed	to highlight NAME field.
Press	← ENTER	Adds NAME field to Selected Output list.
Press	↑ or ↓ as needed	to highlight PAY_RATE field.
Press	← ENTER	Adds PAY_RATE field to Selected Output list.
Press	TAB as needed	until OK button is highlighted.
Press	← ENTER	Returns to RQBE window.
Press	Q	Selects DO QUERY button; performs query.

6 **Return to the Command window.**

Press	ESC	

A warning box appears asking whether or not you want to save the query.

Press	N	Selects No; returns to Command window.

7 **Return to the previous work area.**

Press	ALT, W, V	Selects Window, View.
Press	↓ as needed	Highlights EMPLOYEE work area.
Press	SPACEBAR	Selects EMPLOYEE work area.
Press	ALT, F, C	Selects File, Close.

PROCEDURE SUMMARY

CREATING A QUERY

Select a New Query.	ALT, F, N, Q
Highlight the OK button.	TAB or (arrow keys)
Open the RQBE window.	← ENTER

APPLYING A QUERY

Select the DO QUERY button and perform the query.	Q

PRINTING THE RESULTS

While in the RQBE window, highlight the Output To box.	TAB
Display the RQBE Display Options dialog box.	← ENTER
Select Report.	R
Select Quick Report.	Q
Select the defaulted columnar report.	← ENTER
Uncheck the screen preview option.	P
Select the printer as the destination.	T

Topic 5: Querying a Database

	Highlight the OK button.	TAB or (arrow keys)
	Return to the RQBE window.	ENTER
	Print the report.	Q
	If needed, overwrite the previous query.	Y
DISPLAYING ALL FIELDS	If all the fields were not previously selected, enter the Select Fields option box from the RQBE window.	F
	Select all the fields.	A
DISPLAYING ONLY CERTAIN FIELDS	Remove all the fields from the Selected Output list.	L
	Identify the desired fields to add to the Selected Output list by highlighting each field in the appropriate order.	(arrow keys)
	Select each item to be placed in the Selected Output list.	ENTER
RETURNING TO THE COMMAND WINDOW	Close the RQBE window.	ESC
	If a warning box appears to save the query, respond with No.	N
RETURNING TO THE PREVIOUS WORK AREA	Select the View window.	ALT, W, V
	Highlight the desired work area.	↑ or ↓ (as needed)
	Select the work area.	SPACEBAR
	Close the window.	F, C

EXERCISES

All exercises should be performed twice, first directing output to the Browse window and then to the printer using Quick Report.

1. Display all the records and all the fields in the CHECK database file.
2. Display the Check Number, Date, Payee, and the Check Amount fields for all checks.
3. Display the Date field, and then the Check Number, Payee, and Check Amount fields for all checks.

TOPIC 6

Using Conditions

CONCEPTS In many cases, when you query a database, you are only interested in those records that satisfy some condition. (A condition is an expression that is either true or false.) Suppose, for example, that you only wanted information about those employees whose pay rate is greater than $6.00. What you really want is to display only those employees for whom the condition "pay rate is greater than 6.00" is true. It would be very cumbersome to have to scan through a report containing all the records just to find those that satisfy your condition. Thus the ability to display only those records that satisfy a condition is crucial in the query process.

Using a Condition

To enter a condition on the RQBE window, use the TAB key to move to the bottom portion of the window under the Field Name column. The basic elements of a condition are a field, a comparison operator, and a value. Pressing ENTER displays a list of fields available for use within the condition. Pick the desired field by highlighting it with the UP or DOWN ARROW keys and pressing ENTER. The highlight automatically moves to the next column, which is the NOT checkbox. You can invert the condition for record selection by pressing ENTER, which places an X in this box and advances to the Operators column. ◀

Using Operators

Six operators are available for CHARACTER or NUMERIC fields: like, exactly like, more than, less than, between, and in. Table 6.1 defines these operators, giving the circumstances that must exist in order for the given record to be included in the query output. ◀

> **TIP:** Pressing ENTER not only moves from one condition column to the next, but it also selects columns if they are checkboxes (NOT or Up=Lo). Use the TAB key to move from a checkbox if you do not want to select this column.

> **TIP:** Although the operators can be selected for all field type conditions, not all operators would be desirable for certain field types such as Between or In for LOGICAL field type conditions. Also, Like and Exactly Like would provide the same query result for NUMERIC field type conditions.

Table 6.1
Operators Available for Conditions

Operator	Definition
Like	The field must match the example text (e.g., "EMPLOYEE.NAME Like M" would match records from Mary, Matthew, and Morgan). This is the default option.
Exactly Like	The field must exactly match the example text, character for character.
More Than	The field must be greater than the value in the example text.
Less Than	The field must be less than the value in the example text.

Between	The field must be greater than or equal to the lower value and less than or equal to the higher value in the example text (e.g., "employee.pay_rate Between 6,10" would match records for the employees who earn between $6.00 and $10.00 per hour).
In	The field must match one of several comma-delineated examples in the example text.

Entering an Example

After selecting an operator, the next condition column is the example. The example entry can only be values if used for a condition involving a NUMERIC field. Conditions involving CHARACTER fields may use any string of characters or values for the example. Unlike you would in other databases, do not enclose character strings in quotes nor include dates in braces ({}) for DATE field conditions. If LOGICAL fields are used in conditions, specify the example entry as either .T. or .F. (using the periods to enclose the character). These are the only choices available for LOGICAL field conditions.

Table 6.2 lists the comparison operators and indicates which records would be selected, assuming the selected field is PAY_RATE, a NUMERIC field. If the selected field is DEPARTMENT, a CHARACTER field, the effect of the various operators would be as shown in Table 6.3. (In this case, since the only departments in the database are Accounting, Marketing, Production, and Shipping, the table indicates the specific departments that would be selected.) Note that "More Than" for CHARACTER fields effectively means "comes later alphabetically." ◀

> **TIP**
> When you type example entries for CHARACTER field conditions, be careful to use the same combination of upper- and lowercase as was used in the data that was entered into the database. If you type MARKETING (all uppercase) FoxPro ignores the case sensitivity of example entries, unless you select the Up=Lo checkbox by pressing ENTER.

Table 6.2
Effect of Comparison Operators When Field Is PAY_RATE

Operator	Example	True for records on which pay rate is
Like or Exactly Like	6.75	equal to 6.75
More Than	6.75	above 6.75
Less Than	6.75	below 6.75
Between	5,7	above 5 and below 7
In	6,10,11	only 6, 10, or 11

Table 6.3
Effect of Comparison Operators When Field Is DEPARTMENT

Operator	Example	True for records on which department is
Like	M	Marketing
Exactly Like	Marketing	Marketing
More Than	Marketing	Production or Shipping
Less Than	Marketing	Accounting
Between	Accounting, Shipping	Marketing or Production
In	Accounting, Shipping	Accounting or Shipping

Combining Conditions with AND

⬚50

The conditions discussed so far are called **simple conditions**. They consist of a single field, a comparison operator, and a value. (In the special case of LOGICAL fields, they consist solely of a single field.) In some cases, simple conditions are not sufficient for your needs. Suppose, for example, you want to list all the employees in the Accounting department whose pay rate is $11.00. This involves more than just a simple condition.

Fortunately simple conditions can be extended by placing additional conditions in the list to form compound conditions. This is exactly what you need. You want all employees for whom the compound condition "DEPARTMENT equals Accounting and pay rate equals 11.00" is true. This compound condition would appear as two separate conditions in the condition area of the RQBE window. Each condition is added below the next by pressing TAB after the checkbox.

Combining Conditions with OR

⬚52

Adding OR conditions is done by pressing O (selects the OR button) when the highlight is on the Up=Lo checkbox. FoxPro recognizes that the next condition is joined with an OR statement. The condition "DEPARTMENT equals Accounting or pay rate is less than 9.00" is true for those employees who are in the Accounting department or whose pay rate is less than $9.00 (or both).

TUTORIAL
In this tutorial, you use conditions to restrict the records that are displayed.

1 **Display all fields for the employee whose number is 1030.**

Press	(ALT), (F), (N), (Q), (TAB) twice, (↵ ENTER)	Selects File, New, Query.
Highlight	EMPLOYEE.DBF	
Press	(↵ ENTER)	

You should now see the RQBE window (Figure 5.1).

Press	(TAB)	until highlight is under Field Name column in condition area.
Press	(↵ ENTER)	Displays Field Name list.
Press	(↑) or (↓) as needed	to highlight EMPLOYEE.NUMBER.
Press	(↵ ENTER)	Places EMPLOYEE.NUMBER in Field Name column.

Topic 6: Using Conditions

Press	TAB twice	Moves to Example column.
Type	1030	
Press	ENTER	Completes condition.
Press	Q	Selects DO QUERY button; performs query.

Now you can print the results.

Press	ESC	Removes Browse window.
Press	TAB	until highlight is within Output To box.

The word "Browse" is highlighted.

Press	ENTER	Displays popup list.
Press	↑ or ↓	Highlights and selects Report/Label.
Press	ENTER	Report/Label is placed in Output To box.
Press	TAB	Highlights Options checkbox.
Press	ENTER	Displays RQBE Display Options dialog box.
Press	R, Q, ENTER	Selects Report and column formatted Quick Report.
Press	P, T	Removes screen preview option; selects printer as destination.
Press	TAB	until OK button is highlighted.
Press	ENTER	Returns to RQBE window.
Press	Q	Selects DO QUERY button; performs query.

A warning box may appear asking whether you want to overwrite the query. If this appears, press Y to select the YES button. The report begins printing on the printer.

Press	ESC	Closes RQBE window; displays warning box for saving query.
Press	N	Declines query save.

If you go back to the Command window after you have seen the results of your query and later begin a new query, you start fresh — no conditions are in place. If, however, you go to the Browse window after closing the RQBE window, the conditions you entered previously are still there. You must close the query by entering a command in the Command window. If you do not, you may get unexpected results.

Type	SET FILTER TO	
Press	⏎ ENTER	Selects system prompt command; deactivates query.

2 **Display all fields for all employees whose pay rate is 6.00.**

Press	ALT , F , N , Q , TAB twice, ⏎ ENTER	Selects File, New, Query.

Unless you need to open a database file, you should now see the RQBE window (Figure 5.1).

Press	TAB	until highlight is under Field Name column in condition area.
Press	⏎ ENTER	Displays Field Name list.
Press	↑ or ↓ as needed	to highlight EMPLOYEE.PAY_RATE.
Press	⏎ ENTER	Places EMPLOYEE.PAY_RATE in Field Name column.
Press	TAB twice	Moves to Example column.
Type	6.00	
Press	⏎ ENTER	Completes condition.
Press	Q	Selects DO QUERY button; performs query.

This automatically prints the report since Report/Label was previously selected in the Output To box.

Press	ESC	
Press	N	Declines query save; returns to Command window.

Topic 6: Using Conditions   **43**

3. Display all fields for all employees whose pay rate is greater than 9.00.

Press	ALT , F , N , Q , TAB twice, ↵ ENTER	Selects File, New, Query.

Unless you need to open a database file, you should now see the RQBE window (Figure 5.1).

Press	TAB	until highlight is under Field Name column in condition area.
Press	↵ ENTER	Displays Field Name list.
Press	↑ or ↓ as needed	to highlight EMPLOYEE.PAY_RATE.
Press	↵ ENTER	Places EMPLOYEE.PAY_RATE in Field Name column.
Press	TAB	Moves to Operators column.
Press	↵ ENTER	Displays list of operators.
Press	↑ or ↓ as needed	to highlight More Than.
Press	↵ ENTER	Selects More Than operator; advances to Example column.
Type	9.00	
Press	↵ ENTER	Completes condition.
Press	Q	Selects DO QUERY button; performs query.

This automatically prints the report since Report/Label was previously selected in the Output To box.

Press	ESC	
Press	N	Declines query save; returns to Command window.

4. Display the name, department, and pay rate for those employees whose department is Shipping.

Press	ALT , F , N , Q , TAB twice, ↵ ENTER	Selects File, New, Query.

You should now see the RQBE window (Figure 5.1).

FoxPro

Press	F	Selects SELECT FIELDS button.
Press	L	Deselects all fields from being entered in report.
Press	↑ four times	Highlights EMPLOYEE.NAME.
Press	↵ ENTER	Selects EMPLOYEE.NAME as field to include in queried report.
Press	↑ or ↓ as needed	to highlight EMPLOYEE.DEPART-MENT field in left list.
Press	↵ ENTER	Selects EMPLOYEE.DEPARTMENT as field to include in queried report.
Press	↑ or ↓ as needed	to highlight EMPLOYEE.PAY_RATE field in left list.
Press	↵ ENTER	Selects EMPLOYEE.PAY_RATE as field to include in queried report.
Press	TAB	until highlight is in OK button.
Press	↵ ENTER	Returns to RQBE window.
Press	TAB	until highlight is under Field Name column.
Press	↵ ENTER	Displays Field Name list.
Press	↑ or ↓ as needed	to highlight EMPLOYEE.DEPART-MENT.
Press	↵ ENTER	Places EMPLOYEE.DEPARTMENT in Field Name column.
Press	TAB twice	Selects Like operator; advances to Example column.
Type	"Shipping"	
Press	↵ ENTER, TAB	Completes condition.
Press	Q	Selects DO QUERY button; performs query.

This automatically prints the report since Report/Label was previously selected in the Output To box.

Press	ESC	
Press	N	Declines query save; returns to Command window.

Topic 6: Using Conditions **45**

5 **Display all the fields for employees named Sandy.**

Press	ALT, F, N, Q, TAB twice, ↵ ENTER	Selects File, New, Query.

You should now see the RQBE window (Figure 5.1).

Press	TAB	until highlight is under Field Name column in condition area.
Press	↵ ENTER	Displays Field Name list.
Press	↑ or ↓ as needed	to highlight EMPLOYEE.NAME.
Press	↵ ENTER	Places EMPLOYEE.NAME in Field Name column.
Press	TAB twice	Highlight is under Example column.
Type	"Sandy"	
Press	↵ ENTER	Completes condition.
Press	Q	Selects DO QUERY button; performs query.

This automatically prints the report since Report/Label was previously selected in the Output To box.

Press	ESC	
Press	N	Declines query save; returns to Command window.

6 **Display all the fields for employees who are in the union (UNION is true).**

Press	ALT, F, N, Q, TAB twice, ↵ ENTER	Selects File, New, Query.

You should now see the RQBE window (Figure 5.1).

Press	TAB	until highlight is under Field Name column in condition area.
Press	↵ ENTER	Displays Field Name list.
Press	↑ or ↓ as needed	to highlight EMPLOYEE.UNION.

Press	⏎ ENTER	Places EMPLOYEE.UNION in Field Name column.
Press	TAB twice	Highlight is under Example column.
Type	.T.	
Press	⏎ ENTER , TAB	Completes condition.
Press	Q	Selects DO QUERY button; performs query.

This automatically prints the report since Report/Label was previously selected in the Output To box.

Press	ESC	
Press	N	Declines query save; returns to Command window.

7 Display all the fields for employees who were hired after March 1, 1993.

Press	ALT , F , N , Q , TAB twice, ⏎ ENTER	Selects File, New, Query.

Unless you need to open a database file, you should now see the RQBE window (Figure 5.1).

Press	TAB	until highlight is under Field Name column in condition area.
Press	⏎ ENTER	Displays Field Name list.
Press	↑ or ↓ as needed	to highlight EMPLOYEE.DATE.
Press	⏎ ENTER	Places EMPLOYEE.DATE in Field Name column.
Press	TAB , ⏎ ENTER	Opens Operator popup.
Press	↑ or ↓ as needed	to highlight More Than.
Press	⏎ ENTER	Selects More Than operator.
Type	3/1/93	
Press	⏎ ENTER	Completes condition.
Press	Q	Selects DO QUERY button; performs query.

This automatically prints the report since Report/Label was previously selected in the Output To box.

Topic 6: Using Conditions

Press	ESC	
Press	N	Declines query save; returns to Command window.

8. Display the employees who are in the Accounting department and whose pay rate is more than 9.00.

Press	ALT, F, N, Q, TAB twice, ↵ ENTER	Selects File, New, Query.

Unless you need to open a database file, you should now see the RQBE window (Figure 5.1).

Press	TAB	until highlight is under Field Name column in condition area.
Press	↵ ENTER	Displays Field Name list.
Press	↑ or ↓ as needed	to highlight EMPLOYEE.DEPARTMENT.
Press	↵ ENTER	Places EMPLOYEE.DEPARTMENT in Field Name column.
Press	TAB twice	Highlight is under Example column.
Type	Accounting	
Press	↓	Moves to next row.
Press	↵ ENTER	Displays Field Name list.
Press	↑ or ↓ as needed	to highlight EMPLOYEE.PAY_RATE.
Press	↵ ENTER	Places EMPLOYEE.PAY_RATE in Field Name column.
Press	TAB	Advances highlight to Operators column.
Press	↵ ENTER	Opens Operator popup.
Press	↑ or ↓ as needed	to highlight More Than.
Press	↵ ENTER	Selects More Than as operator; advances to next column.
Type	9	
Press	↵ ENTER	Accepts 9 as example.
Press	Q	Selects DO QUERY button; performs query.

This automatically prints the report since Report/Label was previously selected in the Output To box.

| Press | ESC | |
| Press | N | Declines query save; returns to Command window. |

9 **Display the employees who are in the Accounting department or who belong to the union (or both).** Because this condition involves OR, you must select the OR button before entering the next condition.

| Press | ALT, F, N, Q, TAB twice, ↵ ENTER | Selects File, New, Query. |

Unless you need to open a database file, you should now see the RQBE window (Figure 5.1).

Press	TAB	until highlight is under Field Name column in condition area.
Press	↵ ENTER	Displays Field Name list.
Press	↑ or ↓ as needed	to highlight EMPLOYEE.DEPARTMENT.
Press	↵ ENTER	Places EMPLOYEE.DEPARTMENT in Field Name column.
Press	TAB twice	Highlight is under Example column.
Type	Accounting	
Press	TAB	Accepts input; moves to Hi=Lo column.
Press	O	Selects OR button; advances to next condition.
Press	↵ ENTER	Displays Field Name list.
Press	↑ or ↓ as needed	to highlight EMPLOYEE.UNION.
Press	↵ ENTER	Places EMPLOYEE.UNION in Field Name column.
Press	TAB twice	Highlight is under Example column.
Type	.T.	Indicates True condition.
Press	↵ ENTER	Completes condition.
Press	Q	Selects DO QUERY button; performs query.

This automatically prints the report since Report/Label was previously selected in the Output To box.

Topic 6: Using Conditions

| Press | ESC | |
| Press | N | Declines query save; returns to Command window. |

PROCEDURE SUMMARY

USING A CONDITION

Move to the column for the condition under the field name.	TAB or SHIFT-TAB
Call up the field name list.	ENTER
Highlight the desired field.	↑ or ↓
Select the field.	ENTER
Take one of the following steps.	
Fill the checkbox if the inverse condition is desired.	ENTER
Advance without filling in the checkbox.	TAB
Open the Operators popup.	ENTER
Highlight the desired operator.	↑ or ↓
Select the operator.	ENTER
Type in the Example column.	(your input)
Accept the input.	ENTER
Take one of the following steps.	
Fill the checkbox to ignore case sensitivity.	ENTER
Advance without filling in the checkbox.	TAB
Select the DO QUERY button and perform the query.	Q

COMBINING CONDITIONS WITH AND

Move to the column for the condition under the field name.	TAB or SHIFT-TAB
Call up the Field Name list.	ENTER
Highlight the desired field.	↑ or ↓
Select the field.	ENTER

FoxPro

Take one of the following steps.		
	Fill the checkbox if the inverse condition is desired.	↵ ENTER
	Advance without filling in the checkbox.	TAB
Open the Operators popup.		↵ ENTER
Highlight the desired operator.		↑ or ↓
Select the operator.		↵ ENTER
Type in the Example column.		(your input)
Accept the input.		↵ ENTER
Take one of the following steps.		
	Fill the checkbox if the inverse condition is desired.	↵ ENTER
	Advance without filling in the checkbox.	TAB
Continue with the next condition.		
Call up the Field Name list.		↵ ENTER
Highlight the desired field.		↑ or ↓
Select the field.		↵ ENTER
Take one of the following steps.		
	Fill the checkbox if the inverse condition is desired.	↵ ENTER
	Advance without filling in the checkbox.	TAB
Open the Operators popup.		↵ ENTER
Highlight the desired operator.		↑ or ↓
Select the operator.		↵ ENTER
Type in the Example column.		(your input)
Accept the input.		↵ ENTER
Take one of the following steps.		
	Fill the checkbox if the inverse condition is desired.	↵ ENTER
	Advance without filling in the checkbox.	TAB
Select the DO QUERY button and perform the query.		Q

Topic 6: Using Conditions

COMBINING CONDITIONS WITH OR

Move to the column for the condition under the Field Name.	`TAB` or `SHIFT`-`TAB`
Call up the Field Name list.	`↵ ENTER`
Highlight the desired field.	`↑` or `↓`
Select the field.	`↵ ENTER`
Take one of the following steps.	
Fill the checkbox if the inverse condition is desired.	`↵ ENTER`
Advance without filling in the checkbox.	`TAB`
Open the Operators popup.	`↵ ENTER`
Highlight the desired operator.	`↑` or `↓`
Select the operator.	`↵ ENTER`
Type in the Example column.	(your input)
Accept the input.	`↵ ENTER`
Take one of the following steps.	
Fill the checkbox to ignore case sensitivity.	`↵ ENTER`
Advance without filling in the checkbox.	`TAB`
Select the OR button.	`O`
Enter the next condition.	

EXERCISES

1. Display the record for Check Number 108.
2. Display the record that contains the check written in the amount of $69.50.
3. Display the records for all checks written for Entertainment in a Browse window. Include the Check Number, Payee, Check Amount, and Expense Type fields.
4. Display the records for all checks written for Sav-Mor Groceries.
5. Display the records for all checks written to a payee whose name contains the word "Oil."
6. Display the records for all checks written that are tax deductible.
7. Display the records of all checks written for Entertainment with a check amount greater than $25.00.
8. Display the records for all checks written for Household Expenses or checks that were written for Food Expense.

TOPIC 7

Calculating Statistics

CONCEPTS Three types of statistical calculations, also called summary operators, are available in FoxPro: count, sum, and average. To use one of these operators, select it from the Database menu.

Counting Records
[57]

Sometimes you need to count all the records in a database file. At other times, you need to count only those records that satisfy some condition. For example, you might need to find out how many employees are currently in the Accounting department.

Calculating a Sum
[57]

Another statistic you need to be able to calculate is a sum (total). You often need to calculate the total of values in a certain field. Sometimes you need to calculate the total for all records; in other cases, you want only those records that satisfy a given condition. To find out the total payroll cost for one hour's work in the Accounting department, for example, you would like to find the sum of the pay rates for those records on which the department is Accounting.

Calculating an Average
[57]

Although in some cases it is important to calculate a sum, in others it is more important to calculate an average. Rather than the total of the pay rates of all employees in the Accounting department, for example, you might prefer to calculate the average pay rate.

TUTORIAL In this tutorial, you calculate a variety of statistics concerning the EMPLOYEE database file.

1 Count the number of employees in the Accounting department.

Open	EMPLOYEE	unless already activated.
Press	ALT , D , O	Selects Database, Count.
Press	F	Selects FOR checkbox.
Press	SHIFT - TAB	Moves to Field Name list.
Press	↓ as needed, ↵ ENTER	Selects DEPARTMENT.

Topic 7: Calculating Statistics   **53**

Press	CTRL - L	Selects Logical popup.
Press	↓ three times, ← ENTER	Selects = symbol.
Press	TAB as needed	Moves to Expression window.
Type	"Accounting"	
Press	SHIFT - TAB three times, ← ENTER	Selects OK button.
Press	TAB three times, ← ENTER	Selects OK button.

Your screen should then look like Figure 7.1. The count is displayed in the Logon screen.

Figure 7.1
Sum Logon Screen

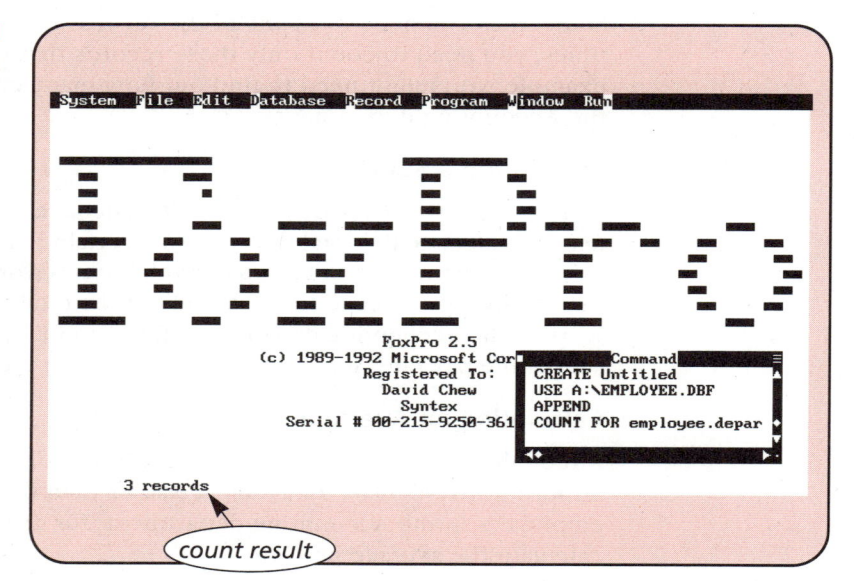

count result

2 Calculate the sum of all the pay rates.

Press	ALT , D , M	Selects Database, Sum.

Your screen should look like Figure 7.2.

Press	E	Selects EXPRESSION checkbox.
Press	SHIFT - TAB	Moves to Field Name list.
Press	↓ as needed, ← ENTER	Selects PAY_RATE.

Figure 7.2
Sum Dialog Box

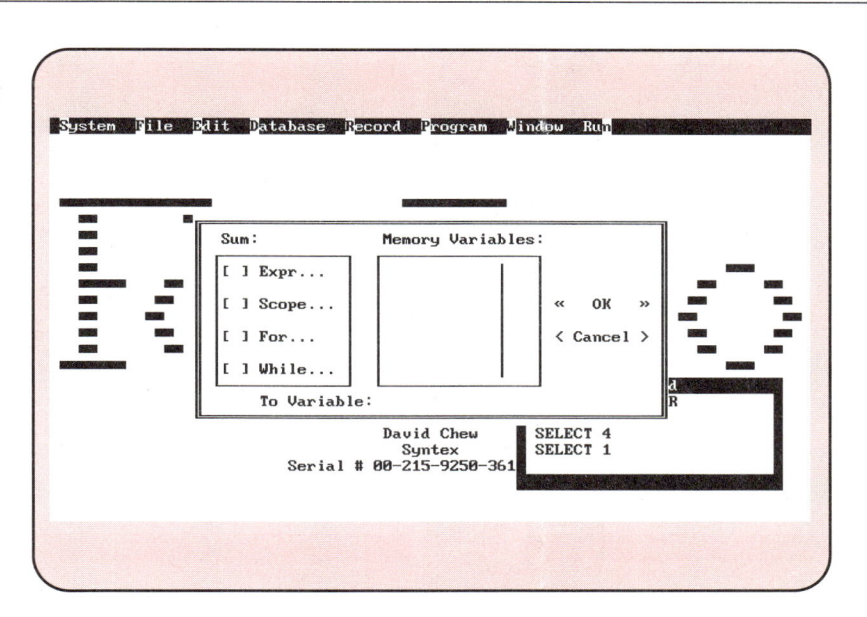

Press	SHIFT - TAB three times, ↵ ENTER	Selects OK button.
Press	SHIFT - TAB twice, ↵ ENTER	Selects OK button.

3 **Calculate the sum of all the pay rates for the employees in the Accounting department.**

Press	ALT , D , M	Selects Database, Sum.
Press	E	Selects EXPRESSION checkbox.
Press	SHIFT - TAB	Moves to Field Name list.
Press	↓ as needed, ↵ ENTER	Selects PAY_RATE.
Press	SHIFT - TAB three times, ↵ ENTER	Selects OK button.
Press	F	Selects FOR checkbox.
Press	SHIFT - TAB	Moves to Field Name list.
Press	↓ as needed, ↵ ENTER	Selects DEPARTMENT.
Press	CTRL - L	Selects Logical popup.
Press	↓ three times, ↵ ENTER	Selects = symbol.
Press	TAB as needed	Moves to Expression window.
Type	"Accounting"	

Your screen should look like Figure 7.3.

Topic 7: Calculating Statistics

Figure 7.3
Expression Dialog Box

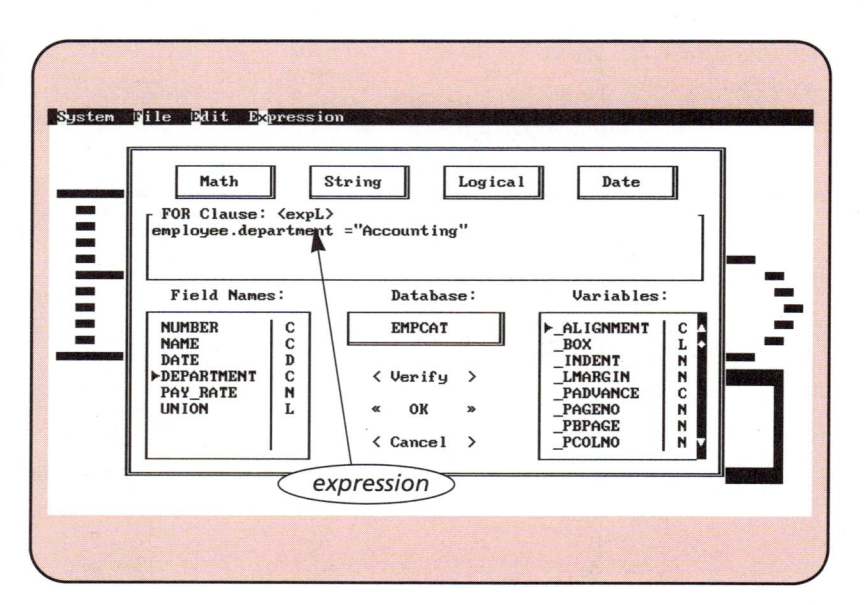

[Figure 7.3: Expression Dialog Box showing FOR Clause: <expL> with expression employee.department ="Accounting", with Field Names, Database (EMPCAT), and Variables lists]

Press	SHIFT - TAB three times, ← ENTER	Selects OK button.
Press	TAB three times, ← ENTER	Selects OK button.

4 Calculate the average pay rate for employees in the Accounting department.

Press	ALT, D, V	Selects Database, Average.
Press	E	Selects EXPRESSION checkbox.
Press	SHIFT - TAB	Moves to Field Name list.
Press	↓ as needed, ← ENTER	Selects PAY_RATE.
Press	SHIFT - TAB three times, ← ENTER	Selects OK button.
Press	F	Selects FOR checkbox.
Press	SHIFT - TAB	Moves to Field Name list.
Press	↓ as needed, ← ENTER	Selects DEPARTMENT.
Press	CTRL - L	Selects Logical popup.
Press	↓ three times, ← ENTER	Selects = symbol.
Press	TAB as needed	Moves to Expression window.
Type	"Accounting"	

56   *FoxPro*

Press	SHIFT - TAB three times, ↵ ENTER	Selects OK button.
Press	SHIFT - TAB three times, ↵ ENTER	Selects OK button.

PROCEDURE SUMMARY

COUNTING RECORDS

Select Database, Count.	ALT, D, O
Select FOR expression.	F
Enter any desired condition.	(your input)

CALCULATING A SUM

Select Database, Sum.	ALT, D, M
Enter the field to total in the expression.	E, (your input)
Select FOR expression.	F
Enter any desired condition.	(your input)

CALCULATING AN AVERAGE

Select Database, Average.	ALT, D, V
Enter the field to total in the expression.	E, (your input)
Select FOR expression.	F
Enter any desired condition.	(your input)

EXERCISES

1. Count the number of records in the CHECK database file.
2. Sum the check amount for all checks written.
3. Sum the amounts for the checks written for Household expenses.
4. Average the check amount for all checks written.
5. Average the check amount for all checks written for Entertainment.

Topic 7: Calculating Statistics

Checkpoint 1
What You Should Know

- ✓ An individual unit of information, such as an employee number or name, is called a **field**. A group of related fields is called a **record**. A collection of records is called a **file**. Sometimes **table**, **row**, and **column** are used in place of file, record, and field, respectively.

- ✓ In FoxPro, each individual file (table) is called a **database file**. Thus, in FoxPro, a database can actually be a collection of database files.

- ✓ **CHARACTER fields** may be used to store any printable character. **DATE fields** can only be used to store dates. **NUMERIC fields** can only be used to store numbers. Arithmetic operations can only be applied to NUMERIC fields. **LOGICAL fields** consist of a single value representing a true or false condition. They can hold only T (True), F (False), Y (Yes), or N (No). **MEMO fields** can be used to store large blocks of text such as words or sentences.

- ✓ The **menu** is where you begin your work. A menu is a list of actions from which you can choose. Each **menu pad** contains **menu popups**.

- ✓ To use menus, press the ALT key. Use the LEFT and RIGHT ARROWs to move from one menu to another. Use the UP and DOWN ARROWs to move from one selection within a menu to another. When you have the choice you want highlighted, press ENTER.

- ✓ The **system prompt** is a mode of operating with FoxPro in which a single dot, called the **dot prompt**, appears in the **Command window**. FoxPro automatically defaults to the Command window on startup and returns to the Command window when a menu task is completed.

- ✓ To exit FoxPro, select ALT, File, Quit.

- ✓ To get help, use the F1 key.

- ✓ To create a database file, select ALT, File, New, Database and describe each of the fields that make up the database file. When done, select the OK button and indicate the name of the database file you have created.

- ✓ To add or change records, select the Database, Change command from the menu. You then open the Change window. The Browse menu allows you to move between the Change and Browse windows. If the file contains no records, you will automatically be adding records. If the file contains records, you will be editing existing records. To add new ones, select the Record, Append command.

- ✓ To move between records when entering or editing data, use the PAGE UP and PAGE DOWN keys if you are on the Change window.

- ✓ A **backup copy** of a database file is a copy that is made and stored as a safety measure. If problems occur in the database file that is actively being used, called the **live copy**, copying the backup version over the live version returns the database file to the state it was in when the backup was made.

- ✓ You can make a backup copy of a database file by using the System, Filer command within FoxPro. In the event of a problem, you can copy the backup copy over the live version by using a similar System, Filer command.
- ✓ To open a database file, select ALT, File, Open. Make sure that "Database" is displayed in the file type popup.
- ✓ To access select data in a database, create a **query** by selecting ALT, Run, New Query and then indicating the conditions that the records you want must satisfy. Optionally you can select to include only certain fields using the Select Fields checkbox.
- ✓ The **RQBE window** contains a conditions list in which you select the records to be found in the query and several checkboxes in which you indicate the output, ordering, and grouping of the fields in the query. To move within a window, press TAB to move clockwise and SHIFT-TAB to move counterclockwise. Use the UP ARROW and DOWN ARROW keys to move within selections.
- ✓ To see the results of a query, select the DO QUERY push button. In technical terms, you are **applying** the query.
- ✓ To print the results of a query, select Report/Label from the Output To popup. Select Quick Report under the Display Options dialog box.
- ✓ To change the outputted field in a query, choose the Select Fields checkbox. Move or remove fields from the Selected Output list.
- ✓ A **simple condition** consists of a single field, an operator, and a single value or example. To enter a simple condition, complete the information in the conditions list.
- ✓ To enter a **compound condition** using AND, enter the second condition on the next line. Continue to add AND conditions by entering them on the remaining lines in the conditions list.
- ✓ To enter a compound condition using OR, enter the first condition and select the OR push button before entering the second condition.

Review Questions

1. How do you load FoxPro?
2. How do you select an option from a menu?
3. How do you escape from some task you have begun? Why might you want to do so?
4. How do you exit FoxPro?
5. How do you get help on some specific option?
6. How do you create a database file? Describe the rules for naming a database file. How do you assign a field type? Describe the possible field types.
7. How do you activate a database file? Why must you do so?
8. Which option do you use to add records to a database file? How do you indicate that you are finished adding records?

9. How do you change records in a database file? How can you move to a record you need to change?
10. How do you delete records from a database file? When are records permanently removed from a database file?
11. How do you list records in a database file?
12. How do you make a backup copy? Why should you do so?
13. How do you restore a database file from a backup copy?
14. How do you display all the records in a database file?
15. How can you include only certain fields in a display?
16. How can you create a condition to limit the records included in a display?
17. How can you use a LOGICAL field in a condition?
18. How can you use a DATE field in a condition?
19. How can you find the records that contain a particular string of characters in some field?
20. How can you find records if you only want those between a range of dates?
21. How do you combine simple conditions with AND?
22. How do you combine simple conditions with OR?
23. How would you count the records in a database file that satisfy some condition?
24. How do you calculate a sum?
25. How do you calculate an average?

CHECKPOINT EXERCISES

You are to create a database file to store information about a music library. The music is on cassette tape (CS), long-playing records (LP), or compact disk (CD), as indicated by the entry under the heading TYPE. A list of available music and field characteristics is as follows. The date field represents the date the music was obtained.

NAME	NAME	ARTIST	TYPE	COST	CATEGORY
02/22/91	Greatest Hits	Panache, Milo	LP	8.95	Classical
02/15/91	America	Judd, Mary	CS	5.95	Vocal
01/02/91	Rio Rio	Duran, Ralph	LP	8.95	Rock
02/15/91	Passione	Panache, Milo	LP	6.99	Classical
01/02/91	Country Hill	Lager, Ricky	CD	11.95	Country
02/22/91	Rockin'	Brady, Susan	CS	5.95	Rock
02/22/91	Pardners	Hudson, Randy	CS	5.95	Country
01/02/91	Private Love	Toner, Arlene	CD	11.95	Vocal
02/22/91	Moods	Silver, Sandy	CD	11.95	Rock

Checkpoint 1

FIELD DESCRIPTION	FIELD NAME	FIELD TYPE	WIDTH	DECIMAL POSITIONS
DATE	DATE	DATE	8	
MUSIC NAME	NAME	CHARACTER	14	
ARTIST	ARTIST	CHARACTER	14	
TYPE	TYPE	CHARACTER	2	
COST	COST	NUMERIC	5	2
CATEGORY	CATEGORY	CHARACTER	9	

Perform the following tasks:

1. Insert your data disk into drive A and then load FoxPro.
2. Create the database file. Use the name MUSIC for the database file.
3. Enter the six fields in the preceding table.
4. Enter the preceding data. When you enter the third record, enter the name as Reeo Reeo and the price as 9.85.
5. After you have entered the records, enter two additional records. You may make up whatever entries you want for the fields in these records.
6. Type LIST TO PRINT in the Command window to print a list of all the data.
7. Correct the third record by changing the name to Rio Rio and the price to 8.95.
8. Delete one of the extra records that you added. Permanently remove the record from the database file.
9. Type LIST TO PRINT in the Command window to print a list of all the data.
10. Make a backup copy of this database file. Call it MUSICBCK.DBF.
11. Open the database file so that it can be accessed.
12. Display all the fields and all the records.
13. Display the Name of the Music, Artist, Type, and Cost.
14. Display the music Category first and then the other fields in the record.
15. Display the records for the music in the Classical category.
16. Display the records for all music that costs $5.95.
17. Display the records for the music performed by an artist named Susan.
18. Display the records for all music whose dates are between 1/1/92 and 1/16/92.
19. Display the records for all music on cassette tape (CS in Type).
20. Display the records for all music on compact disk (CD in type). Include the Type, Music Name, Artist, and Cost.
21. Display the records for all the music by the artist Milo Panache.

22. Display the records for all music that is in the Classical category and costs less than 8.95.
23. Display the records for all music that is in the Rock category and costs less than 8.95.
24. Display the Artist name and the Name of the music for all the Rock category that is unavailable on cassette tape.
25. Count the number of records in the database file.
26. Count the number of music selections in the Vocal category.
27. Sum the total cost of all types of music.
28. Sum the total cost of the music in the Country category.
29. Determine the average cost for types of music in the Country category.

TOPIC 8

Locating a Record

CONCEPTS Before you can work on a record, you must be positioned on it. With small database files, you can usually find the records you want by pressing PAGE UP or PAGE DOWN while you are on the Change window. For large databases, this is very impractical. You would like to be able to easily locate a record just by knowing some condition that the record must satisfy.

Locating a Record That Satisfies a Condition

Remember that you can change the record pointer on the Change window by pressing PAGE UP (to move back to the previous record) and PAGE DOWN (to move to the next one). However, unless you only need to move a record or two, this method can be very cumbersome. It is quicker to use the Record, Goto dialog box (Figure 8.1). The first option of the dialog box, "Top," moves you directly to the first record in the database file. The next option, "Bottom," moves you to the last record. If you pick the third option, "Record," FoxPro asks you for the number of the record to which you want to move. When you enter the number you want, you are taken directly to that record. The fourth option, "Skip," allows you to specify some number of records that you want FoxPro to bypass.

What if you don't know the record number of the record you want? What if you only know something about the record? For example, suppose you want to make some change to the data for employee 1016, but you don't know where this employee is located in the file. This is where the Record, Locate option can be very helpful. It allows you to locate a record on the basis of some condition.

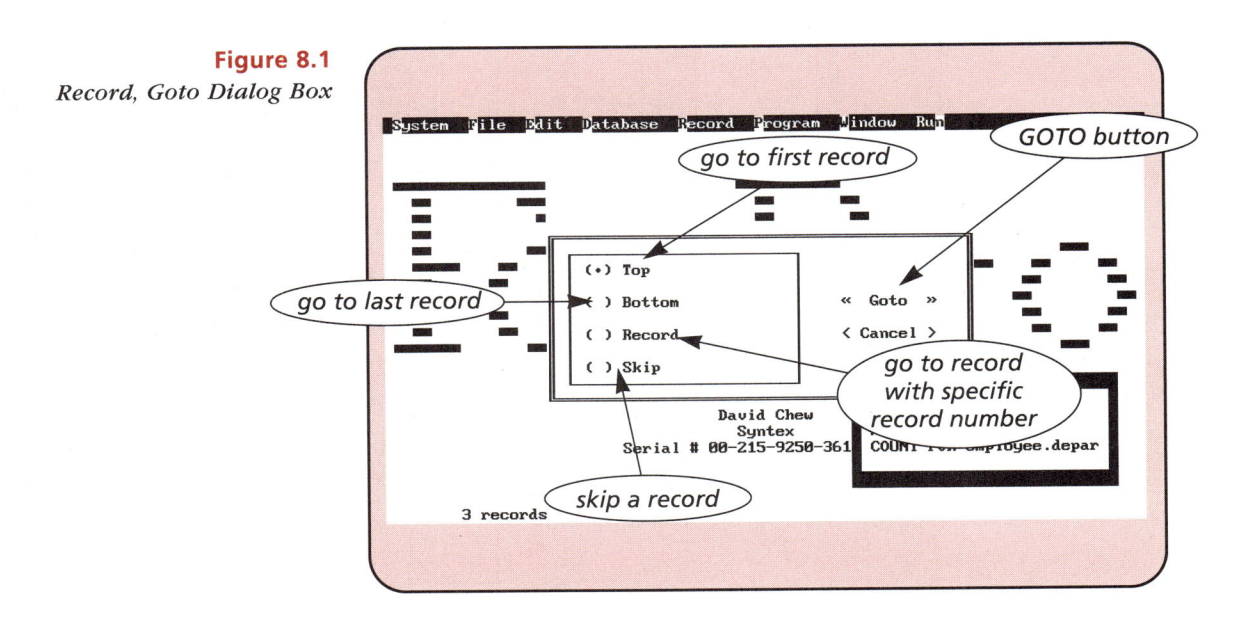

Figure 8.1
Record, Goto Dialog Box

Topic 8: Locating a Record

65

> **TIP** You can press CTRL-K in place of the Record, Continue option.

Finding the Next Record That Satisfies a Condition

(68)

In some cases, you may not want the first record meeting a condition. You may want the second or the third or the tenth. For example, you may want to find the second employee in the Accounting department, or you may want to step through all employees in the Accounting department, one after the other. To do so, you use the Record, Locate option to find the first one. After you have done that, you can use the Record, Continue option to find the next one. ◀

TUTORIAL In this tutorial, you use the Record, Locate command to find records that satisfy certain conditions.

1 Locate the employee whose number is 1016.

| Open | EMPLOYEE | unless already activated. |
| Press | ALT, R, L, F | Selects Record, Locate, For. |

You are then asked to enter a search expression, that is, the particular value you are looking for (Figure 8.2).

Figure 8.2
Search Expression

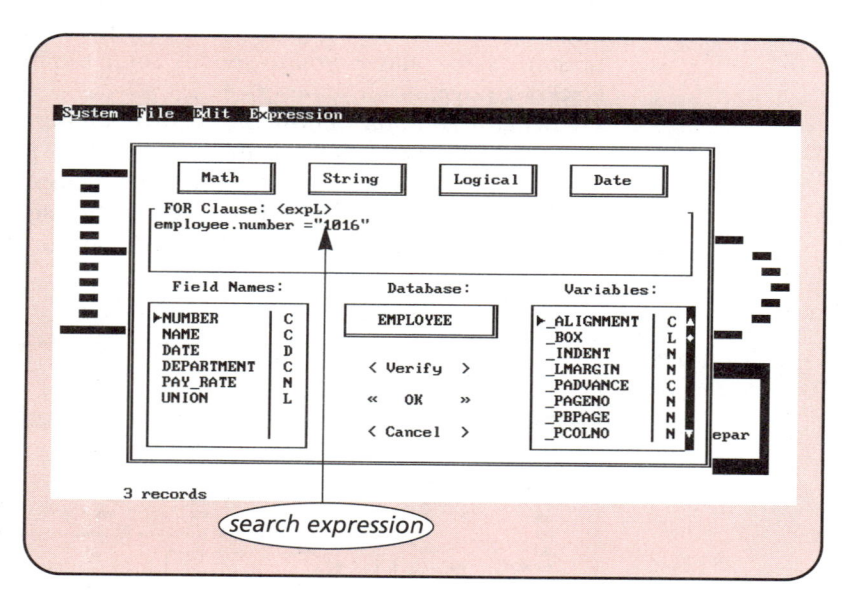

Press	SHIFT-TAB	Highlights NUMBER field of Field Name list.
Press	← ENTER	Inserts NUMBER field in Expression window.
Press	CTRL-L	Logical operators appear in popup list.

66

FoxPro

Press	↓ as needed	Selects = symbol.
Type	'1016'	
Press	SHIFT - TAB three times, ↵ ENTER	Selects OK button.
Press	TAB twice, ↵ ENTER	Selects LOCATE button.

FoxPro then locates this employee for you (Figure 8.3). FoxPro searches only the field that you included in the locate expression.

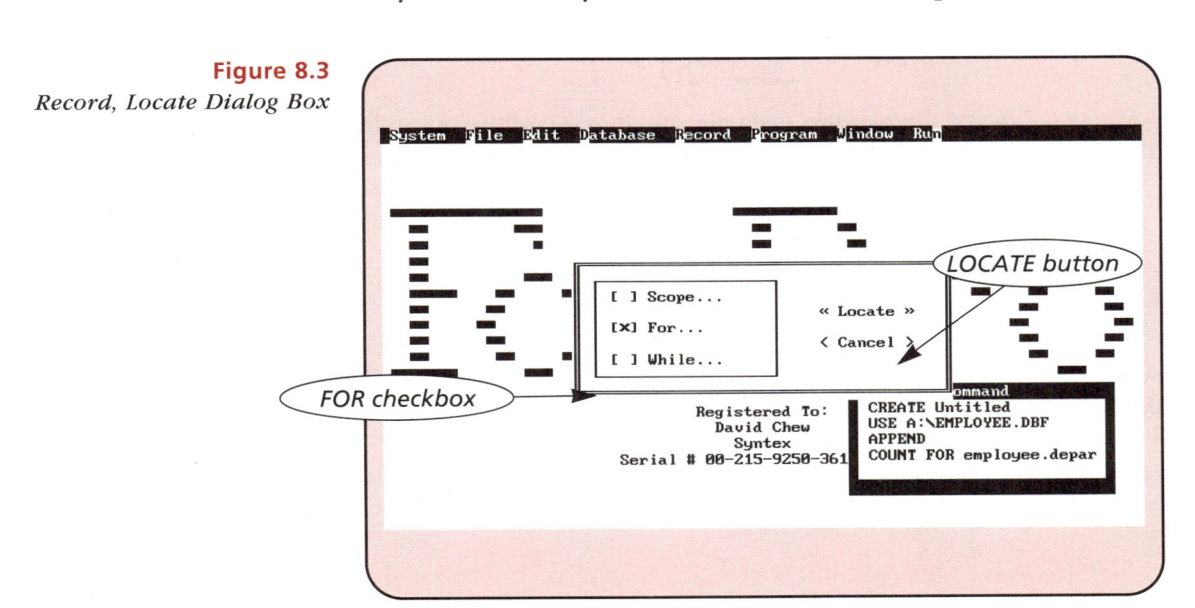

Figure 8.3
Record, Locate Dialog Box

2 Locate the first employee in the Accounting department. Make sure you are at the beginning of the EMPLOYEE database file. (If not, select the Record, Goto, Top command.)

Open	EMPLOYEE	unless already activated.
Press	ALT, R, L, F	Selects Record, Locate, For.
Press	SHIFT - TAB	Moves pointer to Field Name list.
Press	↓ as needed	Highlights DEPARTMENT.
Press	↵ ENTER	Inserts DEPARTMENT field in Expression window.
Press	CTRL - L	Opens Logical operator popup.
Press	↓ as needed, ↵ ENTER	Selects = symbol.

Topic 8: Locating a Record **67**

Press	"Accounting"	
Press	SHIFT - TAB three times, ↵ ENTER	Selects OK button.
Press	TAB twice, ↵ ENTER	Selects LOCATE button.

FoxPro then locates the first employee in the Accounting department.

3 **Locate the next employee in the Accounting department.**

Press	ALT, R, C	Selects Record, Continue.

FoxPro uses the previous search string to locate the next employee in the Accounting department. If there are no more employees in the Accounting department, FoxPro moves you back to the first employee in the department.

PROCEDURE SUMMARY

LOCATING A RECORD THAT SATISFIES A CONDITION

Select Record, Locate, For.	ALT, R, L, F
Select the search field.	SHIFT - TAB, ↓ (as needed), ↵ ENTER
Select the operator.	CTRL-M, CTRL-L, CTRL-S, or CTRL-D
Move to the Expression window.	TAB or SHIFT - TAB (as needed)
Enter the value for which you want to search.	(your input)

FINDING THE NEXT RECORD THAT SATISFIES A CONDITION

Select Record, Continue.	ALT, R, C

EXERCISES

1. Use the CHECK database file and the Record, Locate command to find the check whose number is 110.
2. Use the Record, Locate command to find the first check in the CHECK database file written for Food.
3. Use the appropriate option to locate the next check written for Food.

TOPIC 9

Using the Browse Window

CONCEPTS You can add, change, and delete records using the Change window. On the Change window, you see a few records at a time, depending on the size of your window. Sometimes you might prefer to see several records at a time, presented in the form of a list.

Updating Records with the Browse Window

To edit data in list form, use the Browse window rather than the Change window. The number of records displayed in a Browse window may vary depending the size of the window (Figure 9.1).

The current active record is highlighted. You can move the highlight to any other record by pressing the DOWN ARROW or UP ARROW (which move one record), PAGE DOWN or PAGE UP (which move one windowful), or by using the Record, Goto command. Once you have moved to the record to be changed, you then move the cursor to the field to be changed. You can move the cursor one field to the right by pressing the TAB key and one field to the left by pressing SHIFT-TAB. You can then edit the information.

Figure 9.1
Browse Window

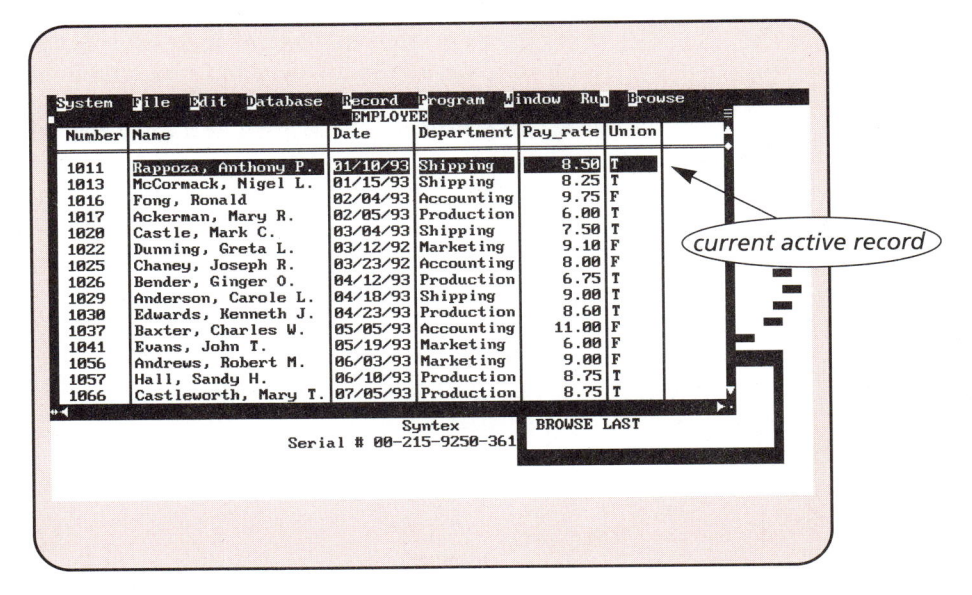

Adding Records with the Browse Window

71

While you are using the Browse window to view your records, you may decide to add new records. This can be done by selecting the Browse, Append Record command or pressing CONTROL-N. A blank record is added to the end of the database.

TUTORIAL In this tutorial, you use the Browse window to update records.

1 **Change Ginger Bender's pay rate to $7.00.**

Open	EMPLOYEE	as done previously.
Press	ALT, D, B	Selects Database, Browse; opens Browse window.
Press	↓ or PAGE DOWN as needed	Moves to Ginger Bender's record.
Press	TAB four times	Moves to PAY_RATE.
Type	7.00	Changes pay rate.
Press	ALT, F, C	Selects File, Close; closes Browse window. ◄

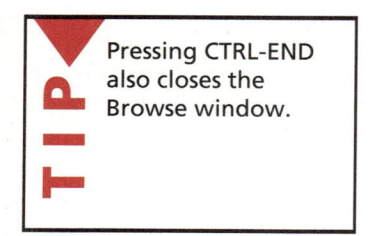

> **TIP:** Pressing CTRL-END also closes the Browse window.

The change is then saved, and you are returned to the Command window. If you needed to make changes to several records, you would probably want to make all the changes before exiting.

2 **Add Andrea Thompson as a new record.**

Press	ALT, D, B	Selects Database, Browse; opens Browse window.
Press	CTRL-N	Adds a new record to end of list.
Type	1070	
Press	TAB	Accepts input; advances to NAME.
Type	Thompson, Andrea K.	
Press	TAB	Accepts input; advances to DATE.
Type	051693	
Press	TAB	Accepts input; advances to DEPARTMENT.

70 *FoxPro*

Type	Marketing	
Press	TAB	Accepts input; advances to PAY_RATE.
Type	10.25	
Press	TAB	Accepts input; advances to UNION.
Type	F	
Press	ALT, F, C	Selects File, Close; closes Browse window.

PROCEDURE SUMMARY

UPDATING RECORDS WITH THE BROWSE WINDOW

Select Database, Browse.	ALT, D, B
Move to the record to be changed.	↑, ↓, PAGE UP or PAGE DOWN
Move the cursor to the field to be changed.	TAB or SHIFT-TAB
Enter the new data.	(your input)
Make any other changes in the same manner.	(your input)
Close the Browse window.	ALT, F, C

ADDING RECORDS WITH THE BROWSE WINDOW

Select Database, Browse.	ALT, D, B
Add a new record.	ALT, B, N
Enter the new data.	(your input)
Accept the new data.	TAB
Close the browse window.	ALT, F, C

EXERCISES

1. Use the Browse window to change the amount for check 102 to $95.00.
2. Use the Browse window to change the payee for check 108 to Amble Inn. In addition, change the amount to $25.00 and change TAXDED to false.
3. List all the records in the CHECK database file.

Topic 9: Using the Browse Window

TOPIC 10

Using Conditions to Change Records

CONCEPTS The Change and Browse windows allow you to make changes to the data in a database file by moving to the appropriate field in the appropriate record and then typing the new data. In some cases, you might need to make the same change to all the records that satisfy some condition. It would be very cumbersome to use the Change or Browse windows and make all these changes individually. It would be far more convenient to specify a condition that identifies the record or records to be changed and then simply indicate the new values.

Using the Record, Replace Command

Fortunately, by using the Record, Replace command, you can update a database file in this fashion. To illustrate the benefits to this approach, suppose you needed to give each employee in the Marketing department a 50-cent raise. To do so using the Change window or the Browse window, you would need to move through the entire EMPLOYEE database file. Whenever you came to an employee with the value "Marketing" in the DEPARTMENT field, you would need to move the cursor to the PAY_RATE field, calculate what the new pay rate should be, and then type the new value. By contrast, with the Record, Replace command, you only need to enter a condition that identifies the records to be updated and then enter the replacement value.

The replacement value you enter can be a specific number (like 6.75) or an expression (like PAY_RATE + .50). Such expressions can involve + (addition), − (subtraction), * (multiplication), or / (division).

TUTORIAL In this tutorial, you use the Record, Replace command to change all the records that satisfy some condition.

1 **Use a condition to change the pay rate of employee 1026 (Helen Bender) from 7.00 back to 6.75.** This reverses the change you made earlier.

Press	ALT, F, O	Displays File Open dialog box.
Select	EMPLOYEE	
Press	↵ ENTER	Opens EMPLOYEE file.
Press	ALT, R, P	Selects Record, Replace.

Topic 10: Using Conditions to Change Records 73

The Replace dialog box appears. (Figure 10.1). Proceed by selecting the field that contains the data to be changed, defining the criteria for the records to be change, and defining the new replacement data.

Figure 10.1
Replace Dialog Box

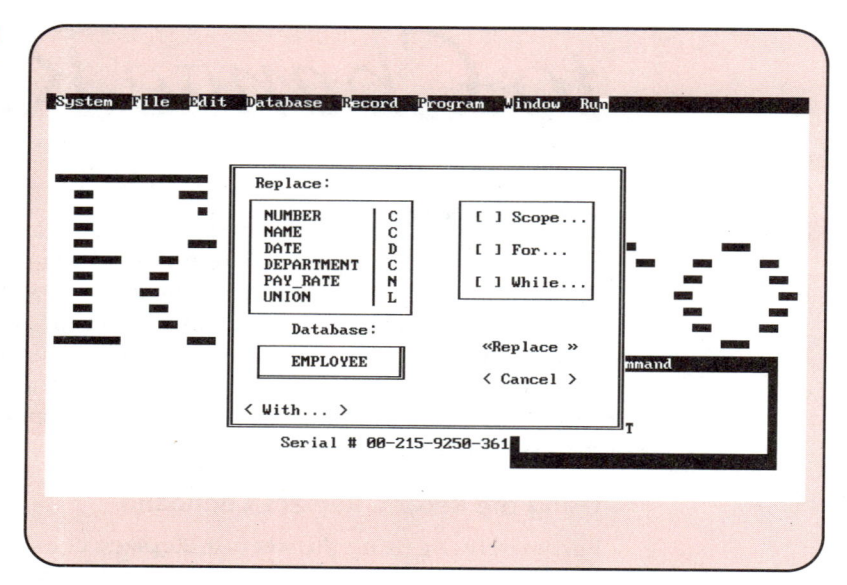

Press	↓ four times	Selects PAY_RATE.
Press	S , A	Selects Scope, All.
Press	SHIFT - TAB twice, ← ENTER	Returns to Replace dialog box.
Press	F	Builds FOR search expression.
Press	CTRL - F	Moves to Field Name list.
Press	← ENTER	Selects NUMBER as search field.
Press	CTRL - L	Logical function/operator popup appears.
Press	↓ three times, ← ENTER	Selects = symbol.
Type	"1026"	

Notice that the values for character fields must be enclosed in quotes.

Press	SHIFT - TAB three times	Highlights and selects OK button.
Press	T	Selects WITH expression dialog builder.
Type	6.75	

74

FoxPro

Press	SHIFT - TAB three times, ↵ ENTER	Highlights and selects OK button; returns to Replace dialog box.
Press	SHIFT - TAB three times, ↵ ENTER	Highlights REPLACE button.

Your update is made, and you should see the screen shown in Figure 10.2. The phrase, "REPLACE NEXT 1 employee" appears in the Command window. Also, the message, "1 replacements" appears in the Logon screen since only one record was replaced.

Figure 10.2
Replace Dialog Box

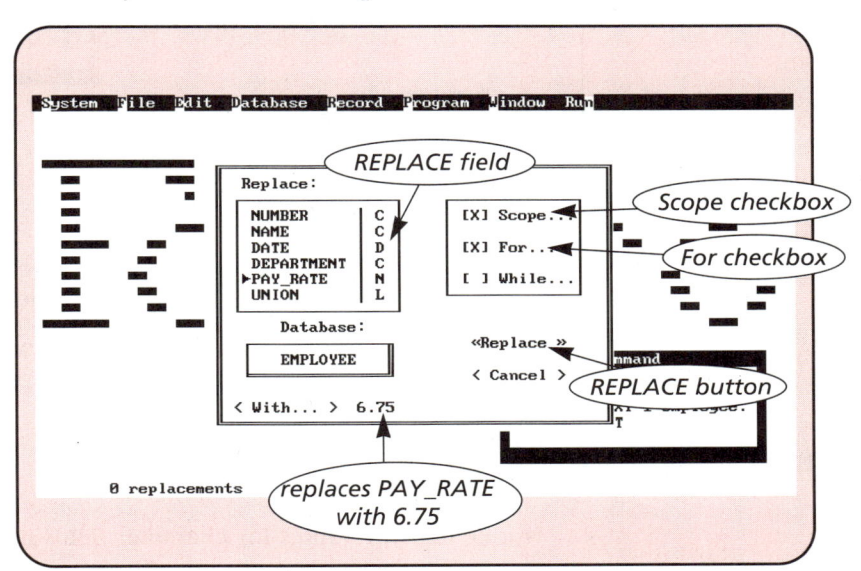

2 Give all Marketing department employees a 50 cent raise.

Press	ALT , R , P	Selects Record, Replace.

The Replace dialog box appears. (Figure 10.3). Proceed by selecting the field that contains the data to be changed, defining the criteria for the records to be change, and defining the new replacement data.

Press	↓ four times	Selects PAY_RATE.
Press	S , A	Selects Scope, All.
Press	SHIFT - TAB twice, ↵ ENTER	Returns to Replace dialog box.
Press	F	Builds FOR search expression
Press	CTRL - F	Moves to Field Name list.

Topic 10: Using Conditions to Change Records

Figure 10.3
Logon Screen

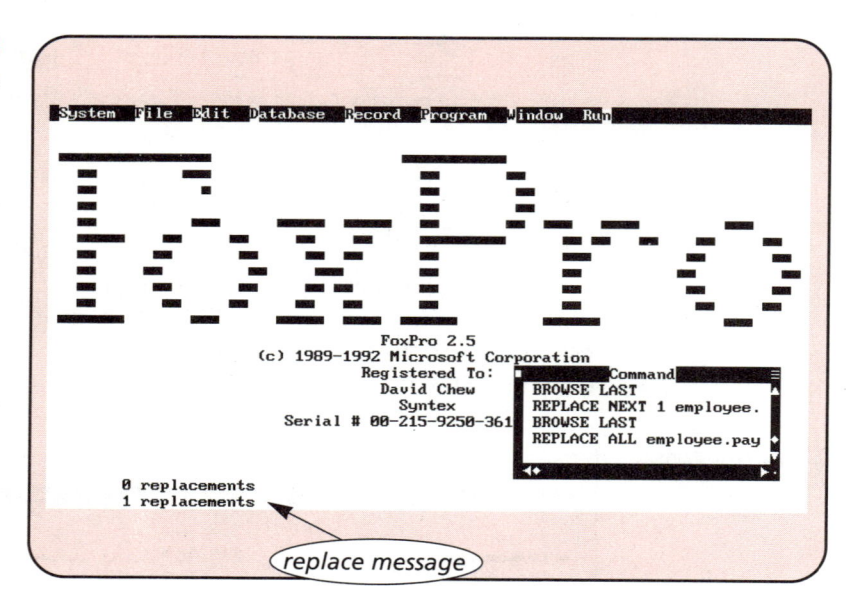

Press	↓ three times, ↵ ENTER	Selects DEPARTMENT as search field.
Press	CTRL-L	Logical function/operator popup appears.
Press	↓ three times, ↵ ENTER	Selects = symbol.
Type	"Marketing"	

Notice that the values for character fields must be enclosed in quotes.

Press	SHIFT-TAB three times	Highlights OK button.
Press	↵ ENTER	
Press	T	Selects WITH expression dialog builder.
Press	CTRL-F	Moves to Field Name list.
Press	↓ four times, ↵ ENTER	Selects PAY_RATE as search field.
Press	CTRL-M	Math function/operator popup appears.
Press	↓, ↵ ENTER	Selects + symbol.
Type	.50	
Press	SHIFT-TAB three times	Highlights OK button.

FoxPro

Press	⏎ ENTER		Returns to Replace dialog box.
Press	SHIFT - TAB	three times	Highlights REPLACE button.
Press	⏎ ENTER		

Returns to the Command window. Your update is made.

PROCEDURE SUMMARY

USING THE RECORD REPLACE COMMAND TO UPDATE RECORDS

Open the database file unless it is already open.	ALT , F , O
Select Record, Replace.	ALT , R , P
Select the replacement field.	↑ or ↓ (as needed)
Select the Scope clause.	S
Select the Scope range.	A , N , R , or T
Select a For or While clause.	F or W
Select the search field.	CTRL - F , ↑ or ↓ (as needed), ⏎ ENTER
Select the operator popup.	CTRL - M , CTRL - S , CTRL - L , or CTRL - D
Select the operator.	↑ or ↓ (as needed), ⏎ ENTER
Enter the search value.	(your input)
Select the OK button.	SHIFT - TAB three times, ⏎ ENTER
Enter the replacement expression.	T
Enter the replacement value or build an expression.	(your input)
Select the OK button.	SHIFT - TAB three times, ⏎ ENTER
Select the REPLACE button.	SHIFT - TAB three times, ⏎ ENTER

Topic 10: Using Conditions to Change Records

EXERCISES

1. Use the Record, Replace command to subtract $0.50 from the pay rate of all employees in the EMPLOYEE database who are in the Marketing department.
2. Use the Record, Replace command to change the check amount on check 105 in the CHECKS database to $24.75.
3. Use the Record, Replace command to add $1.00 to the amount of all checks written to Sav-Mor Groceries.
4. List all the records in the CHECK database file.

TOPIC 11

Deleting Records

CONCEPTS It is sometimes necessary to delete records from a file. For example, if an employee no longer works for the company, the employee's record should be removed (deleted) from the EMPLOYEE file. You have already seen how to delete records using the Change window by moving to the record to be marked and then pressing CONTROL-T. You can delete records on the Browse window in exactly the same way.

When you delete records from a database file using either of these options, the records are not actually removed from the file at that time. Instead, FoxPro merely marks them as being deleted. You must use the Pack command of the Database menu to physically remove these records from the file. Until you do so, the records are still in the file. FoxPro, however, indicates which records have been marked. When records are being edited and the current active record happens to be one that has been marked for deletion, dots appear along the left of the field names as in Figure 11.1.

Figure 11.1
Record Marked for Deletion

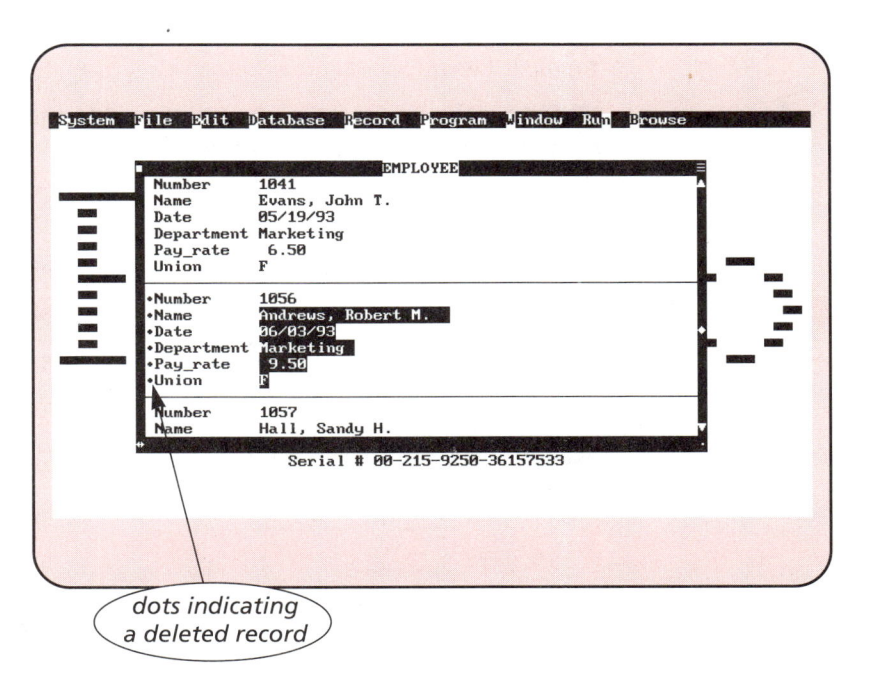

dots indicating a deleted record

Topic 11: Deleting Records

79

Using Conditions to Mark Records for Deletion [81]

Sometimes you need to delete all the records that satisfy a certain condition. For example, if you had a database file of orders placed by the customers of your organization, periodically you would want to delete all the orders that had been paid (that is, all orders on which the balance owed was zero). This process would certainly be cumbersome using the Change or the Browse window. Fortunately you can use the Record, Delete command to mark all the records that satisfy certain conditions. When you have marked all the records you want to delete, you can then select the appropriate option to permanently remove the marked records.

Using Conditions to Unmark Records [82]

Just as it is useful to have an option to mark all the records that satisfy a certain condition, it is also useful to have an option to unmark such records. This is especially important if you inadvertently create the wrong condition when you marked the records. You need an easy way to unmark them. Fortunately you can use the Record, Recall command to unmark all records satisfying certain conditions. Then such records will no longer be marked for deletion.

TUTORIAL

In this tutorial, you use the Record, Delete command to mark all the records that satisfy some condition for deletion. You also use the Record, Recall command to unmark records.

1 Use the Record, Delete command to mark the employee whose name is Robert M. Andrews for deletion.

Open	EMPLOYEE	unless already activated.
Press	ALT, R, D	Selects Record, Delete.
Press	S, A	Selects Scope, All.
Press	SHIFT-TAB twice, ↵ENTER	Returns to Delete dialog box.
Press	F	Builds For expression.
Press	CTRL-F, ↓, ↵ENTER	Selects NAME for search field.
Press	CTRL-L, ↓ three times, ↵ENTER	Selects = symbol.
Type	"Andrews, Robert M."	
Press	SHIFT-TAB three times, ↵ENTER	Selects OK button.
Press	TAB twice, ↵ENTER	Selects DELETE button.

Marks record for deletion. Returns to the Command window. Normally, if you only have a single record to delete, you can use either the Change or

Browse window. If you need to delete all the records that satisfy a certain condition (such as all the employees in a given department), the Record, Delete command is ideal.

2 **Use the Record, Recall command to unmark the record on which the employee name is Robert M. Andrews.**

Press	ALT , R , R	Selects Record, Recall.
Press	S , A	Selects Scope, All.
Press	SHIFT - TAB twice, ↵ ENTER	Returns to Recall dialog box.
Press	F	Builds For expression.
Press	CTRL - F , ↓ , ↵ ENTER	Selects NAME for search field.
Press	CTRL - L , ↓ three times, ↵ ENTER	Selects = symbol.
Type	"Andrews, Robert M."	
Press	SHIFT - TAB three times, ↵ ENTER	Selects OK button.
Press	TAB twice, ↵ ENTER	Selects RECALL button.

Returns to the Command window.

PROCEDURE SUMMARY

USING CONDITIONS TO MARK RECORDS FOR DELETION

Open the database file unless it is already open.	ALT , F , O
Select Records, Delete.	ALT , R , D
Select the Scope clause.	S
Select the Scope range.	A , N , R , or T
Select For or While.	F or W
Select the delete field.	CTRL - F , ↑ or ↓ (as needed), ↵ ENTER
Select the operator popup.	CTRL - M , CTRL - S , CTRL - L , or CTRL - D

Topic 11: Deleting Records

Select the operator.	`↑` or `↓` (as needed), `↵ ENTER`
Enter the delete value.	(your input)
Select the OK button.	`SHIFT`-`TAB` three times, `↵ ENTER`
Select the DELETE button.	`TAB` twice, `↵ ENTER`

USING CONDITIONS TO UNMARK RECORDS

Open the database file unless it is already open.	`ALT`, `F`, `O`
Select Records, Recall.	`ALT`, `R`, `R`
Select the Scope clause.	`S`
Select the Scope range.	`A`, `N`, `R`, or `T`
Select For or While.	`F` or `W`
Select the recall field.	`CTRL`-`F`, `↑` or `↓` (as needed), `↵ ENTER`
Select the operator popup.	`CTRL`-`M`, `CTRL`-`S`, `CTRL`-`L`, or `CTRL`-`D`
Select the operator.	`↑` or `↓` (as needed), `↵ ENTER`
Enter the recall value.	(your input)
Select the OK button.	`SHIFT`-`TAB` three times, `↵ ENTER`
Select the RECALL button.	`TAB` twice, `↵ ENTER`

EXERCISES

1. Use the Record, Delete command to mark all checks written to Sav-Mor Groceries for deletion.
2. Use the Record, Recall command to unmark all checks written to Sav-Mor Groceries.
3. Use the Change window to mark check 111 for deletion.
4. Use the Browse window to mark check 110 for deletion.
5. Pack the CHECK database file.
6. List all the records in the CHECK database file.

TOPIC 12

Creating and Using a Custom Screen

CONCEPTS You have already used the Change window to add new records to a database file and to change existing records. When you did, you used a window on the screen to enter data. Although the window did provide you with some assistance in the task, the window was not particularly attractive or helpful. The fields were simply stacked on top of each other. The names shown on the window were the names of the fields, which are not as descriptive as they might be.

In this section, you see how to create custom screens like the one shown in Figure 12.1. Notice that the names that appear in front of the fields (often called **prompts** since they prompt the user to enter a particular item of data) are more descriptive and that the prompts and fields are located near the center of the screen. FoxPro also allows you to generate graphic buttons for manuevering through records using a mouse or the keyboard.

Figure 12.1
Change Window

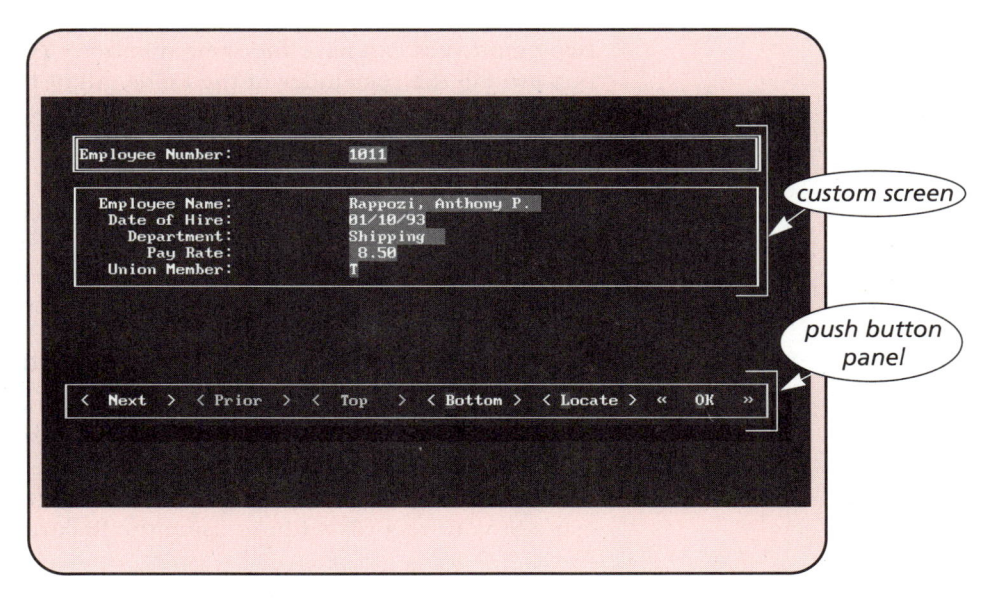

custom screen

push button panel

Topic 12: Creating and Using a Custom Screen   83

Creating an Initial Screen [93]

The simplest way to begin creating custom screens is to let FoxPro create an initial screen for you. To do so, you use a special option called "Quick screen." This option creates an initial screen that looks exactly like the one you normally see when you use the Change window. You then modify this screen, gradually transforming it into the one you want.

Adding Blank Lines [94]

One way to improve the appearance of a screen is to add blank lines. This helps related fields to be seen together and unrelated fields to be separated.

Changing the Prompts [94]

Making the prompts more descriptive is another way to improve a screen. The prompt "Employee number:" is more descriptive, for example, than "NUMBER." The user has a clearer idea of what to enter.

Repositioning Fields and Prompts [94]

Often a screen looks better if the contents are approximately centered on the screen. This requires repositioning the fields and prompts. Unlike other databases, FoxPro offers a more **object-oriented approach** to designing a screen. Each field and prompt is treated as an object that can be moved freely anywhere in the window using the cursor keys or a mouse, if available.

Adding Boxes [95]

Boxes can often improve the look of a screen. For example, you could place a double box around the primary key to emphasize its special nature. (The primary key is the field that uniquely identifies a record. The employee number field, for example, in the EMPLOYEE database file is the primary key since no two employees can have the same number.) You could then place a single box around the remainder of the fields. All of these features combine to give the screen a much more pleasing appearance.

Saving a Screen [95]

When you have completed the design of the screen, you need to save your work. If, by some chance, you do not like the screen you have created, you can instead abandon your work. If you choose this option, all your work will be lost. You could then begin designing the screen again from scratch.

Generating Screen Code and Using a Screen [95]

To use a screen you have created, you must first open the database file. Then you must also open the screen. When you finish the screen, it must be generated into a **screen code file**. The database file contains the FoxPro program code used for generating the screen. Through the Run, Forms command, you can edit your records without using the Record, Change command.

Modifying a Screen

96

You can modify a screen design at any time. You make any changes to the design in the same way you did when you created the design in the first place. When you have finished, save the changes. You must regenerate the screen code each time you make a change in your screen.

TUTORIAL In this tutorial, you create a custom screen. You then use the screen to update records.

1 **Create an initial screen.** Begin creating the screen shown in Figure 12.1.

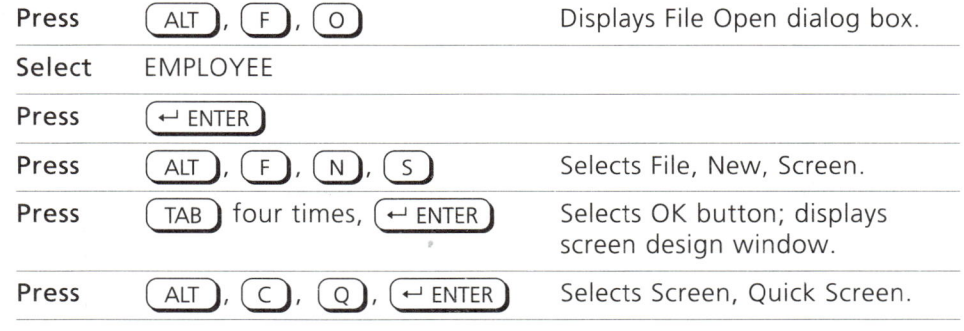

Press	ALT, F, O	Displays File Open dialog box.
Select	EMPLOYEE	
Press	ENTER	
Press	ALT, F, N, S	Selects File, New, Screen.
Press	TAB four times, ENTER	Selects OK button; displays screen design window.
Press	ALT, C, Q, ENTER	Selects Screen, Quick Screen.

> **TIP** Although the screen selected through Quick Screen looks exactly like the Change view, a column or tabular layout may also be chosen through the Quick Screen dialog box.

At this point, FoxPro creates the screen shown in Figure 12.2. It is precisely the screen you normally see on the Change window. You now modify this screen, gradually turning it into precisely what you want. ◀

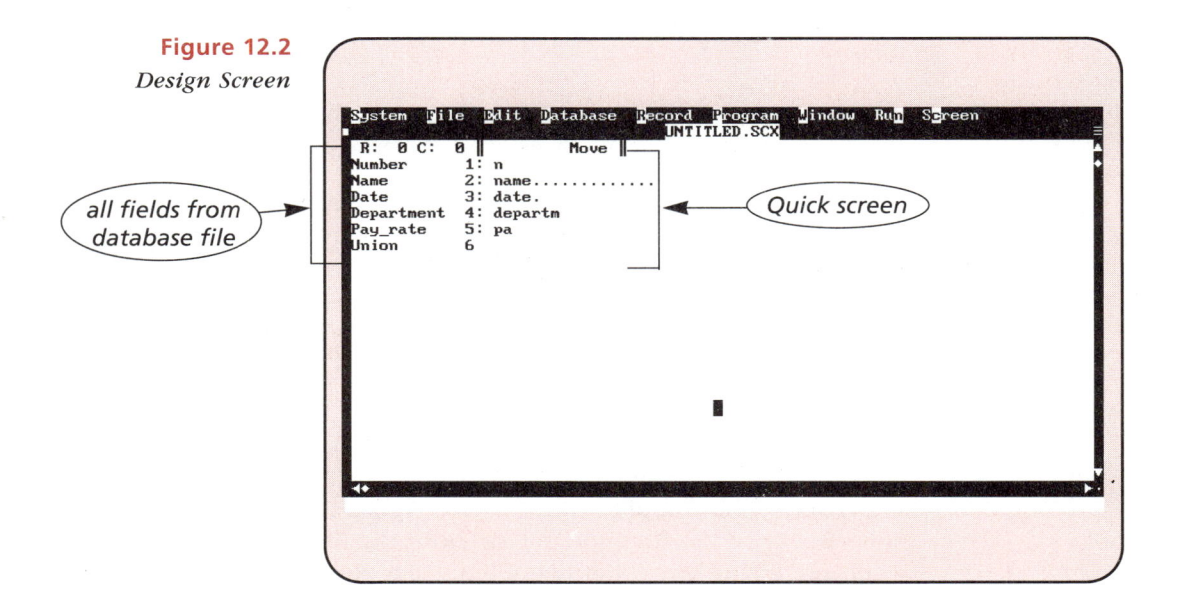

Figure 12.2
Design Screen

```
System File Edit Database Record Program Window Run Screen
                           UNTITLED.SCX
 R:  0 C:  0       Move
Number        1: n
Name          2: name............
Date          3: date.
Department    4: departm
Pay_rate      5: pa
Union         6:
```

all fields from database file →

← *Quick screen*

Topic 12: Creating and Using a Custom Screen   **85**

> **TIP:** You may also move objects by positioning mouse pointer over object and holding left mouse button down. Drag object to desired destination and release mouse button. Select multiple objects by holding SHIFT key down while clicking left mouse button once for each object to be moved. If prompts and fields are in a block (next to and below each other), you may select multiple objects by "rubberbanding" them. Position mouse pointer slightly above and to left of first field and hold left mouse button down while dragging to the right bottom corner of the selected objects. A "band" of dots surrounds objects. When you release the mouse button, all objects are highlighted. When all objects are selected, position mouse pointer over a selected object and hold left mouse button down while dragging all objects to desired destination.

2 Modify the EMPLOYEE screen by adding blank lines.

Press	SPACEBAR	Highlights Number field name indicating it is selected object.

Using the arrow keys, you can move the selected object anywhere in the window. This is done by pressing the SPACEBAR when the cursor is within an object. In order to select the other objects to be moved, hold down the SHIFT key and do not release it until all the objects have been selected. Each object is highlighted when selected.

Hold down	SHIFT	continuously for entire operation.
Press	↓ , SPACEBAR	Selects Name.
Press	↓ , SPACEBAR	Selects Date.
Press	↓ , SPACEBAR	Selects Department.
Press	↓ , SPACEBAR	Selects Pay_rate.
Press	↓ , SPACEBAR	Selects Union.
Release	SHIFT	
Press	HOME	Cursor returns to Number field name.

Your screen should now look like the one shown in Figure 12.3.

Hold down	SHIFT	continuously for entire operation.
Press	→ twelve times, SPACEBAR	Selects NUMBER field.
Press	↓ , SPACEBAR	Selects NAME field.
Press	↓ , SPACEBAR	Selects DATE field.
Press	↓ , SPACEBAR	Selects DEPARTMENT field.
Press	↓ , SPACEBAR	Selects PAY_RATE field.
Press	↓ , SPACEBAR	Selects UNION field.
Release	SHIFT	
Press	↓	Blank line appears at top.

Your screen should now look like Figure 12.4. You now add two blank lines between the first line (NUMBER in the figure) and the second (NAME). Feel free to add any other blank lines that you think enhance the look of your screen.

Figure 12.3
Design Screen

highlighted objects

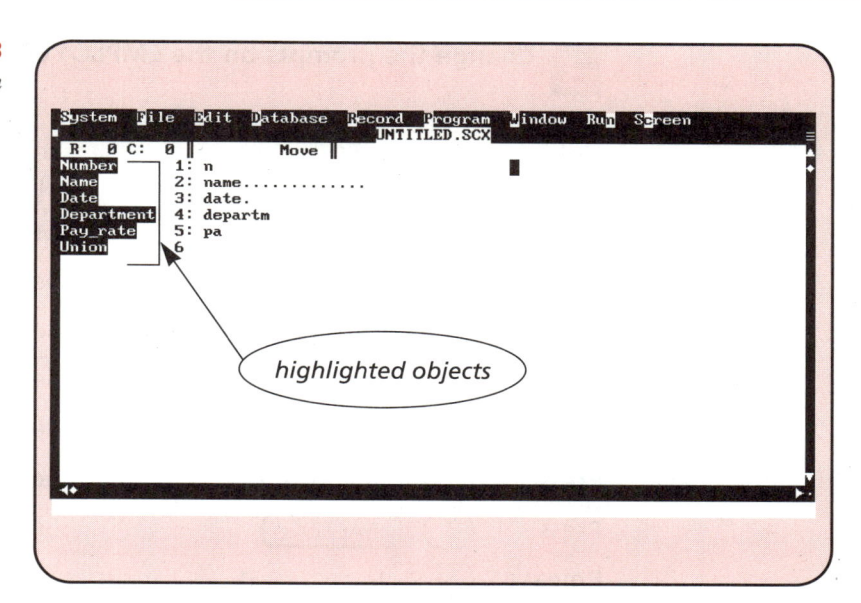

Figure 12.4
Design Screen

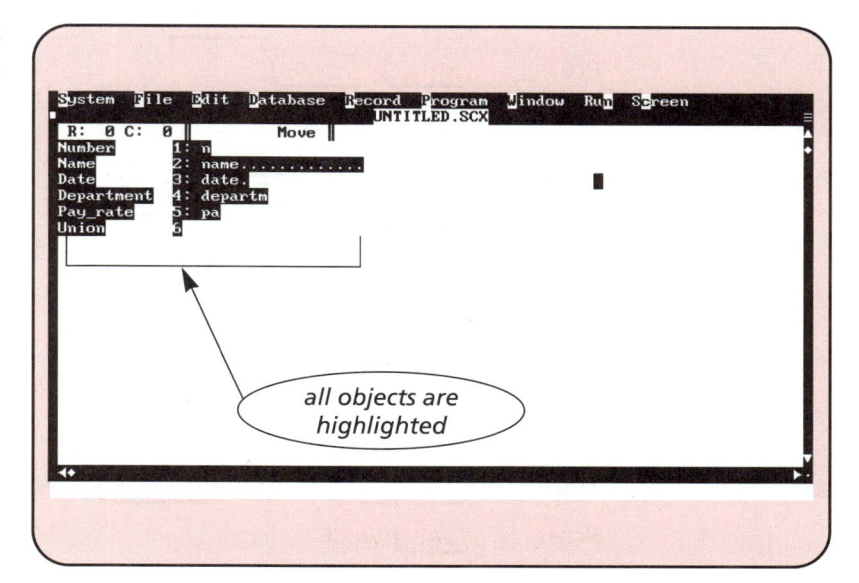

all objects are highlighted

Hold down	SHIFT	continuously for entire operation.
Press	HOME	Cursor returns to Number field name.
Press	SPACEBAR	Deselects Name prompt.
Press	→ twelve times, SPACEBAR	Deselects NUMBER field.
Release	SHIFT	
Press	↓ twice, ← ENTER	Two blank lines appear between Number and Name lines.

Topic 12: Creating and Using a Custom Screen   **87**

3 **Change the prompts on the EMPLOYEE screen.**

Hold down	`SHIFT`	continuously for entire operation.
Press	`TAB` twice	Moves to NUMBER field.
Press	`SPACEBAR`	Selects NUMBER field.
Press	`↓` three times, `SPACEBAR`	Selects NAME field.
Press	`↓`, `SPACEBAR`	Selects DATE field.
Press	`↓`, `SPACEBAR`	Selects DEPARTMENT field.
Press	`↓`, `SPACEBAR`	Selects PAY_RATE field.
Press	`↓`, `SPACEBAR`	Selects UNION field.
Release	`SHIFT`	
Press	`→` ten times, `↵ ENTER`	Moves fields to right.
Press	`CTRL`-`HOME`, `↓` three times	Moves to Number prompt.
Type	Employee `SPACEBAR`, `CTRL`-`→`, `:`, `↵ ENTER`	Revises prompt.
Press	`TAB` twice	Moves to Name prompt.
Type	Employee `SPACEBAR`, `CTRL`-`→`, `:`, `↵ ENTER`	Revises prompt.
Press	`TAB` twice	Moves cursor to Date prompt.
Press	`CTRL`-`→`	Moves to end of Date prompt.
Type	`SPACEBAR` of Hire: `↵ ENTER`	Revises prompt.
Press	`TAB` twice	Moves to Department prompt.
Press	`CTRL`-`→`, `:`, `↵ ENTER`	Revises prompt.
Press	`TAB` twice, `SPACEBAR`, `DELETE`	Moves cursor to Pay_rate prompt and deletes.
Type	Pay Rate: `↵ ENTER`	Creates new prompt.
Press	`TAB` twice	Moves cursor to Union prompt.
Type	`CTRL`-`→`, `SPACEBAR`, Member: `↵ ENTER`	Revises prompt.

4 Move the fields on the EMPLOYEE screen.

Press	CTRL - HOME , TAB twice	Moves cursor into NUMBER field.
Press	SPACEBAR	Selects field.
Hold down	SHIFT	continuously for entire operation.
Press	↓ three times, SPACEBAR	Selects NAME field.
Press	↓ , SPACEBAR	Selects DATE field.
Press	↓ , SPACEBAR	Selects DEPARTMENT field.
Press	↓ , SPACEBAR	Selects PAY_RATE field.
Press	↓ , SPACEBAR	Selects UNION field.
Release	SHIFT	
Press	→ ten times, ← ENTER	Moves fields to right.

Your screen should now look like the one shown in Figure 12.5.

Figure 12.5
Screen Layout Window

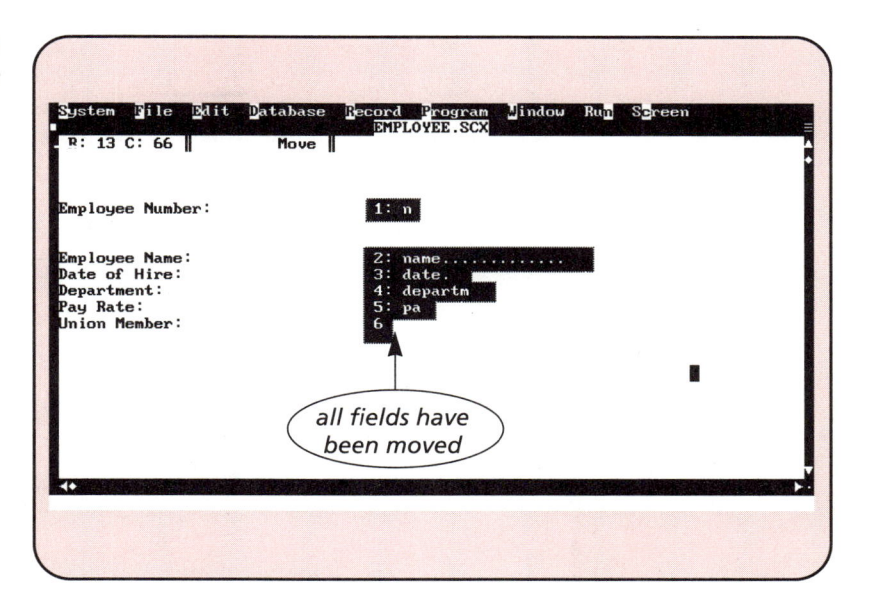

all fields have been moved

5 Reposition the prompts on the EMPLOYEE screen.

Press	SHIFT - TAB	Moves cursor to E in Employee Number.
Press	SPACEBAR	Selects prompt.
Press	→ four times, ← ENTER	Moves prompt.

Topic 12: Creating and Using a Custom Screen

Press	TAB twice	Moves cursor to E in Employee Name.
Press	SPACEBAR	Selects prompt.
Press	→ six times, ↵ ENTER	Moves prompt.
Press	TAB twice	Moves cursor to D in Date of Hire.
Press	SPACEBAR	Selects prompt.
Press	→ seven times, ↵ ENTER	Moves prompt.
Press	TAB twice	Moves cursor to D in Department.
Press	SPACEBAR	Selects prompt.
Press	→ nine times, ↵ ENTER	Moves prompt.
Press	TAB twice	Moves cursor to P in Pay Rate.
Press	SPACEBAR	Selects prompt.
Press	→ eleven times, ↵ ENTER	Moves prompt.
Press	TAB twice	Moves cursor to U in Union Member.
Press	SPACEBAR	Selects prompt.
Press	→ seven times, ↵ ENTER	Moves prompt.

Your screen should now look like Figure 12.6.

Figure 12.6
Design Screen

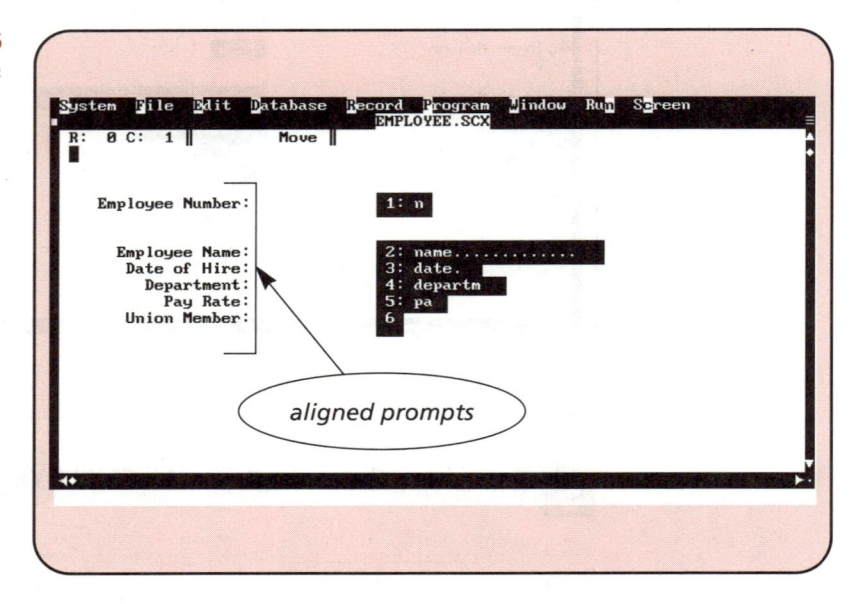

[Design screen showing aligned prompts: Employee Number, Employee Name, Date of Hire, Department, Pay Rate, Union Member]

6 **Add boxes to the EMPLOYEE screen.**

Press	ALT, F, O	Select File, Open.

> **TIP**
> The left corner of the design screen displays the row and column coordinates of your cursor position. Use this to position your box to column 74 rather than counting the number of times you press the RIGHT ARROW.

> **TIP**
> If you put the box in the wrong place, you can move the box. You can also delete the box and start over again if the size is incorrect. Move the box by placing your cursor on any border of the box and pressing SPACEBAR. Now move the box with the arrow keys and press ENTER. Delete the box by placing your cursor on any border of the box and pressing SPACEBAR. Press DELETE to remove the box.

Press	SHIFT - TAB twice, ← ENTER	Selects file type popup.
Press	↓ as needed, ← ENTER	Selects screen type.
Press	↓ as needed, ← ENTER	Selects EMPLOYEE.SCX file.
Press	→ three times, ↓ twice	Moves cursor to third column of line above line containing "Employee Number."
Press	CTRL - B	Selects box.
Press	↓, → seventy times	Moves cursor to 74th column of line below line containing "Employee Number." ◀
Press	← ENTER	Displays single line box.
Press	← ENTER	Displays Box Attribute dialog box.
Press	D, SHIFT - TAB three times	Changes box to double lines. ◀
Press	TAB, ← three times, ↑	Moves cursor to third column on line above "Employee Name."
Press	CTRL - B	Selects box.
Press	↓ five times, → seventy times	Moves cursor to 74th column on line below "Union Member."
Press	← ENTER	Displays single box.

See the previous tip if you make a mistake. Your screen should look like the one shown in Figure 12.7.

Figure 12.7
Design Screen

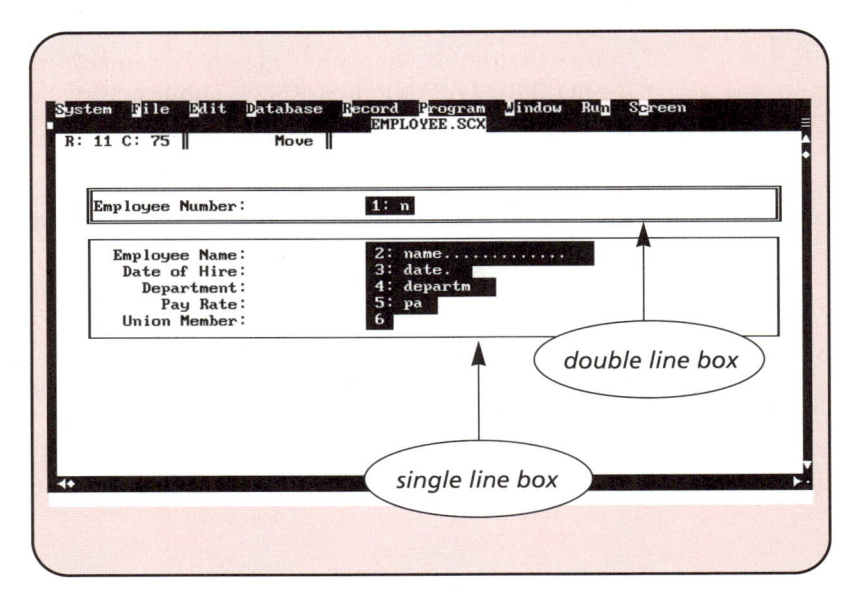

Topic 12: Creating and Using a Custom Screen   **91**

Press	ALT , F , C , Y		Selects File, Close, Yes.

7 **Save the screen.** Call the screen EMPLOYEE. This name emphasizes that it is a screen for the EMPLOYEE database.

Press	ALT , F , C	Selects File, Close.
Press	Y	Selects Yes to save screen.
Type	EMPLOYEE	Names screen.
Press	SHIFT - TAB twice, ← ENTER	Selects OK button.

A dialog box appears with the message, "Save environment information?" Selecting yes creates a view file that records all the open files, indexes, and relations that were being used during the screen design.

Type	N

You may wonder if giving a database file the same name as a screen could cause a problem. After all, both files are stored on your disk, and all the files stored on a disk must have unique names. Fortunately this is not a problem because the files are of different types, and consequently FoxPro assigns them different extensions. Thus, as far as DOS is concerned, they have different names.

8 **Open the screen file, generate the screen code, and use the screen you created.** Before you use a screen, you must generate the screen code. The screen code filename has an extension of .SPR. Also, your database file must be open. In this case, it should already be open because you activated it in the previous task. If it were not open, you would be prompted to open it when activating the screen. You need three files from your instructor for use with this exercise. These files are CONTROL1.SCX, CONTROL1.SCT, and BROWSER.SPR. Copy these files to the data subdirectory that holds your other files. You can also find these files in the \FOXPRO25\SAMPLE\SCREENS subdirectory.

Press	ALT , F , O	Select File, Open.

The screen type may already be selected from the last exercise.

Press	(arrow keys)	to select EMPLOYEE.
Press	← ENTER	Selects OK button.
Press	ALT , P , N	Selects Program, Generate.

A second screen, which handles the record manuevering through push buttons, is attached to the first screen.

Press	A	Selects Add.
Press	(arrow keys)	to highlight CONTROL1.
Press	← ENTER	to select CONTROL1.
Press	SHIFT - TAB twice	Moves to GENERATE button.
Press	← ENTER	Selects GENERATE button.

Now your screen code is generated. You may close the screen design window and activate your screen. Since no changes were made to the EMPLOYEE.SCX file, you may abort this screen.

Press	ESC	Aborts screen design window.
Press	ALT, W, R	Selects Windows, Clear; clears window.
Press	ALT, N, S	Selects Run, Screens.
Press	(arrow keys)	to select EMPLOYEE from file list.
Press	TAB three times, ← ENTER	Selects RUN button.

The normal FoxPro screen is replaced with your own custom screen (Figure 12.1). Notice that the screen being displayed is the one you created with the addition of graphic push buttons. You can use it to make changes as you did before. One advantage of this screen is that it offers different manuevering capabilities which can be integrated into a custom application.

Press	PAGE DOWN	Moves to push button panel.
Press	N	Moves to next record.
Press	I	Moves to previous record.
Press	B	Moves to last record.
Press	T	Moves to first record.
Press	O	Leaves screen and returns to Command window.

PROCEDURE SUMMARY

CREATING AN INITIAL SCREEN

Open the database file.	ALT, F, O
Create the new screen.	ALT, F, N, S, TAB four times, ← ENTER
Select Quick Screen from the Screen menu.	ALT, C, Q, ← ENTER

Topic 12: Creating and Using a Custom Screen

ADDING BLANK LINES

Open the database file.	
Select File and Open.	`ALT`, `F`, `O`
Move to TYPE button.	`TAB` six times
View TYPE list.	`ENTER`
Highlight DATABASE type.	(arrow keys)
Select DATABASE type.	`ENTER`
Select the filename.	(arrow keys)
Make any changes you want to make.	
Save the screen.	`ALT`, `F`, `C`, `Y`
Open the screen file.	
Select File and Open.	`F`, `O`
Move to TYPE button.	`TAB` six times
View TYPE list.	`ENTER`
Highlight SCREEN type.	(arrow keys)
Select SCREEN type.	`ENTER`
Select the filename.	(arrow keys)
Move to OK button.	`TAB` three times
Select the OK button.	`ENTER`
Highlight the fields starting at the position where the new line is to be inserted.	`SPACEBAR`
Move the highlighted fields down to open a line(s).	`↓` (as needed)
Save the screen.	`ALT`, `F`, `C`, `Y`

CHANGING THE PROMPTS

Move the cursor to the first letter in the prompt that is to be changed.	(arrow keys)
Delete the entry.	`DELETE`
Type the new prompt.	(your input), `ENTER`

REPOSITIONING FIELDS AND PROMPTS

To select a field:

Position the cursor within the field.	(arrow keys)
Select the field.	`SPACEBAR`

FoxPro

To select a prompt (or other character string):

Move the cursor into the prompt.	(arrow keys)
Select the prompt.	SPACEBAR

To reposition a field or prompt:

Select the field or prompt.	(your choice)
Move the cursor to the new position.	(arrow keys)
Complete the move.	ENTER

ADDING BOXES

Move the cursor to the upper left corner of the box.	(arrow keys)
Select the Box command.	CTRL - B
Move the cursor to the lower right corner of the box.	(arrow keys)
Select the lower right corner.	ENTER
Select the box attributes (single or double line).	ENTER, S or D
Move to the OK button.	TAB (as needed)
Select the OK button.	ENTER

SAVING A SCREEN

Save the new screen.	ALT, F, C, Y
If this is the first time you have saved your screen, type the name of the screen.	(your input)
Move to the OK button.	SHIFT - TAB twice, ENTER

GENERATING SCREEN CODE

Open the database file.	(your choice)
Open the screen file.	(your choice)
Select the Generate dialog box.	ALT, P, N
Add other screens.	A, (your input)
Start screen code generation.	SHIFT - TAB twice

Topic 12: Creating and Using a Custom Screen

USING A SCREEN

Clear the Logon screen.	`W`, `R`
Start the screen.	`N`, `S`, (your input)

MODIFYING A SCREEN

Open the database file.	
Select File and Open.	`ALT`, `F`, `O`
Move to TYPE button.	`TAB` six times
View TYPE list.	`ENTER`
Highlight DATABASE type.	(arrow keys)
Select DATABASE type.	`ENTER`
Select the filename.	(arrow keys)
Move to OK button.	`TAB` three times
Select the OK button.	`ENTER`
Open the screen file.	
Select File and Open.	`ALT`, `F`, `O`
Move to TYPE button.	`TAB` six times
View TYPE list.	`ENTER`
Highlight SCREEN type.	(arrow keys)
Select SCREEN type.	`ENTER`
Select the filename.	(arrow keys)
Move to OK button.	`TAB` three times
Select the OK button.	`ENTER`
Make any changes you want to make.	(your input)
Save the screen.	`ALT`, `F`, `C`, `Y`

EXERCISES

1. Create a screen for the CHECK database file that is similar to the screen you created for the EMPLOYEE database file. Call it CKFORM.

2. Generate the screen code file and run the screen. (Select the OK button of the push button panel to leave the screen once you have finished viewing it.)

TOPIC 13

Sorting a Database File

CONCEPTS Sometimes you would like to see the data in a database file in a particular order. It may be helpful, for example, to see the employees listed alphabetically by name. In another case, it might be better to see them in order of employee number, or, perhaps, in order of pay rate. In still another, you might prefer to see them in order of department, so that all the employees in the Accounting department appear first, then the employees in Marketing, and so on. You can accomplish this by sorting the database file. **Sorting** a database file means rearranging the records on the basis of the values in some field or combination of fields. Such fields are called **sort keys**.

In FoxPro, when you sort, you create a brand new file. The new file contains the same records as the original. The only difference is that the records have been rearranged in the desired order.

Sorting a Database File on a Single Field

To illustrate the process, suppose the data in the EMPLOYEE file is sorted by name. In other words, NAME is the sort key. (CHARACTER, NUMERIC, and DATE fields can be sorted. LOGICAL and MEMO fields cannot be sorted. Because NAME is a CHARACTER field, there is no problem using it as the key field.) The results of sorting the employees by name are shown in Figure 13.1.

Figure 13.1
Employee Records Sorted by Name

Record#	NUMBER	NAME	DATE	DEPARTMENT	PAY_RATE	UNION
1	1017	Ackerman, Mary R.	02/05/93	Accounting	6.00	.T.
2	1029	Anderson, Carole L.	04/18/93	Shipping	9.00	.T.
3	1056	Andrews, Robert M.	06/03/93	Marketing	9.00	.F.
4	1037	Baxter, Charles W.	05/05/93	Accounting	11.00	.F.
5	1026	Bender, Ginger O.	04/12/93	Production	6.75	.T.
6	1020	Castle, Mark C.	03/04/93	Shipping	7.50	.T.
7	1066	Castelworth, Mary T.	07/05/93	Production	8.75	.T.
8	1025	Chaney, Joseph R.	03/23/93	Accounting	8.00	.F.
9	1022	Dunning, Greta L.	03/12/93	Marketing	9.10	.T.
10	1030	Edwards, Kenneth J.	04/23/93	Production	8.60	.T.
11	1041	Evans John T.	05/19/93	Marketing	6.00	.F.
12	1016	Fong, Ronald	02/04/93	Accounting	9.75	.T.
13	1057	Hall, Sandy H.	06/10/93	Production	8.75	.T.
14	1013	McCormack, Nigel L.	01/15/93	Shipping	8.25	.T.
15	1011	Rapoza, Anthony P.	01/10/93	Shipping	8.50	.T.

Topic 13: Sorting a Database File

Using a Sorted File

When you sort a database file, you produce another database file that contains the sorted data. The original, unsorted file is still active, however. Thus, in order to use a sorted database file, you must activate it. Once you have done so, you have the data in the order you want.

Sorting on More Than One Field

Sometimes you need to sort on more than one field. For example, you might want the employees sorted by department and all the employees in a given department sorted by name. In this case, you would have two sort keys, DEPARTMENT and NAME. Figure 13.2 illustrates the employee records sorted by name within department.

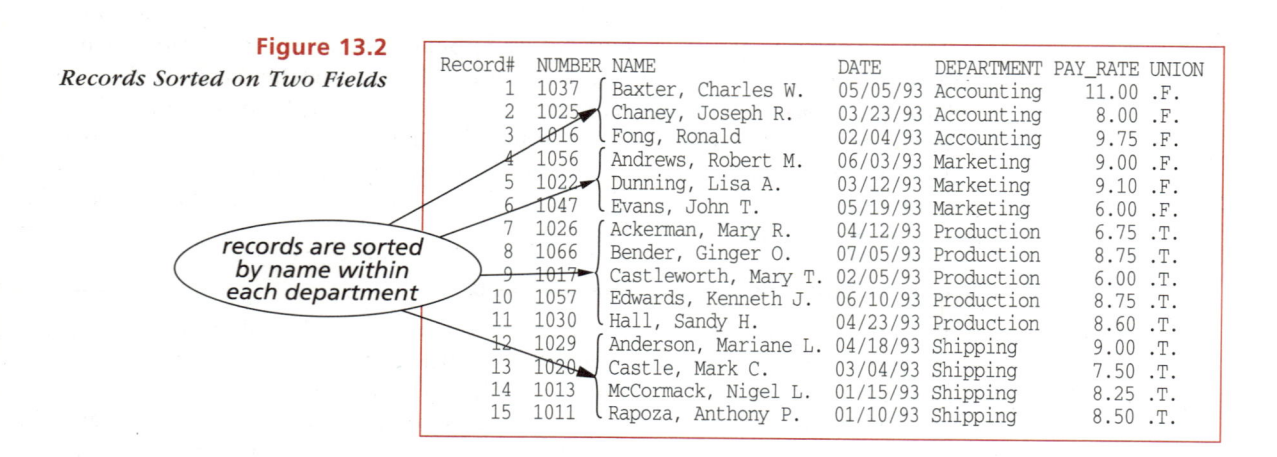

Figure 13.2
Records Sorted on Two Fields

Record#	NUMBER	NAME	DATE	DEPARTMENT	PAY_RATE	UNION
1	1037	Baxter, Charles W.	05/05/93	Accounting	11.00	.F.
2	1025	Chaney, Joseph R.	03/23/93	Accounting	8.00	.F.
3	1016	Fong, Ronald	02/04/93	Accounting	9.75	.F.
4	1056	Andrews, Robert M.	06/03/93	Marketing	9.00	.F.
5	1022	Dunning, Lisa A.	03/12/93	Marketing	9.10	.F.
6	1047	Evans, John T.	05/19/93	Marketing	6.00	.F.
7	1026	Ackerman, Mary R.	04/12/93	Production	6.75	.T.
8	1066	Bender, Ginger O.	07/05/93	Production	8.75	.T.
9	1017	Castleworth, Mary T.	02/05/93	Production	6.00	.T.
10	1057	Edwards, Kenneth J.	06/10/93	Production	8.75	.T.
11	1030	Hall, Sandy H.	04/23/93	Production	8.60	.T.
12	1029	Anderson, Mariane L.	04/18/93	Shipping	9.00	.T.
13	1020	Castle, Mark C.	03/04/93	Shipping	7.50	.T.
14	1013	McCormack, Nigel L.	01/15/93	Shipping	8.25	.T.
15	1011	Rapoza, Anthony P.	01/10/93	Shipping	8.50	.T.

records are sorted by name within each department

Sorting on two (or more) keys is very similar to sorting on a single key. The only difference concerns the sort key. Instead of selecting one key, you must select two. Further, you must select the more important sort key (called the **major key**) first. Then you select the less important sort key (called the **minor key**). In the example, you would select DEPARTMENT and then NAME.

Removing Files

Sometimes you want to remove a file from your catalog and delete it from your disk. If you never remove files, your disk and your catalogs can become cluttered quickly. Thus, if you have files that you don't think you will need again, it's a good idea to remove them. In your case, the sorted file is a good candidate for removal once you have used it to display the sorted data. After all, once you make any further changes in EMPLOYEE, the data in this file is out of date. If you need it again later, you can re-create it using the new data in EMPLOYEE.

TUTORIAL

In this tutorial, you sort a database file and then display the sorted data.

1 **Sort the EMPLOYEE database file on the NAME field.** Call the sorted file SORTFLE.

Open	EMPLOYEE	unless already activated.
Press	ALT , D , S	Displays Sort window.

Your screen should then look like Figure 13.3. FoxPro is now prompting you to indicate the sort keys. You can highlight the field to sort by and press ENTER. This produces a list of selected sort keys in the right portion of the Sort window.

Figure 13.3
Sort Window

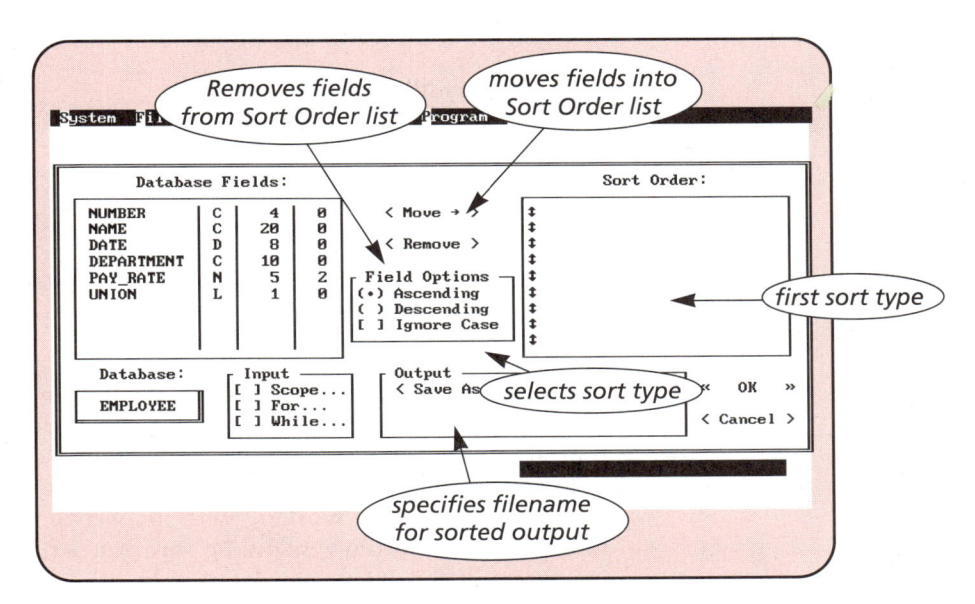

Database Fields:
- NUMBER   C   4   0
- NAME   C   20   0
- DATE   D   8   0
- DEPARTMENT C 10   0
- PAY_RATE N   5   2
- UNION   L   1   0

< Move >
< Remove >

Field Options
(•) Ascending
( ) Descending
[ ] Ignore Case

Sort Order:

Database: EMPLOYEE

Input
[ ] Scope...
[ ] For...
[ ] While...

Output
< Save As >

« OK »
< Cancel >

- Removes fields from Sort Order list
- moves fields into Sort Order list
- first sort type
- selects sort type
- specifies filename for sorted output

Highlight	NAME	
Press	← ENTER	Selects sort key.

Next you indicate the type of sort you want. The entry in the Field Options dialog box describes this sort. FoxPro can sort records in ascending or descending order. To change from one to another, press the TAB key until an item in the Field Options dialog box is highlighted. The ascending and descending items are **radio buttons**. Selecting one of these items automatically deselects the opposite choice. Use the arrow keys to highlight the desired radio button. In this text, unless you are specifically told otherwise, select "Ascending." This sequence is already on the screen. You may also select the option to Ignore Case. Selecting this option ignores whether the field begins with upper- or lowercase characters.

You could now enter a second sort key if you wanted. In this example, you have no second sort key.

Topic 13: Sorting a Database File

Press	V	Opens Save As dialog box.
Type	SORTFLE	
Press	SHIFT-TAB twice, ↵ENTER	Selects SAVE button; names sorted file.
Press	TAB three times, ↵ENTER	Selects OK button.

If FoxPro indicates that the file exists and asks if it is all right to overwrite the existing file, press Y. (This only happens if you have previously created a file named SORTFLE.) The data will now be sorted. During the sort operation, FoxPro displays the percentage of the file that has been sorted and the number of records sorted. When the message indicates that the file has been 100% sorted, the sort is completed.

You are returned to the Command window.

2 Display all the sorted records.

Press	ALT, F, O	Selects File, Open.
Highlight	SORTFLE	
Press	TAB	until OK button is highlighted.
Press	↵ENTER	

Remember that the Database, Sort command simply creates the file; it does not open it. If after completing a sort you immediately display records, they are not in the order you have specified. You may think that the sort has not even worked or that you must have made a mistake. The only thing wrong is that you are working with the wrong file: your original database file rather than the sorted version. Be sure you activate the sorted version before you attempt to display your data.

Press	ALT, D, B	Selects Database, Browse; opens Browse window.

Your screen should look like Figure 13.4. Notice that the records are indeed sorted by name.

Press	ALT, F, C	Selects File, Close.

You are returned to the Command window.

3 Sort the EMPLOYEE database file on the NAME field within the DEPARTMENT field. Call the sorted file SORTFLE. Close the previous SORTFLE database file.

Press	ALT, D, S	Selects Database, Sort.

Figure 13.4
Browse Window

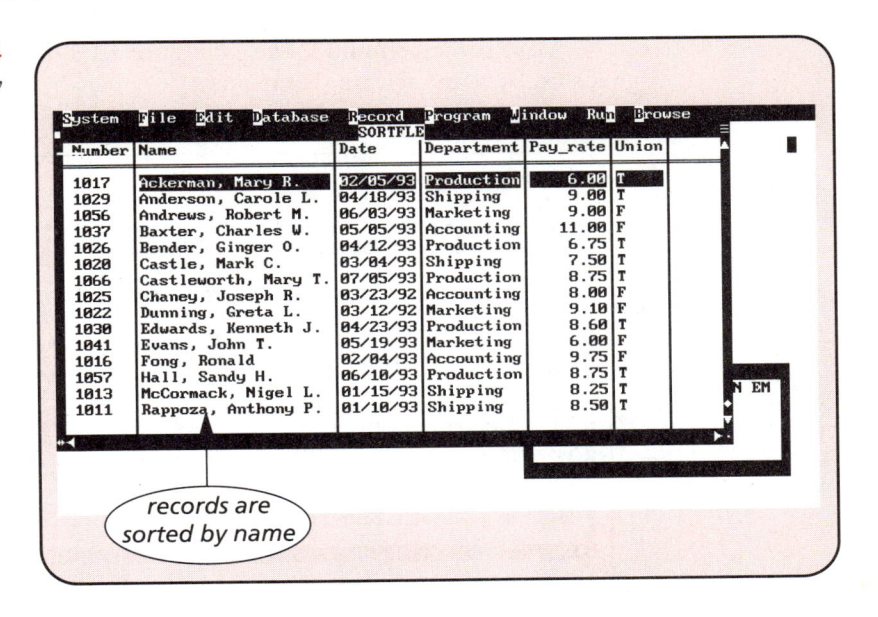

```
System  File  Edit  Database  Record  Program  Window  Run  Browse
                    SORTFLE
Number  Name                Date      Department  Pay_rate  Union
1017    Ackerman, Mary R.   02/05/93  Production      6.00  T
1029    Anderson, Carole L. 04/18/93  Shipping        9.00  T
1056    Andrews, Robert M.  06/03/93  Marketing       9.00  F
1037    Baxter, Charles W.  05/05/93  Accounting     11.00  F
1026    Bender, Ginger O.   04/12/93  Production      6.75  T
1020    Castle, Mark C.     03/04/93  Shipping        7.50  T
1066    Castleworth, Mary T.07/05/93  Production      8.75  T
1025    Chaney, Joseph R.   03/23/92  Accounting      8.00  F
1022    Dunning, Greta L.   03/12/92  Marketing       9.10  F
1030    Edwards, Kenneth J. 04/23/93  Production      8.60  T
1041    Evans, John T.      05/19/93  Marketing       6.00  F
1016    Fong, Ronald        02/04/93  Accounting      9.75  F
1057    Hall, Sandy H.      06/10/93  Production      8.75  T
1013    McCormack, Nigel L. 01/15/93  Shipping        8.25  T
1011    Rappoza, Anthony P. 01/10/93  Shipping        8.50  T
```

records are sorted by name

Press	(arrow keys)	to select DEPARTMENT.
Press	↵ ENTER	Adds DEPARTMENT to Sort Order list as first sort key.
Press	(arrow keys)	to select NAME.
Press	↵ ENTER	Adds NAME to Sort Order list as second sort key.
Press	V	Moves to Save As entry.
Type	SORTFLE	
Press	SHIFT - TAB twice, ↵ ENTER	Names sorted file.
Press	Y	Overwrites existing file.
Press	TAB three times, ↵ ENTER	Selects OK button.

You are returned to the Command window.

4 Display all the sorted records.

Press	ALT , F , O	Selects File, Open.
Highlight	SORTFLE	
Press	TAB	until OK button is highlighted.
Press	↵ ENTER	
Press	ALT , D , B	Opens Browse window.

Topic 13: Sorting a Database File

Your screen should look like Figure 13.5. Notice that the records are sorted by name within department.

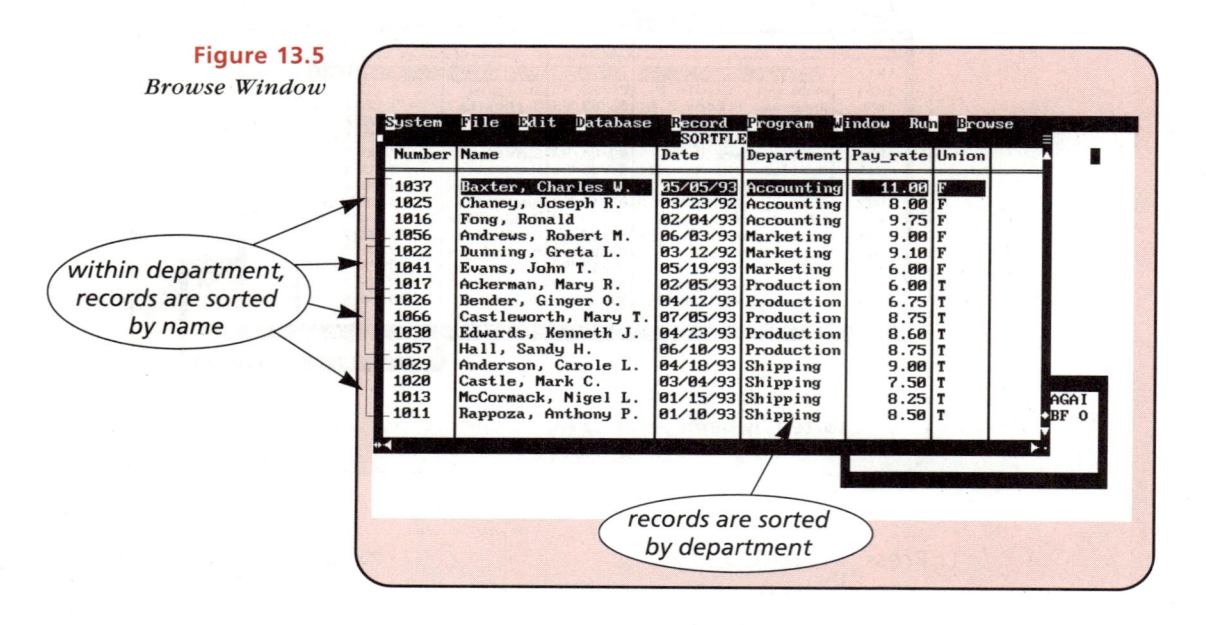

Figure 13.5
Browse Window

```
 System  File  Edit  Database  Record  Program  Window  Run  Browse
                             SORTFLE
 Number  Name                Date      Department  Pay_rate  Union
 1037    Baxter, Charles W.  05/05/93  Accounting    11.00    F
 1025    Chaney, Joseph R.   03/23/92  Accounting     8.00    F
 1016    Fong, Ronald        02/04/93  Accounting     9.75    F
 1056    Andrews, Robert M.  06/03/93  Marketing      9.00    F
 1022    Dunning, Greta L.   03/12/92  Marketing      9.10    F
 1041    Evans, John T.      05/19/93  Marketing      6.00    F
 1017    Ackerman, Mary R.   02/05/93  Production     6.00    T
 1026    Bender, Ginger O.   04/12/93  Production     6.75    T
 1066    Castleworth, Mary T.07/05/93  Production     8.75    T
 1030    Edwards, Kenneth J. 04/23/93  Production     8.60    T
 1057    Hall, Sandy H.      06/10/93  Production     8.75    T
 1029    Anderson, Carole L. 04/18/93  Shipping       9.00    T
 1020    Castle, Mark C.     03/04/93  Shipping       7.50    T
 1013    McCormack, Nigel L. 01/15/93  Shipping       8.25    T
 1011    Rappoza, Anthony P. 01/10/93  Shipping       8.50    T
```

within department, records are sorted by name

records are sorted by department

| Press | ALT , F , C | Selects File, Close. |

You are returned to the Command window.

5 **Remove SORTFLE from your disk.** To delete a file, it must not be active. If it is (that is, if it appears above the line), you must deactivate it.

Type	USE	in the Command window; closes database.
Press	ALT , S , F	Selects System, Filer.
Press	SPACEBAR	Selects SORTFLE.DBF.
Press	(arrow keys)	to highlight SORTFLE.DBF.
Press	SHIFT - TAB seven times, ↵ ENTER	Selects DELETE button; deletes file.

FoxPro asks you if you also want to remove the file from the disk.

| Press | D | Deletes file from disk. |
| Press | ALT , F , C | Closes Filer. |

FoxPro

PROCEDURE SUMMARY

SORTING A DATABASE FILE ON A SINGLE FIELD

Select the database file to sort.	`ALT`, `D`, `S`
Select the sort key.	(arrow keys), `↵ ENTER`
Select the desired type of sort.	`A` or `D`
Move to the Save As entry.	`V`
Type the name of the sorted file.	(your input)
Move to the OK button.	`SHIFT`-`TAB` three times
Select the OK button.	`↵ ENTER`
If you are asked if it is all right to overwrite the existing file and you don't mind, select Y. If you don't want to overwrite the file, select N and the sort will not take place.	
Sort the file.	`TAB` three times, `↵ ENTER`

USING A SORTED FILE

Open the sorted file.	`ALT`, `F`, `O`

SORTING ON MORE THAN ONE FIELD

Select the database file to sort.	`ALT`, `D`, `S`
Select the sort key.	(arrow keys), `↵ ENTER`
Select the desired type of sort.	`A` or `D`
Select the next sort key.	(arrow keys), `↵ ENTER`
Move to the Save As entry.	`V`
Type the name of the sorted file.	(your input), `SHIFT`-`TAB` three times, `↵ ENTER`
If you are asked if it is all right to overwrite the existing file and you don't mind, select Y. If you don't want to overwrite the file, select N and the sort will not take place.	
Sort the file.	`TAB` three times, `↵ ENTER`

Topic 13: Sorting a Database File

REMOVING FILES

Select Filer	`ALT`, `S`, `F`
Select the file.	(arrow keys)
Select the DELETE button.	`TAB` seven times, `↵ ENTER`
Confirms deletion of the file from disk.	`D`
Close Filer.	`ALT`, `F`, `C`

EXERCISES

1. Sort the records in the CHECK database file by Check Number. Use SORTFLE as the filename for the sorted file.

2. After the records have been sorted, display the Check Number, Date, Payee, and Check Amount fields for all records.

3. Sort the records in the CHECK database file in alphabetical order by Payee within Expense type. Use SORTFLE as the filename for the sorted file.

4. After the records have been sorted, display the Expense Type, Payee, Amount, Date, and Check Number fields for all records.

TOPIC 14

Creating and Using Indexes

CONCEPTS You are already familiar with the concept of an index. The index in the back of a book contains important words or phrases together with a list of pages on which the given words or phrases can be found. An index for a database file is similar. Figure 14.1, for example, shows the EMPLOYEE database file along with an index built on employee names. (In technical terms, NAME is the **index key.**) In this case, the items of interest are employee names rather than key words or phrases. Each employee name occurs in the index along with the number of the record on which the employee name is found. If you were to use this index to find Helen Bender, for example, you would find her name in the index, look at the corresponding record number (8), and then go immediately to record 8 in the EMPLOYEE file, thus finding her much more rapidly than if you had had to look at each employee one at a time. This is precisely what FoxPro does when using an index. Thus indexes make the process of retrieving an employee much more efficient.

Figure 14.1
Use of an Index

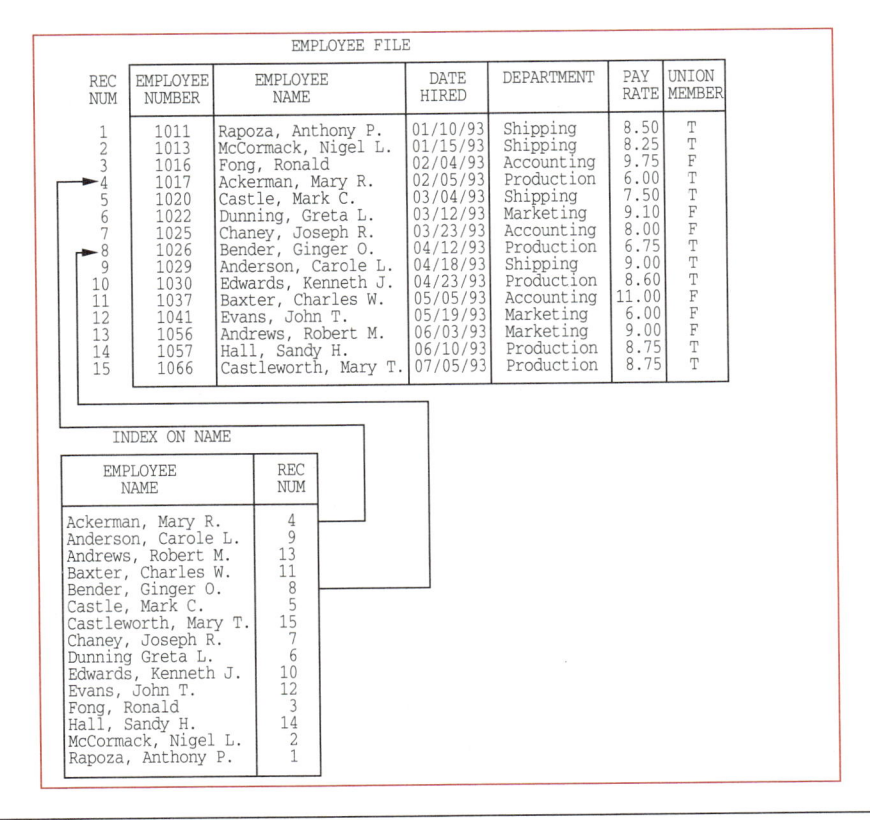

EMPLOYEE FILE

REC NUM	EMPLOYEE NUMBER	EMPLOYEE NAME	DATE HIRED	DEPARTMENT	PAY RATE	UNION MEMBER
1	1011	Rapoza, Anthony P.	01/10/93	Shipping	8.50	T
2	1013	McCormack, Nigel L.	01/15/93	Shipping	8.25	T
3	1016	Fong, Ronald	02/04/93	Accounting	9.75	F
4	1017	Ackerman, Mary R.	02/05/93	Production	6.00	T
5	1020	Castle, Mark C.	03/04/93	Shipping	7.50	T
6	1022	Dunning, Greta L.	03/12/93	Marketing	9.10	F
7	1025	Chaney, Joseph R.	03/23/93	Accounting	8.00	F
8	1026	Bender, Ginger O.	04/12/93	Production	6.75	T
9	1029	Anderson, Carole L.	04/18/93	Shipping	9.00	T
10	1030	Edwards, Kenneth J.	04/23/93	Production	8.60	T
11	1037	Baxter, Charles W.	05/05/93	Accounting	11.00	F
12	1041	Evans, John T.	05/19/93	Marketing	6.00	F
13	1056	Andrews, Robert M.	06/03/93	Marketing	9.00	F
14	1057	Hall, Sandy H.	06/10/93	Production	8.75	T
15	1066	Castleworth, Mary T.	07/05/93	Production	8.75	T

INDEX ON NAME

EMPLOYEE NAME	REC NUM
Ackerman, Mary R.	4
Anderson, Carole L.	9
Andrews, Robert M.	13
Baxter, Charles W.	11
Bender, Ginger O.	8
Castle, Mark C.	5
Castleworth, Mary T.	15
Chaney, Joseph R.	7
Dunning Greta L.	6
Edwards, Kenneth J.	10
Evans, John T.	12
Fong, Ronald	3
Hall, Sandy H.	14
McCormack, Nigel L.	2
Rapoza, Anthony P.	1

There is another benefit to indexes, however. Indexes provide an efficient alternative to sorting. Look at the record numbers in the index and suppose you used them to list all employees. That is, you simply followed down the record number column, listing the corresponding employees as you went. In this example, you would first list the employee on record 3 (David Ackerman), then the employee on record 9 (Mariane Anderson), then the employee on record 13 (Robert Andrews), and so on. You would be listing the employees in name order without sorting the file. Provided you have such an index in place, there is no need to take the time to create a separate sorted version of the EMPLOYEE file.

Creating an Index on a Single Field [112]

To gain the benefits from an index, you must first create one. Usually an index is created on a single field (like NAME). In other words, the index key is usually a single field. When you create such an index, you must specify a name (also called a **tag**) for the index along with the field that will be the index key.

Creating an Index on More Than One Field [112]

Although the index key is usually a single field, it can be a combination of fields. The steps in creating such an index are very similar to those used when the index is a single field. The only difference is that when you enter the index key, you must enter an expression that combines the fields.

Using an Index to Order Records [112]

One use for indexes is as an efficient alternative to sorting. If you decide to use the index on the NAME field, for example, the records in the database file will appear to be in name order. If you instead use the index on the combination of the DEPARTMENT and NAME fields, the records will appear to be sorted by name within department. This allows you to have the records in the order you want without going through the process of sorting your database file.

Using an Index to Find a Record [113]

The other use for indexes is to allow you to rapidly find records. Using an index to locate a record is much more efficient than finding the record with the Record, Locate command. With the Record, Locate command, FoxPro must examine each record in turn, until it finds the one you want. With an index, it can go directly to the desired record. To use an index in this way, you must open it as the master index. Then you will be able to find records using the Record, Seek command.

Removing Unwanted Indexes [113]

Occasionally you might find that you created an index that you now never use. You should probably get rid of such an index because it occupies disk space. In addition, FoxPro must keep this index up to date; that is, when you change the data in your database file, FoxPro must make the appropriate changes to the index. If you are not going to use the index, there is no point in wasting the space or in having FoxPro do the extra work.

TUTORIAL In this tutorial, you create and use a variety of indexes for a database file.

1 **Create an index on the NAME field of the EMPLOYEE database file.**

Press	ALT, F, O	Selects File, Open; displays File Open dialog box.

Confirm that the Database type is selected. If not, you need to press the TAB key several times to move to the type popup and change it to Database.

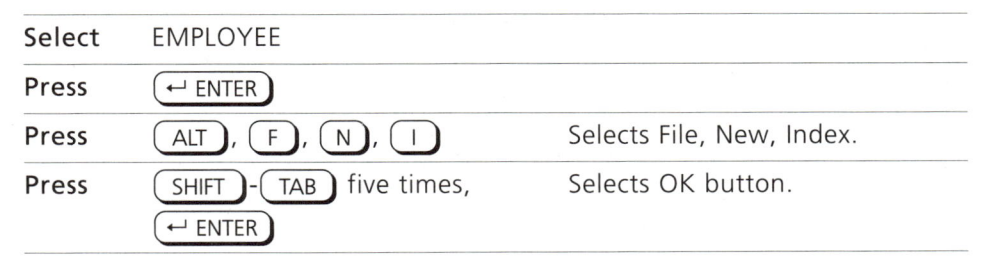

Select	EMPLOYEE	
Press	ENTER	
Press	ALT, F, N, I	Selects File, New, Index.
Press	SHIFT-TAB five times, ENTER	Selects OK button.

When you select File, New, Index, you see the screen shown in Figure 14.2. Use this screen to specify the details of your index. To specify an index, you must give it a name, also called a tag. You must also specify the index key, that is, the expression on which the index is created.

Figure 14.2
Index Dialog Box

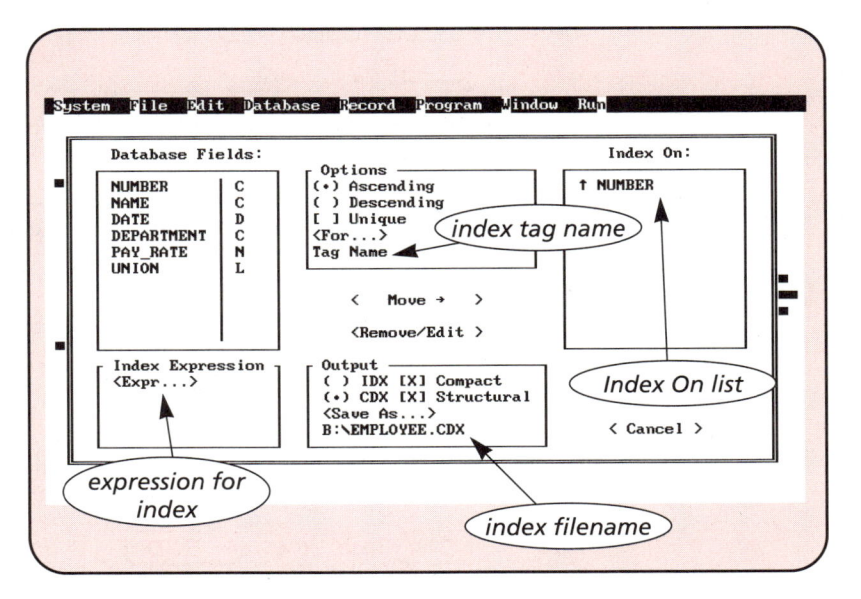

Topic 14: Creating and Using Indexes

107

> **TIP:** If your index expression is a single field, it's a good idea to use this field name as the index tag also, as has been done here.

Press	↓ , SPACEBAR	Selects NAME from Fields list; assigns it as tag name. ◄
Press	M	Moves NAME into Index On list.
Press	TAB four times, ↵ ENTER	Selects OK button.

You are returned to the Command window.

2 Create an index on the combination of the DEPARTMENT field and the NAME field in the EMPLOYEE database file.

Press	ALT , F , N , I	Selects File, New, Index.
Press	SHIFT - TAB five times, ↵ ENTER	Selects OK button.
Press	TAB , ↵ ENTER	Selects EXPRESSION button.
Press	DELETE , SHIFT - TAB	Deletes previous expression; moves to Fields list.
Press	↓ three times, ↵ ENTER	Places DEPARTMENT in Expression window.
Press	CTRL - M , ↓ , ↵ ENTER	Adds + symbol to Expression window.
Press	SHIFT - TAB , ↑ twice, ↵ ENTER	Moves to Fields lists; adds NAME to Expression window.

This index expression indicates the combination of DEPARTMENT and NAME.

Press	SHIFT - TAB three times, ↵ ENTER	Selects OK button.
Press	TAB seven times	Moves to Tag entry.
Type	DPTNAME	
Press	↵ ENTER	Gives DPTNAME as index tag.
Press	↵ ENTER	Moves Expression into Index On list.
Press	TAB four times, ↵ ENTER	Selects OK button.

You are returned to the Command window.

Unfortunately, to build an index on a combination of fields, both fields must be of CHARACTER type. This means that you could not use the same technique to build an index on the combination of department and pay rate, for example. There are ways around this problem, but they are beyond the scope of this text. Fortunately the situations in which you would need to do this are not very common. If you ever find yourself in such a situation, consult the FoxPro manual.

3 Use an index to list the employees alphabetically by NAME.

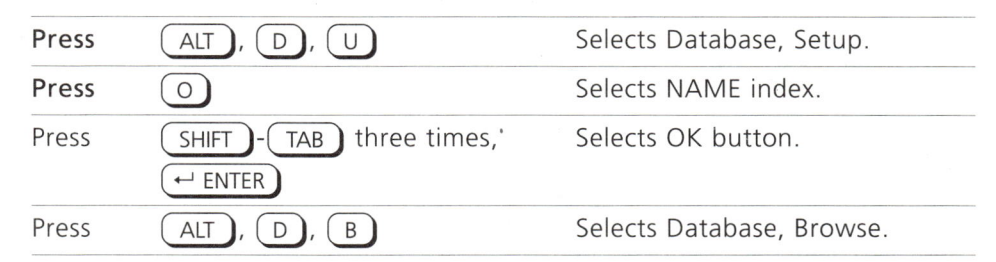

Press	ALT, D, U	Selects Database, Setup.
Press	O	Selects NAME index.
Press	SHIFT-TAB three times,' ENTER	Selects OK button.
Press	ALT, D, B	Selects Database, Browse.

The Change window would have worked just as well. It is more common to use this feature on the Browse window, however, since that is where you will view the records. This index is now used to order the records. Your display should look like Figure 14.3. Note that the records appear to be sorted by name.

Figure 14.3
Browse Window

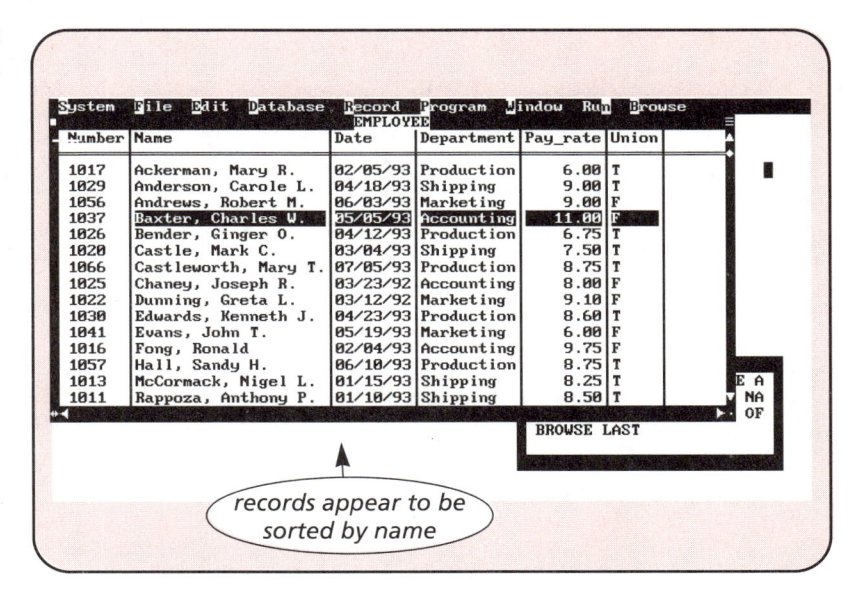

```
System  File  Edit  Database  Record  Program  Window  Run  Browse
                       EMPLOYEE
 Number  Name              Date      Department  Pay_rate  Union
 1017    Ackerman, Mary R.  02/05/93  Production   6.00     T
 1029    Anderson, Carole L.04/18/93  Shipping     9.00     T
 1056    Andrews, Robert M. 06/03/93  Marketing    9.00     F
 1037    Baxter, Charles W. 05/05/93  Accounting  11.00     F
 1026    Bender, Ginger O.  04/12/93  Production   6.75     T
 1020    Castle, Mark C.    03/04/93  Shipping     7.50     T
 1066    Castleworth, Mary T.07/05/93 Production   8.75     T
 1025    Chaney, Joseph R.  03/23/92  Accounting   8.00     F
 1022    Dunning, Greta L.  03/12/92  Marketing    9.10     F
 1030    Edwards, Kenneth J.04/23/93  Production   8.60     T
 1041    Evans, John T.     05/19/93  Marketing    6.00     F
 1016    Fong, Ronald       02/04/93  Accounting   9.75     F
 1057    Hall, Sandy H.     06/10/93  Production   8.75     T
 1013    McCormack, Nigel L.01/15/93  Shipping     8.25     T
 1011    Rappoza, Anthony P.01/10/93  Shipping     8.50     T
                                              BROWSE LAST
```

records appear to be sorted by name

Press	ALT, F, C	Select File, Close.

You are returned to the Command window.

4 Use an index to list the employees by NAME within DEPARTMENT.

Press	ALT, D, U	Selects Database, Setup.
Press	↓, O	Selects DPTNAME index.

Topic 14: Creating and Using Indexes

Press	SHIFT - TAB three times, ↵ ENTER	Selects OK button.
Press	ALT, D, B	Selects Database, Browse.

This index is now used to order the records. Note that the records are sorted by name within department.

Press	ALT, F, C	Selects File, Close.

You are returned to the Command window.

5 Create and use an index to locate employee 1037.

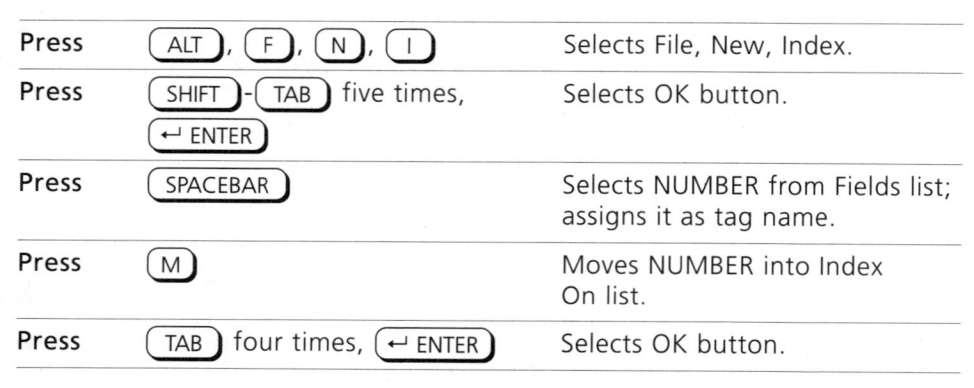

Press	ALT, F, N, I	Selects File, New, Index.
Press	SHIFT - TAB five times, ↵ ENTER	Selects OK button.
Press	SPACEBAR	Selects NUMBER from Fields list; assigns it as tag name.
Press	M	Moves NUMBER into Index On list.
Press	TAB four times, ↵ ENTER	Selects OK button.

You are returned to the Command window.

This index is now used to order the records. It can also be used to rapidly retrieve records.

Press	ALT, R, S	Selects Record, Seek.

You are now in the Seek dialog box. Enter the data to search for.

Type	"1037"	Enters search data in Expression window.
Press	SHIFT - TAB three times, ↵ ENTER	Selects OK button.

If there were no such employee, FoxPro would display a message indicating this. If, as is the case here, there is such an employee, this employee's record becomes the current active record. Use the Record, Change screen or run the screen that was created in Chapter 12 to view the current record. (Figure 14.4).

Figure 14.4
Change Window

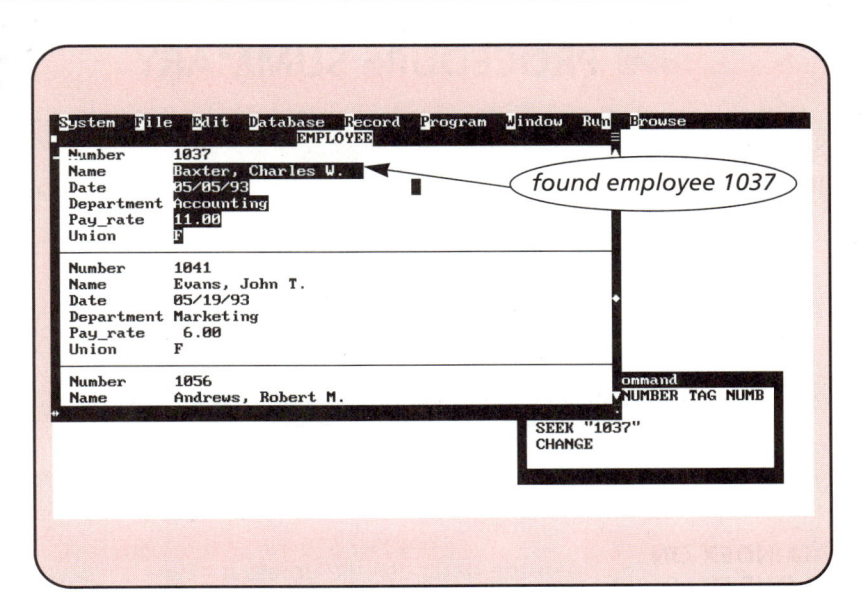

```
 System  File  Edit  Database  Record  Program  Window  Run  Browse
                        EMPLOYEE
 Number      1037
 Name        Baxter, Charles W.  ◄─────      found employee 1037
 Date        05/05/93
 Department  Accounting
 Pay_rate    11.00
 Union       F

 Number      1041
 Name        Evans, John T.
 Date        05/19/93
 Department  Marketing
 Pay_rate     6.00
 Union       F

 Number      1056                                  ommand
 Name        Andrews, Robert M.                    NUMBER TAG NUMB

                                              SEEK "1037"
                                              CHANGE
```

Press	ALT , R , E	Selects Record, Change.
Press	ESC	

You are returned to the Command window.

6 **Remove the index called DPTNAME.** It is no longer needed.

Press	ALT , D , U	Selects Database, Setup.
Press	↓ , M	Highlights DPTNAME index; selects MODIFY INDEX button.
Press	R	Selects REMOVE button.
Press	SHIFT - TAB four times, SPACEBAR	Selects OK button.

Alert box appears with the message, "Remove DPTNAME from the CDX file?"

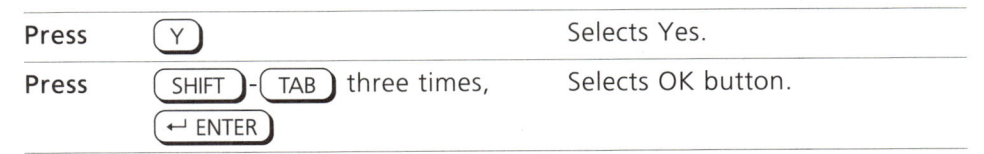

Press	Y	Selects Yes.
Press	SHIFT - TAB three times, ↵ ENTER	Selects OK button.

You are returned to the Command window.

Topic 14: Creating and Using Indexes   **111**

PROCEDURE SUMMARY

CREATING AN INDEX ON A SINGLE FIELD	Open the database.	(your choice)
	Create a new index.	ALT, F, I, SHIFT-TAB five times, ↵ ENTER
	Move to the index field.	(arrow keys)
	Select the index field.	SPACEBAR, M
	Select the OK button.	TAB four times
CREATING AN INDEX ON MORE THAN ONE FIELD	Open the database file unless it is already active.	(your choice)
	Create a new index.	ALT, F, I, SHIFT-TAB five times, ↵ ENTER
	Move to the Expression window.	TAB, ↵ ENTER
	Move to the Fields list.	SHIFT-TAB
	Select the first index key.	↑ or ↓, ↵ ENTER
	Select the + symbol.	CTRL-M, ↓, ↵ ENTER
	Select the second index key.	SHIFT-TAB, ↑ or ↓, ↵ ENTER
	Select the OK button.	SHIFT-TAB three times, ↵ ENTER
	Enter the tag name.	TAB six times, (your input), ↵ ENTER
	Move the expression into the Index On list.	M
	Select OK button.	TAB four times
USING AN INDEX TO ORDER RECORDS	Open the database file unless it is already active.	(your choice)
	Select the Setup dialog box.	ALT, D, U
	Move to the desired index tag.	↑ or ↓

FoxPro

Select the SET ORDER button.	(O)
Select the OK button.	(SHIFT)-(TAB) three times
Open the Browse window.	(ALT), (D), (B)
The records now are ordered by this index.	

USING AN INDEX TO FIND A RECORD

Open the database file unless it is already active.	(your choice)
Select the Setup dialog box.	(ALT), (D), (U)
Move to the desired index tag.	(↑) or (↓)
Select the SET ORDER button.	(O)
Select the OK button.	(SHIFT)-(TAB) three times
Select the Seek command.	(ALT), (R), (S)
Type the search string.	(your input)
Select the OK button.	(SHIFT)-(TAB) three times, (↵ ENTER)
If there is no matching record, FoxPro displays a message indicating this. If there is such a record, it becomes the current active record and displays on the screen.	

REMOVING UNWANTED INDEXES

Open the database file unless it is already active.	(your choice)
Select the Setup dialog box.	(ALT), (D), (U)
Move to the desired index tag.	(↑) or (↓)
Select the MODIFY button.	(M)
Select the REMOVE button.	(R)
Select the OK button.	(SHIFT)-(TAB) twice, (↵ ENTER)
Select Yes.	(Y)

Topic 14: Creating and Using Indexes

EXERCISES

1. Create an index called PAYEE on the PAYEE field in the CHECK database.
2. Create an index called EXPPAY on the combination of the EXPENSE and PAYEE fields in the CHECK database.
3. Use an appropriate index to list the records in CHECK in PAYEE order.
4. Use an appropriate index to list the records in CHECK ordered by EXPENSE within PAYEE.
5. Use an appropriate index to locate the record containing check 107.
6. Remove the index that was created on the combination of the EXPENSE and PAYEE fields.

Checkpoint 2
What You Should Know

- ✓ To position the record pointer on a record containing a certain value, use the Record, Locate command.
- ✓ To change records while viewing several records at a time, use the Browse window.
- ✓ To make the same change to all records satisfying a certain condition, use the Record, Replace command.
- ✓ Deleting records does not remove them from a database file. Rather, such records are marked for deletion. To physically remove such records from the file, use the Database, Pack command.
- ✓ To mark records for deletion, use the Change or the Browse window. In either case, move to the record that is to be deleted and press CONTROL-T. Diamonds appear to the left of the field names indicating that the record has been deleted.
- ✓ To unmark records that have been marked for deletion, use the Change or the Browse window. In either case, move to the deleted record and press CONTROL-T. The diamonds along the left of the record disappear.
- ✓ To mark all records that satisfy a certain condition for deletion, use the Record, Delete command.
- ✓ To unmark all records that satisfy a certain condition, use the Record, Recall command.
- ✓ To create a custom screen, select the File, New, Screen command.
- ✓ To select fields or text on a screen, use the SPACEBAR.
- ✓ To move selected fields or text on a screen, use the arrow keys.
- ✓ To place boxes on a screen, use the Screen, Box command.
- ✓ To use a **custom screen**, select the Run, Screen command.
- ✓ A **key field** is a field that is used as a basis of a **sorting** operation.
- ✓ To sort the records in a database file, producing a new database file, use the Database, Sort command.
- ✓ To sort on multiple keys, select the keys in order of importance.
- ✓ To display the records in a sorted file, the sorted file must be open.
- ✓ An **index key** is the field or combination of fields on which an **index** is built. The name of an index is called a **tag**.
- ✓ To build an index, use the File, New, Index command. Specify a name and expression for the index.
- ✓ To build an index on multiple fields, the fields should be CHARACTER fields. Enter the names of the fields, separated by plus signs.

✓ To make an individual index active, select the Database, Setup, Set Order To command. Records in the database file then appear to be sorted in order of the index key.

✓ An index may be used to allow rapid retrieval of individual records on the basis of the index key.

Review Questions

1. How do you find a record satisfying some condition?
2. How do you find the next record satisfying a condition?
3. How do you use the Browse window to update records?
4. Which option allows you to use conditions to update records?
5. Which option allows you to use conditions to mark records for deletion?
6. How do you create an initial custom screen? What does it look like?
7. How do you add blank lines to a custom screen? Why might you want to do so?
8. How do you change the prompts on a custom screen? Why might you want to do so?
9. How do you reposition prompts and fields on a custom screen?
10. How do you add boxes to a custom screen? What purpose do they serve?
11. How do you save a custom screen?
12. How do you use a custom screen? With which options do you use it?
13. How do you sort a database file on a single field?
14. How do you use a sorted file? At what point is a sorted file active?
15. How can you sort a database file on more than one field?
16. What is an index? What are the advantages associated with indexes? Describe the process of creating an index on a single field.
17. How can you create an index on more than one field?
18. How can you use an index to order records?
19. How can you use an index to find a record?

CHECKPOINT EXERCISES

The following exercises pertain to the MUSIC database file that you created in Checkpoint 1.

1. Use the Record, Locate command to find the music named Rio Rio.
2. Use the Record, Locate command to find the first record in the MUSIC database file that is of type CS.
3. Use the appropriate option to locate the next record of type CS.
4. Use the Browse window to change the cost of Rio Rio to $9.95.
5. Use the Browse window to change the price for Pardners to $6.95. In addition, change the type to LP and change the date to 2/24/92.

6. Use the Record, Replace command to change the price of the music named Country Hills to $12.95.
7. Use the Record, Replace command to add $1.00 to the amount of all records of type CD.
8. Use the Record, Replace command to mark all records of type CD for deletion.
9. Use the Record, Replace command to unmark all records of type CD.
10. Use the Change window to mark Passione for deletion.
11. Use the Browse window to mark Moods for deletion.
12. Physically remove the marked records from the MUSIC database file.
13. List all the records in the MUSIC database file.
14. Create a screen for the MUSIC database file that is similar to the screen you created for the EMPLOYEE database file. Call it MUSFORM.
15. Activate this screen. Select the Run, Screen command.
16. Sort the records stored in the MUSIC database file in alphabetical order by Artist Name. Use SORTFLE as the filename for the sorted file.
17. After the records have been sorted, print a list of all records using Quick Report.
18. Sort the records in the database file in alphabetical order by Music Name within Category. Use SORTFLE as the filename of the sorted file.
19. After the records have been sorted, print a list of all records using Quick Report.
20. Create an index on the Artist field in the MUSIC database. Use it to list the records in MUSIC in Artist order.
21. Create an index on the combination of the ARTIST and NAME fields in the MUSIC database. Use it to list the records in MUSIC ordered by NAME within ARTIST.
22. Use an index to locate the record on which the music name is Rio Rio.
23. Remove the index that was created on the combination of the ARTIST and NAME fields.

TOPIC 15

Creating a Report Layout

CONCEPTS In previous examples, you have looked at data using the Browse window. You have also printed the data using Quick Report. The format of the displayed output was very restrictive. Fortunately FoxPro allows you to produce nicely formatted reports containing such items as a page number, date, page and column headings, and totals. Reports can thus be given a very professional appearance.

The report in Figure 15.1 lists the name, department, pay rate, and weekly pay amount for all employees. (The weekly pay amount is the pay rate multiplied by 40.) The top area of the report is called the **page header**. A page header appears at the top of each page in the report. The body of the report consists of **detail lines**. One of these is printed for each record. The bottom area, the one containing the total of the weekly pay amounts, is called the **report summary**. It appears once at the end of the report. Even if this report were 50 pages long, there would still be only one report summary and it would appear at the very end.

Figure 15.1
Weekly Payroll Report

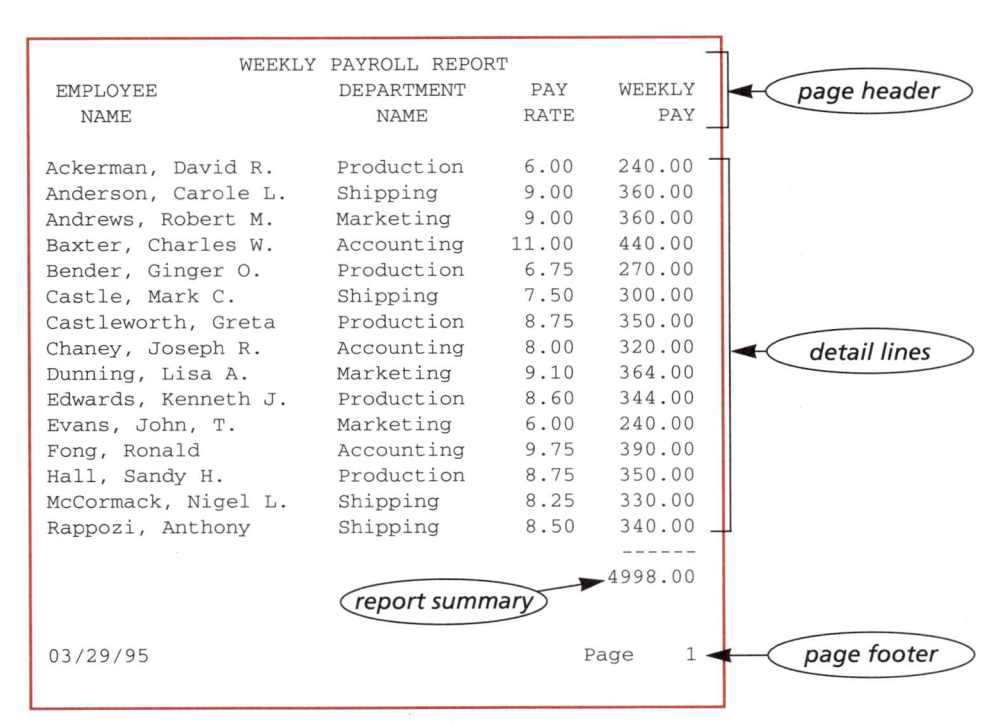

```
                    WEEKLY PAYROLL REPORT
EMPLOYEE               DEPARTMENT       PAY      WEEKLY
  NAME                    NAME          RATE      PAY

Ackerman, David R.     Production       6.00     240.00
Anderson, Carole L.    Shipping         9.00     360.00
Andrews, Robert M.     Marketing        9.00     360.00
Baxter, Charles W.     Accounting      11.00     440.00
Bender, Ginger O.      Production       6.75     270.00
Castle, Mark C.        Shipping         7.50     300.00
Castleworth, Greta     Production       8.75     350.00
Chaney, Joseph R.      Accounting       8.00     320.00
Dunning, Lisa A.       Marketing        9.10     364.00
Edwards, Kenneth J.    Production       8.60     344.00
Evans, John, T.        Marketing        6.00     240.00
Fong, Ronald           Accounting       9.75     390.00
Hall, Sandy H.         Production       8.75     350.00
McCormack, Nigel L.    Shipping         8.25     330.00
Rappozi, Anthony       Shipping         8.50     340.00
                                                 ------
                                                4998.00

03/29/95                                       Page    1
```

- page header
- detail lines
- report summary
- page footer

Topic 15: Creating a Report Layout — 119

Figure 15.1 is quite typical of simple reports. The page header contains the date the report was produced, the title of the report, the page number, and headings for the various columns in the report. The detail lines contain values in various fields. The report summary contains a statistic, in this case, the sum of all the weekly pay amounts.

Sometimes you want to group records in a report; that is, you want to create separate collections of records sharing some common characteristic. In Figure 15.2, for example, the records are grouped by department. There are four groups: Accounting, Marketing, Production, and Shipping.

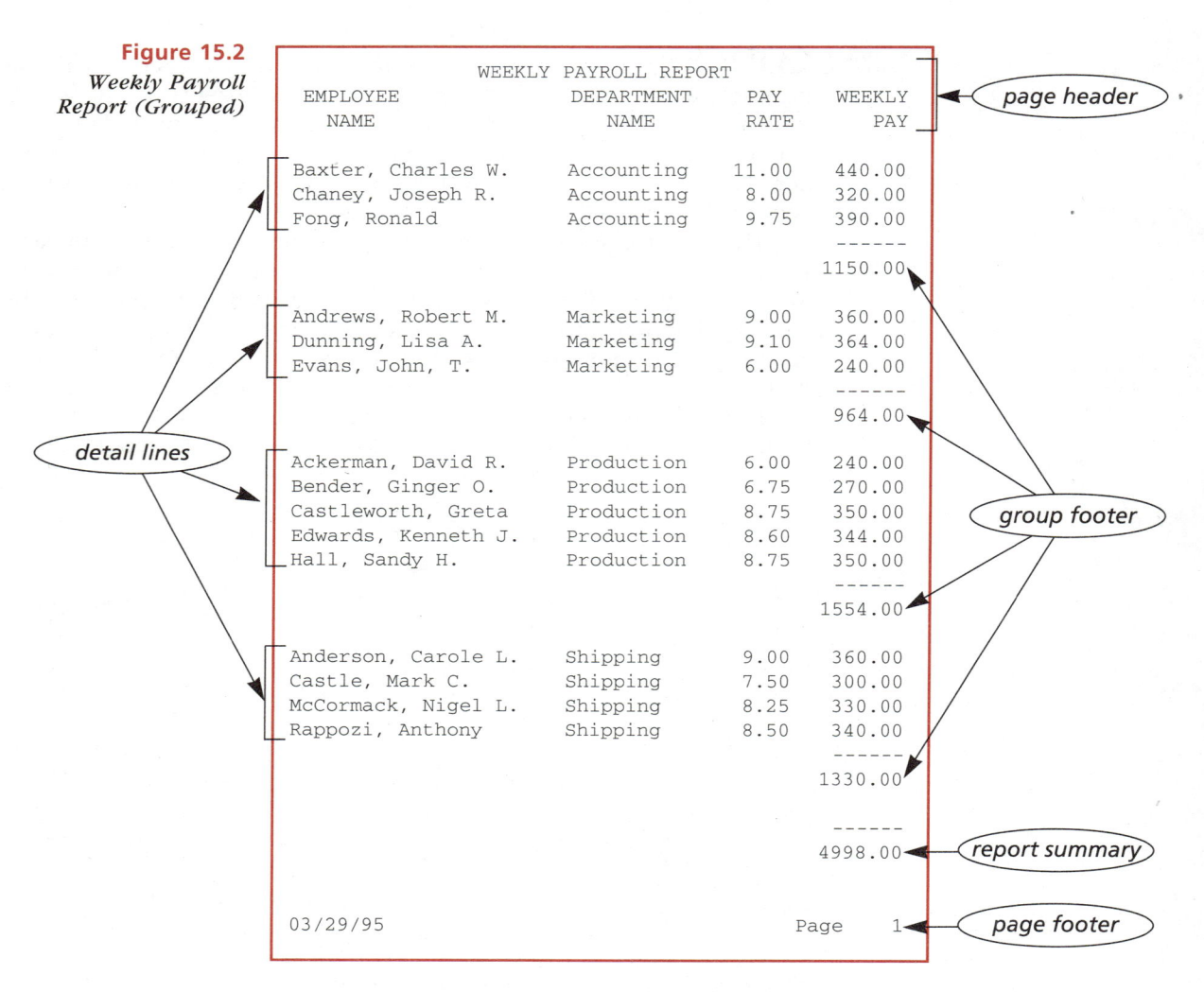

Figure 15.2
Weekly Payroll Report (Grouped)

```
                    WEEKLY PAYROLL REPORT
EMPLOYEE            DEPARTMENT          PAY      WEEKLY
NAME                NAME                RATE     PAY

Baxter, Charles W.  Accounting          11.00    440.00
Chaney, Joseph R.   Accounting           8.00    320.00
Fong, Ronald        Accounting           9.75    390.00
                                                 ------
                                                 1150.00

Andrews, Robert M.  Marketing            9.00    360.00
Dunning, Lisa A.    Marketing            9.10    364.00
Evans, John, T.     Marketing            6.00    240.00
                                                 ------
                                                  964.00

Ackerman, David R.  Production           6.00    240.00
Bender, Ginger O.   Production           6.75    270.00
Castleworth, Greta  Production           8.75    350.00
Edwards, Kenneth J. Production           8.60    344.00
Hall, Sandy H.      Production           8.75    350.00
                                                 ------
                                                 1554.00

Anderson, Carole L. Shipping             9.00    360.00
Castle, Mark C.     Shipping             7.50    300.00
McCormack, Nigel L. Shipping             8.25    330.00
Rappozi, Anthony    Shipping             8.50    340.00
                                                 ------
                                                 1330.00

                                                 ------
                                                 4998.00

03/29/95                                         Page    1
```

- page header
- detail lines
- group footer
- report summary
- page footer

When you group, you might include in your report two other types of objects: a group header and a group footer. A **group header** introduces the records in a particular group. You may also add the field name, such as DEPARTMENT, within this band to identify the group. It has not been added here because it is redundant with the DEPARTMENT column. A **group footer** provides some summary information about the records in the group. In Figure 15.2, the group footer gives the weekly pay totals for all records in the group.

Beginning the Report Creation Process

Quick Report is a useful shortcut to starting a report. This option creates an initial report like the one shown in Figure 15.3. Before moving on, let's use this initial report to examine the screen's general characteristics.

Figure 15.3
Report Layout Window

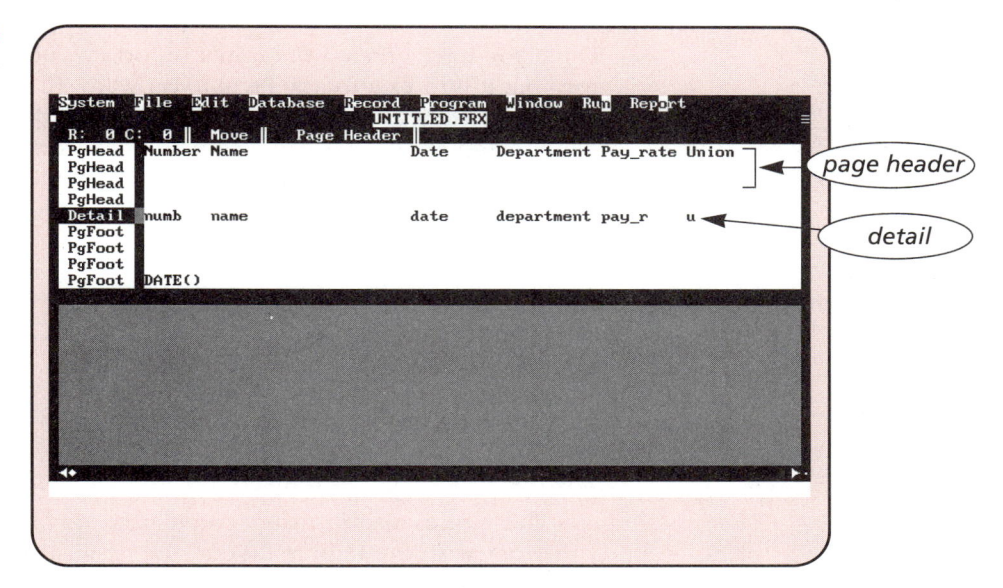

Each portion of the report is described in what is often termed a **band**. The page header band, detail band, and page footer band correspond to sections of the report you wish to create. A page footer appears at the bottom of each page. There are also two other bands: a report title band and a report summary band. A **report title** appears once at the beginning of a report, regardless of how many pages the report contains. A **report summary** appears at then end of a report.

To specify the layout of a report, you must describe each of the bands that you plan to include in the report. Thus you need to indicate the precise position of each item that will appear in the band.

At any given moment during the process, only one band is active. The active band is the band on which the cursor is currently positioned. To move from one band to another, use the UP and DOWN ARROWs. The band in which you are currently positioned is updated on the status bar.

Let's look at the specifics of the layout that FoxPro has created for you (Figure 15.3). The block of lines that are identified along the left column as "PgHead" is the page header, and it prints at the top of each page. There is currently no report title band. The detail band contains all the fields from the database file. The page footer band prints once at the end of each page. The report summary band, which must be added using the Report, Title/Summary command, prints at the end of the report.

In the page header band of the Report Layout window, you see such labels as Number, Name, Date, and so on. These are printed on the page

Topic 15: Creating a Report Layout **121**

header exactly as they are shown here in precisely the same position. The system date and page number print on the footer of each page. You can view the format of each field object by pressing ENTER when the cursor is over the field. This opens the **Field dialog box**, which contains the contents (expression) and format of the field object.

Altering the Report Layout 129

Once you have created the initial report layout, you alter it, gradually transforming it into exactly the layout you want. In the process, you will move fields, delete fields, resize fields, add new fields, and so on. You may also need to add lines to a band or delete lines from a band.

It is usually easiest to transform the detail band first. When the detail band is the way you want it, first transform the report summary band and then the page header band.

Adding or Deleting Lines in a Band 130

The process for adding or deleting lines in a band is very simple. It uses the following rules:

1. Press CONTROL-O to delete the cursor line, the line on which the cursor is located.
2. Press CONTROL-N to insert a blank line before the cursor line.

These rules also furnish a convenient way to correct mistakes. The more you work with the Report Layout, the easier it is to correct mistakes. But, until you become comfortable with the various correction methods, you can use the two preceding rules as follows:

- If you have an extra line you don't want, delete it with CONTROL-O. If you need an additional line, insert one.
- If you have made mistakes on a particular line that you don't know how to fix, use CONTROL-O to delete the line and then CONTROL-N to insert a new line. This combination erases the contents of the line. Now reconstruct the line the way it should be.

Selecting Fields and Text Objects 130

The procedures you learned in Topic 12 for moving screen objects are identical to the procedures for moving report objects. FoxPro allows you to easily move, delete, or resize field objects on the screen. You can also move and delete text objects. Text objects means simply characters. (On the current screen, the entries Page No., NUMBER, NAME, DATE, DEPARTMENT, PAY_RATE, and UNION are all text.) In any case, before you take any of these actions, you must select the portion of the screen with which you want to work. You use SPACEBAR to select the field or text, and then you can take the appropriate action.

Removing Fields from a Report 130

To remove a field from a report, select it as you have done previously and then press the DELETE key.

Moving Fields in a Report 〔130〕

To move a field, you must first select it. Then you can move the field by pressing the SPACEBAR, moving the cursor to the new location, and then pressing ENTER. As you move the cursor, the field object moves along with it. This helps you make sure you get the position you want. In some cases, getting the right position is not a problem. In other cases, though, this feature can be very handy.

Resizing Fields in a Report 〔130〕

In some cases, you want to change the size of a field in a report. You may, for example, not need to allow as much space as FoxPro had originally assigned to the field. If so, you can resize the field by selecting it, pressing ENTER, and then indicating the size you want under the Width entry of the Field dialog box.

Adding Fields 〔131〕

Sometimes you need additional fields. In the weekly pay report, for example, you need to add the weekly pay rate to the detail band. To add a field, move the cursor to wherever you want to place the field and then use the Report, Field command or press CONTROL-F.

Finishing the Report Layout Process 〔132〕

Before saving the report, it's a good idea to preview it on the screen. You can do this whenever you want by using the Report, Page Preview command or pressing CONTROL-I. If you discover something you don't like about the report layout when you preview it, you can change it at this time. Assuming the report is the way you want it, you can save it. The first time you save your report, assign it a name.

Modifying a Report Layout 〔132〕

You can make changes to a report layout whenever you want by selecting File, Open and changing to Report type in the file type popup. You are then returned to the Report Layout window with the current layout displayed. You can then make changes to the design using the same techniques you used when you first created it. Once you have finished, save your work and the changes are made permanent.

TUTORIAL
In this tutorial, you create the weekly pay report.

1 Begin creating the weekly pay report. Call the report REPORT1.

Open	EMPLOYEE	unless already active.
Press	[ALT], [F], [N], [R]	Selects File, New, Report.
Press	[TAB] six times, [↵ ENTER]	Selects OK button.
Press	[ALT], [O], [Q], [↵ ENTER]	Selects Report, Quick Report, OK.

Your screen should now look like Figure 15.3. Do not save your work at this point. Instead proceed directly to the next task.

Topic 15: Creating a Report Layout

2 View the current version of the report on the screen. When you have finished, save your work.

| Press | ALT, O, I | Selects Report, Page Preview. |

After a brief period, the report appears (Figure 15.4). As you can see, it looks just like the Quick Reports you produced earlier. Whenever you view a report on the screen, FoxPro shows you the first screenful and then displays a message indicating that you should press ESCAPE if you do not want to see any more of the report or press the SPACEBAR to see more.

Figure 15.4
Print Preview Screen

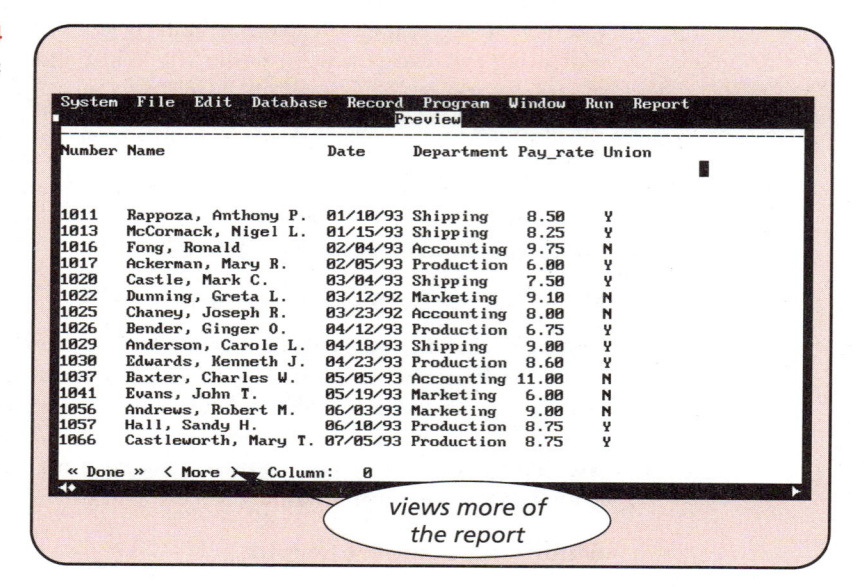

```
System  File  Edit  Database  Record  Program  Window  Run  Report
                         Preview
Number Name                    Date     Department Pay_rate Union

1011   Rappoza, Anthony P.     01/10/93 Shipping     8.50   Y
1013   McCormack, Nigel L.     01/15/93 Shipping     8.25   Y
1016   Fong, Ronald            02/04/93 Accounting   9.75   N
1017   Ackerman, Mary R.       02/05/93 Production   6.00   Y
1020   Castle, Mark C.         03/04/93 Shipping     7.50   Y
1022   Dunning, Greta L.       03/12/92 Marketing    9.10   N
1025   Chaney, Joseph R.       03/23/92 Accounting   8.00   N
1026   Bender, Ginger O.       04/12/93 Production   6.75   Y
1029   Anderson, Carole L.     04/18/93 Shipping     9.00   Y
1030   Edwards, Kenneth J.     04/23/93 Production   8.60   Y
1037   Baxter, Charles W.      05/05/93 Accounting  11.00   N
1041   Evans, John T.          05/19/93 Marketing    6.00   N
1056   Andrews, Robert M.      06/03/93 Marketing    9.00   N
1057   Hall, Sandy H.          06/10/93 Production   8.75   Y
1066   Castleworth, Mary T.    07/05/93 Production   8.75   Y

« Done »  < More >  Column:  0
```

views more of the report

Press	D	Selects DONE button.
Press	ALT, F, C, Y	Selects File, Close, Yes.
Type	REPORT1	
Press	SHIFT-TAB twice, ↵ ENTER	Selects SAVE button.
Press	N	to not save environment.

3 Correct the detail band on the weekly pay report.

Open	EMPLOYEE	unless already active.
Press	ALT, F, O	Selects File, Open.
Press	SHIFT-TAB twice, ↵ ENTER, ↓ five times, ↵ ENTER	Changes file type to Report.

FoxPro

Press	(arrow keys) as needed	Highlights Report1.
Press	TAB three times, ← ENTER	Selects OPEN button; opens REPORT1.

> **TIP:** The mouse operations work exactly the same for moving report objects as they did for screen objects.

The current layout appears on the screen. You can now make changes to this layout in exactly the same manner you did when you first created it. To move, delete, or resize a field, you first need to select the field. Selecting a report object is exactly the same as selecting a screen object. Use the cursor to move to the object, press the SPACEBAR, move the object with the arrow keys, and press ENTER.

> **TIP:** As you remove fields from the detail band, the page header will no longer be accurate. Don't worry about this. You will fix it shortly.

Press	↓ as needed	to move to NUMBER field in detail band.
Press	SPACEBAR	Selects field.
Press	DELETE	Deletes field.

Your screen should then look like Figure 15.5. Note that the field is now removed. Use the same technique to remove the DATE and UNION fields from the detail band. ◀

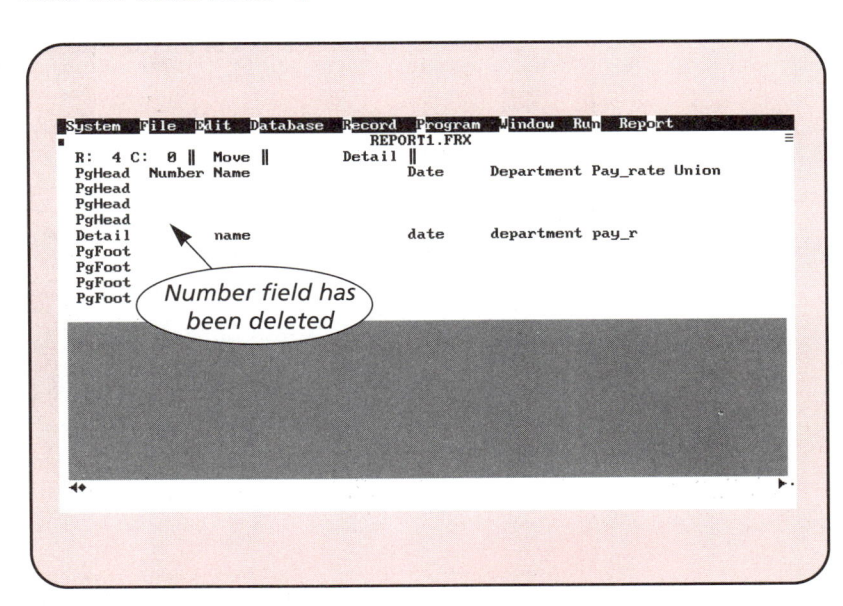

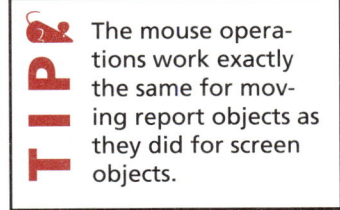

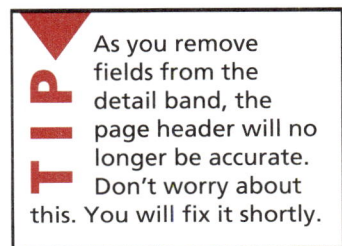

Figure 15.5
Report Layout Window

```
System  File  Edit  Database  Record  Program  Window  Run  Report
                         REPORT1.FRX
R:  4 C:  0 ‖ Move ‖        Detail ‖
PgHead  Number Name          Date       Department Pay_rate Union
PgHead
PgHead
PgHead
Detail         name          date       department pay_r
PgFoot
PgFoot        (Number field has
PgFoot         been deleted)
PgFoot
```

You now need to move the NAME field to the beginning of the band.

Press	SHIFT-TAB as needed	to move to NAME field in detail band.
Press	SPACEBAR	Selects field.
Press	← as needed	Moves to beginning of detail band.

Topic 15: Creating a Report Layout **125**

| Press | ⏎ ENTER | |

Move the DEPARTMENT and PAY_RATE fields in the same manner so that only one space separates each field.

Press	TAB as needed	to move to DEPARTMENT field in detail band.
Press	SPACEBAR	Selects field.
Press	← as needed	Moves DEPARTMENT one space over from NAME.
Press	⏎ ENTER	Sets position of DEPARTMENT.

Now move the pay rate to the position shown in Figure 15.6. The only step that remains is to add the weekly pay rate to the detail band. You need to create an additional field that is calculated from existing fields (weekly pay is equal to PAY_RATE multiplied by 40).

Figure 15.6
Report Layout Window

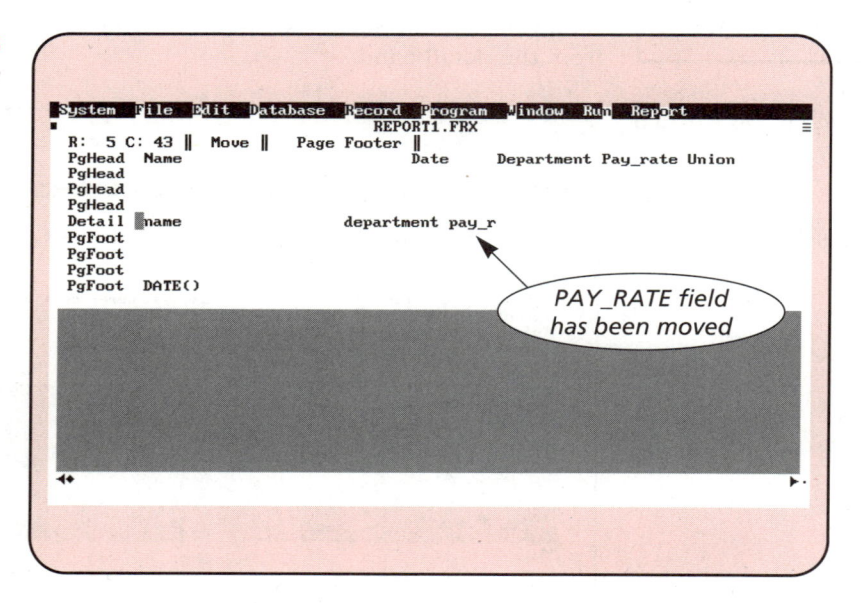

[Screenshot of Report Layout Window showing REPORT1.FRX with PgHead, Detail, and PgFoot bands. Callout: "PAY_RATE field has been moved"]

Press	→ as needed	to move cursor to end of detail band one space past PAY_RATE field.
Press	ALT, O, F	Selects Record, Field.
Press	⏎ ENTER	Selects EXPRESSION button.
Press	SHIFT-TAB	Moves to Field Name list.
Press	↓ four times, ⏎ ENTER	Selects PAY_RATE.
Press	CTRL-M, ↑, ⏎ ENTER	Selects * symbol.

Type	40	
Press	SHIFT - TAB three times, ↵ ENTER	Selects OK button; returns to Field dialog box.
Press	SHIFT - TAB twice, ↵ ENTER	Selects OK button; returns to Report Layout window; inserts a new field.

This indicates that the value of the calculated field for a record is to be obtained by taking the value of PAY_RATE on the record and multiplying it by 40. In these expressions, you can also use the plus sign (+) for addition, the minus sign (-) for subtraction, and a backslash (/) for division.

Resize the field so that it is 6 characters wide rather than 8.

Press	→ as needed	to move cursor into field.
Press	↵ ENTER	Opens Field dialog box.
Press	TAB four times	Moves to Width entry.
Type	6	Replaces 8 with 6.
Press	SHIFT - TAB six times, ↵ ENTER	Selects OK button.

4 **Correct the report summary on the weekly pay report.** Create a Report Summary band and insert a new field for totaling the weekly pay rates.

Press	ALT, O, Y	Selects Report, Title/Summary.
Press	S	Selects Summary checkbox.
Press	TAB twice, ↵ ENTER	Selects OK button.
Press	(arrow keys) as needed	to move to calculated weekly PAY_RATE field.
Press	SPACEBAR	Selects PAY_RATE field.
Press	ALT, E, C	Selects Edit, Copy.
Press	↓ as needed, ↵ ENTER	to move duplicated field to summary band of report.
Press	ALT, E, P	Selects Edit, Paste.

By copying and pasting the field, you did not have to reenter the entire expression that was created earlier. Now convert the field to a summary field.

Topic 15: Creating a Report Layout

Press	`← ENTER`	Opens Field dialog box.
Press	`C`, `S`	Selects Calculate, Sum checkboxes.
Press	`SHIFT`-`TAB` four times, `← ENTER`	Selects OK button; returns to Field dialog box.
Press	`SHIFT`-`TAB` three times	Moves to Width entry.
Type	9	Changes width to 9.
Press	`TAB` five times, `← ENTER`	Selects OK button; returns to Reports Layout window.
Press	`SPACEBAR`, `←` three times	Moves field to align with weekly pay rate field.
Press	`ALT`, `O`, `N`	Selects Report, Add Line; adds another summary line to report.
Type	-------- `← ENTER`	Adds dotted line text object to separate summary from detail numbers.

Make sure that the text object appears directly above the **summary field**. You may need to move the object.

Press	`ALT`, `F`, `C`, `Y`	Selects File, Close, Yes.

5 Correct the page header on the weekly pay report.

Open	EMPLOYEE	unless already active.
Open	Report	as described earlier unless already active.

Now correct the page header so that it looks like the one in **Figure 15.7**. Minor changes such as moving report objects may need to be made in order for the report to look like Figure 15.7.

Press	`CTRL`-`HOME`	Moves cursor to top left corner of report.
Press	`CTRL`-`O` and `Y` twice	Confirms and deletes two lines.
Press	`CTRL`-`N` four times	Inserts four new lines.

Figure 15.7
Report Layout Window

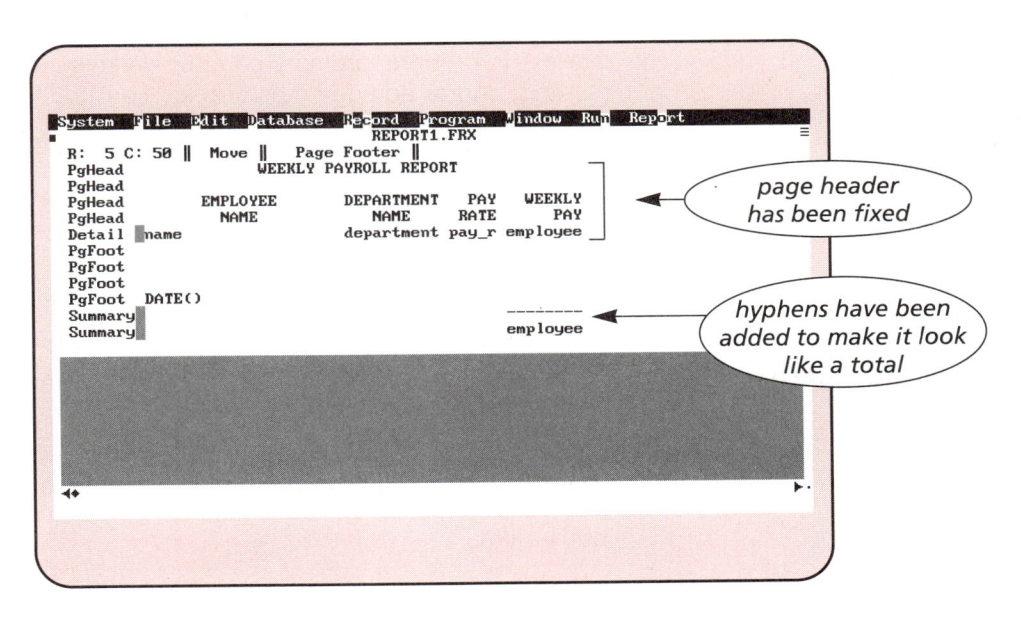

```
System  File  Edit  Database  Record  Program  Window  Run  Report
                         REPORT1.FRX
R:  5 C: 50 ║  Move ║  Page Footer ║
PgHead                WEEKLY PAYROLL REPORT
PgHead
PgHead          EMPLOYEE     DEPARTMENT    PAY    WEEKLY
PgHead            NAME          NAME      RATE     PAY
Detail   name
PgFoot                        department  pay_r  employee
PgFoot
PgFoot
PgFoot   DATE()
Summary                                          --------
Summary                                          employee
```

— page header has been fixed

— hyphens have been added to make it look like a total

This erases all the text objects (column headings) and gives you the right number of lines. To make any of the entries shown in the page header band in the figure, move the cursor to the desired location and type the letters you want. If you make a mistake, move the cursor to within the text object, press CONTROL-RIGHT ARROW, place the cursor on the incorrect letter using the arrow keys, press DELETE, and press ENTER. All text entries must be completed by pressing ENTER.

| Press | ALT , F , C , Y | Selects File, Close, Yes. |

PROCEDURE SUMMARY

BEGINNING THE REPORT CREATION PROCESS

Open the database file.	(your choice)
Create a report.	ALT , F , N , R
Change the file type to Report.	(arrow keys)
Select the OK button.	TAB seven times, ↵ ENTER
Select Quick Report.	ALT , O , Q , ↵ ENTER

ALTERING THE REPORT LAYOUT

Correct the detail band by deleting, resizing, and/or adding fields or text. You may also need to add or delete lines.	(your input)

Topic 15: Creating a Report Layout

129

	Correct the report summary band by deleting, resizing, and/or adding fields or text. You may also need to add or delete lines.	(your input)
	Correct the page header band by deleting, resizing, and/or adding fields or text. You may also need to add or delete lines.	(your input)
ADDING OR DELETING LINES IN A BAND	**To delete the line the cursor is on:**	
	Delete the line.	CTRL-O
	To insert a blank line before the line the cursor is on:	
	Insert a line.	CTRL-N
SELECTING FIELDS AND TEXT OBJECTS	**To select a field:**	
	Move the cursor to the field.	(arrow keys)
	Select the field.	SPACEBAR
	To select text:	
	Move the cursor to anyplace in the text object.	(arrow keys)
	Select the text.	SPACEBAR
REMOVING FIELDS FROM A REPORT	Select the field.	(your choice)
	Delete the field.	DELETE
MOVING FIELDS IN A REPORT	Select the field.	(your choice)
	Move the cursor to the new position for the field.	(arrow keys)
	Complete the move.	↵ ENTER
RESIZING FIELDS IN A REPORT	Select the field.	(your choice)
	Open the Field dialog box.	↵ ENTER

130   *FoxPro*

Move the Width entry.	`TAB` four times
Type the new width number.	(your input)
Select the OK button.	`SHIFT`-`TAB` six times, `↵ ENTER`

ADDING FIELDS

To add an existing field:

Move the cursor to the position for the new field.	(arrow keys)
Select the Field dialog box.	`CTRL`-`F`
Select the Expression dialog box.	`↵ ENTER`
Move to the Field Name list and select the field.	`SHIFT`-`TAB`, `↑` or `↓` as needed, `↵ ENTER`
Select the OK button.	`SHIFT`-`TAB` three times, `↵ ENTER`
Select the OK button.	`SHIFT`-`TAB` twice, `↵ ENTER`

To add a calculated field:

Move the cursor to the position for the new field.	(arrow keys)
Select the Field dialog box.	`CTRL`-`F`
Select the Expression dialog box.	`↵ ENTER`
Move to the Field Name list and select the field.	`SHIFT`-`TAB`, `↑` or `↓` (as needed), `↵ ENTER`
Select the operator popup.	`CTRL`-`M`, `CTRL`-`S`, `CTRL`-`L`, or `CTRL`-`PAGE DOWN`
Select the operator.	`↑` or `↓`, `↵ ENTER`
Complete the expression.	(your input)
Select the OK button.	`SHIFT`-`TAB` three times, `↵ ENTER`
Select the OK button.	`SHIFT`-`TAB` twice, `↵ ENTER`

Topic 15: Creating a Report Layout **131**

To add a summary field:

Select the field to be summarized in the detail.	`SPACEBAR`
Copy the field.	`ALT`, `E`, `C`
Paste the field.	`ALT`, `E`, `P`
Select the duplicate field.	`SPACEBAR`
Move to the summary band.	`↓` (as needed), `↵ ENTER`
Open the Field dialog box.	`↵ ENTER`
Select Calculate, Sum.	`C`, `S`
Select the OK button.	`SHIFT`-`TAB` four times, `↵ ENTER`
Select the OK button.	`TAB` twice, `↵ ENTER`

FINISHING THE REPORT LAYOUT PROCESS

Preview the report on the screen.	`ALT`, `O`, `I`
Save and close the report.	`ALT`, `F`, `C`
If this is the first time you have saved this report, enter a name for the report file.	(your input)

MODIFYING A REPORT LAYOUT

Open the database file.	(your choice)
Open the report.	`ALT`, `F`, `O`
Change the file type to Report.	(arrow keys)
Select the report file to modify.	`↑` or `↓`, `↵ ENTER`
Select the OK button.	`↵ ENTER`

EXERCISES

1. You are to create a report for data in the CHECK database file. The report is to contain page and column headings. Fields to be included on the report include the Check Number, Date, Payee, Check Amount, and Expense type. A final total is to be displayed of the check amount field. Begin the report creation process for this report. Call the report CHKRPT1.
2. Correct the detail band for this report.
3. Correct the report summary for this report.
4. Correct the page header for this report.

TOPIC 16

Printing a Report

CONCEPTS A report file contains information about the layout (design) of a report. It contains details concerning the page heading, the layout of various columns, the totals that are to be calculated, and so on. The value of a report file is that, once it has been created, you can print a report using the layout stored in the report file whenever you want. You do not have to specify the same details every time you print the report. You simply refer to the report file.

Printing a Report

(135)

At any point, you can print a report with the same layout as the one that was shown in Figure 15.1. You simply use the data in the EMPLOYEE database file together with the report file you have created. Certainly the data shown in the report will change. There could be new employees or changes in pay rates, for example. Nevertheless the "look" of the report remains the same. There will always be the same columns with the same column headings; the title will always be the same; the same columns will be totaled; and so on.

Sometimes you would like to have the records in a report ordered in some particular fashion. To do so, you just make sure the records in the database are ordered the way you want them to appear on the report. In this text, you do this by using an appropriate index. Another option would be to first sort the database file and then use the sorted file for the report.

Selecting Records for a Report

(136)

In many cases, you want to include all the records from your database file when you print the report. In other cases, you only want to include those records that satisfy some condition in the report. For example, the manager of the Accounting department may only be interested in employees who are in Accounting. Including other employees in the report would make it unnecessarily long. Further, the manager would need to skim through the report looking for just those employees in Accounting. It would be much simpler if the report included those employees only. Fortunately you can easily restrict the records that appear in a report by using a query.

TUTORIAL In this tutorial, you print the report you have created.

1 Print the report whose description is stored in the report file called REPORT1. Include all the records from the EMPLOYEE database file. The records should be ordered by name.

| Press | ALT , F , O | Selects File, Open; displays File Open dialog box. |

Topic 16: Printing a Report **133**

Confirm that the Database type is selected. If not, you need to press the TAB key several times to move to the type popup and change the type to Database.

Press	(arrow keys) as needed	to highlight EMPLOYEE.
Press	↵ ENTER	Selects EMPLOYEE database file.
Press	ALT , D , U	Selects Database, Setup.
Press	↑ or ↓ as needed	Selects NAME index tag.
Press	O	Selects the SET ORDER button.
Press	SHIFT - TAB three times, ↵ ENTER	Selects OK button.

You are returned to the Command window. The records are ordered by name.

Press	ALT , N , R	Selects Run, Report.
Press	(arrow keys) as needed	to highlight REPORT1.
Press	TAB three times	Selects RUN button.

You now see the Report dialog box. By selecting one of the checkboxes, you determine the destination of your output: Preview, To Print (printer), or To File. You now print the report.

Press	P	Selects To Print.
Press	R	Selects RUN button; prints report.

2 **Print the report whose description is stored in the report file called REPORT1.** Include only the employees in the Shipping department. You can restrict the records that will appear in a report by creating and using an appropriate query. Because you need the query only for this printing of the report, change the output popup to Report.

Open	EMPLOYEE	unless already active.
Press	ALT , N , N	Selects Run, New Query.
Press	SHIFT - TAB	until highlight is under Field Name column in condition area.
Press	↵ ENTER	Displays Field Name list.
Press	↑ or ↓ as needed	to highlight EMPLOYEE.DEPARTMENT.
Press	↵ ENTER	Places EMPLOYEE.DEPARTMENT in Field Name column.

Press	TAB twice	Moves to Example column.
Type	"Shipping"	
Press	← ENTER	Completes condition.
Press	END	Removes Browse window.
Press	TAB	until highlight is within Output To box. The word "Browse" is highlighted.
Press	← ENTER	Displays popup list.
Press	↑ or ↓ as needed	to highlight Report/Label.
Press	← ENTER	Places Report/Label in Output To box.
Press	TAB	Highlights Options checkbox.
Press	← ENTER	Displays RQBE Display Options dialog box.
Press	R, Q, ← ENTER	Selects Report and column formatted Quick Report.
Press	P, T	Removes screen preview option; selects printer as destination.
Press	TAB twice, ← ENTER	Selects OK button; returns to RQBE window.
Press	Q	Selects DO QUERY button; performs query; prints report.
Press	ESC	Closes RQBE window; displays warning box for saving query.
Press	N	Declines query save.

You are returned to the Command window. The query is still active so you need to run another query or exit FoxPro before proceeding to another exercise.

PROCEDURE SUMMARY

PRINTING A REPORT

Open the database file. If an index is required to order the records a particular way, order the records by the index.	(your choice)
Select the Run, Report command.	ALT, R, P
Select the Report file.	↑ or ↓

Topic 16: Printing a Report　　　　　　　　　　　　　　　　　　　　　　　135

Select the destination.	(arrow keys)
Select the OK button.	`TAB` (as needed), `ENTER`

SELECTING RECORDS FOR A REPORT

Open the database file.	
Open the RQBE window.	`ALT`, `R`, `R`
Move to the column for the condition under the field name.	`TAB` or `SHIFT`-`TAB`
Call up the Field Name list.	`ENTER`
Highlight the desired field.	`↑` or `↓`
Select the field.	`ENTER`
Take one of the following steps.	
Fill the checkbox if the inverse condition is desired.	`ENTER`
Advance without filling in the checkbox.	`TAB`
Open the Operators popup.	`ENTER`
Highlight the desired operator.	`↑` or `↓`
Select the operator.	`ENTER`
Type in the Example column.	(your input)
Accept the input.	`ENTER`
Take one of the following steps.	
Fill the checkbox to ignore case sensitivity.	`ENTER`
Advance without filling in the checkbox.	`TAB`
Move to the Output To popup.	`TAB` (as needed)
Open the Output To popup.	`ENTER`
Move to Report/Label.	`↑` or `↓` (as needed)
Display the RQBE Display Options dialog box.	`P`
Select Report.	`R`, `ENTER`
Open the Report file box.	`N`
Select the Report filename.	`↑` or `↓` (as needed)
Select the OK button.	`TAB` twice, `ENTER`
Uncheck the screen preview option.	`P`

FoxPro

Select the printer as the destination.	T
Highlight the OK button.	TAB or (arrow keys)
Return to the RQBE window.	↵ ENTER
Select the DO QUERY button and print the report.	Q
If needed, overwrite the previous query.	Y

EXERCISES

1. Print a report of all the records in the CHECK database file. Use the report layout stored in CHKRPT1.

2. Print a report of those records in the CHECK database file on which amount is more than $50.00. Use the report layout stored in CHKRPT1.

Topic 16: Printing a Report **137**

TOPIC 17

Including Subtotals

CONCEPTS Often you need to group together in a report all the records that have the same value in some field. For example, you might want all the employees in any given department to appear together on the report. When you group records in this fashion, you may be interested in the totals for the records in each group. After the list of employees in a department, for example, you may want to see the total of the pay rates for just those employees. Such totals are called subtotals because they represent a subset of the overall total. The report shown in Figure 15.2, for example, contains subtotals of the weekly pay amounts for the employees in each department.

Grouping

The report in Figure 15.2 included two new types of objects: a group header and a group footer. The group header indicates the department, and the group footer gives the total of the weekly pay amounts for all records in the group. To group records in a report, you need to use a new type of band, called a **group band**.

When you have added group bands to your report, your screen should look like the one in Figure 17.1. Note that two new bands have appeared, the group header band and the group footer band. The collection of all employees in the same department is a group. Whatever you specify in the group header band is displayed immediately before each group (it heads the group). Whatever you specify in the group footer band is displayed immediately after each group (in other words, it is at the foot of each group).

Figure 17.1
Report Layout Window

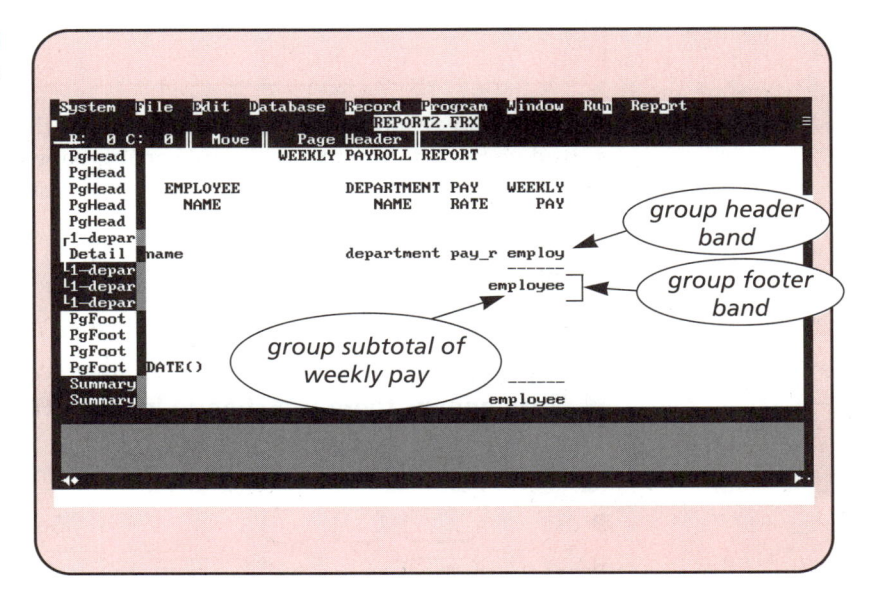

Look at the report title band and the group header band in Figure 17.1. Do you notice a difference? A blank line follows the group header band, but none follows the report title band. Any band that does not have at least one line following it is closed, and the contents of the band, whatever they may be, will not be printed on the report. The other bands are open, and their contents will print. Currently the group header band consists of just a single blank line. This will still appear on the report, however. The group of employees in any given department is preceded by a single blank line. To close a band that is currently open or to open a band that is currently closed, move the cursor to the line that gives the name of the band and press ENTER.

Printing a Report with Subtotals

The only special consideration in printing a report with subtotals is that data must be in the correct order. Figure 17.2 illustrates what can happen if the order is not correct. This report is certainly very strange. There is a group for Accounting, followed by a group for Shipping, one for Marketing, and then another one for Accounting. What's wrong? The problem is that the records are not sorted correctly. All the records for a given department must be together for the report to be correct.

Figure 17.2
Weekly Payroll Report (with Incorrect Grouping)

```
                     WEEKLY PAYROLL REPORT
EMPLOYEE              DEPARTMENT         PAY         WEEKLY
  NAME                  NAME             RATE          PAY
Ackerman, David R.    Production         6.00        240.00
                                                     ------
                                                     240.00

Anderson, Carole L.   Shipping           9.00        360.00
                                                     ------
                                                     360.00

Andrews, Robert M.    Marketing          9.00        360.00
                                                     ------
                                                     360.00

Baxter, Charles W.    Accounting        11.00        440.00
                                                     ------
                                                     440.00

Bender, Ginger O.     Production         6.75        270.00
                                                     ------
                                                     270.00
```

It is your responsibility to make sure that the data used for the report is sorted correctly. You can do so by sorting your database file appropriately and then using the sorted file for the report. Alternatively, you can use an index that orders the records appropriately.

TUTORIAL
In this tutorial, you change the report to include subtotals.

1 Modify the report stored in REPORT1 so that a subtotal is taken whenever there is a change in DEPARTMENT.

Open	EMPLOYEE	unless already active.
Press	ALT , F , O	Selects File, Open.
Press	TAB as needed, ↵ ENTER	Change file type popup to Report.

140   FoxPro

Press	(arrow keys) as needed	Highlights REPORT1.
Press	`TAB` three times, `ENTER`	Selects OPEN button.

To group records in a report, you need to use a new type of band, called a group band. Add the necessary group band to the report.

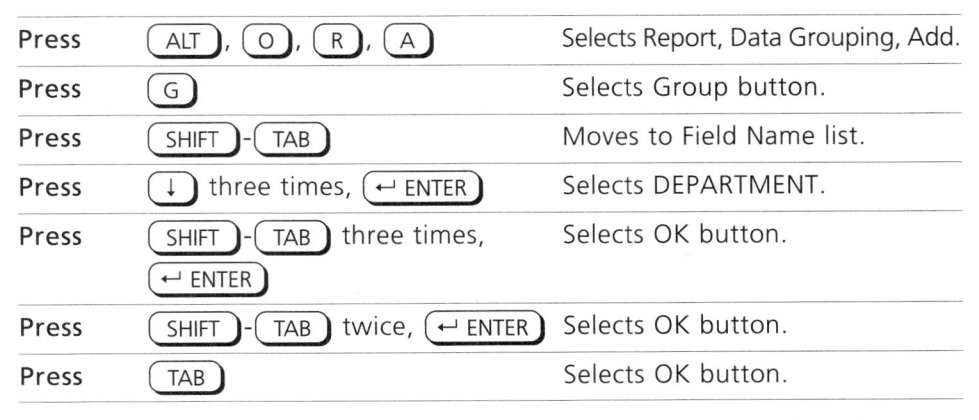

Press	`ALT`, `O`, `R`, `A`	Selects Report, Data Grouping, Add.
Press	`G`	Selects Group button.
Press	`SHIFT`-`TAB`	Moves to Field Name list.
Press	`↓` three times, `ENTER`	Selects DEPARTMENT.
Press	`SHIFT`-`TAB` three times, `ENTER`	Selects OK button.
Press	`SHIFT`-`TAB` twice, `ENTER`	Selects OK button.
Press	`TAB`	Selects OK button.

The group header band follows the page header band. Now let's fix the group footer band.

Press	(arrow keys) as needed	Moves to blank line in group footer band (the line after the detail band).
Press	`CTRL`-`N` twice	Adds two lines.
Press	`←` or `→` as needed	Moves cursor under weekly pay field.

You should be on the first of the three blank lines in the group footer band.

Type	-------- `ENTER`	
Press	`↑`, `SPACEBAR`	Moves up one line; selects weekly pay field object.
Press	`ALT`, `E`, `C`	Copies field.
Press	`SPACEBAR`	Deselects field.
Press	`↓` twice, `ALT`, `E`, `P`	Pastes field below dotted line.
Press	`SPACEBAR`, `ENTER`	Deselects field; opens Field dialog box.
Press	`C`, `S`	Selects Calculate, Sum checkboxes.
Press	`SHIFT`-`TAB` five times, `ENTER`	Opens Reset popup.

Topic 17: Including Subtotals

Press	↑ or ↓ as needed, ↵ ENTER	Selects EMPLOYEE.DEPARTMENT.
Press	TAB , ↵ ENTER	Selects OK button; returns to Field dialog box.

Now you need to resize the field.

Press	SHIFT - TAB three times	Moves cursor to Width entry.
Type	8	Changes width to 8.
Press	TAB five times, ↵ ENTER	Selects OK button; returns to Reports Design screen.
Press	ALT , F , C , Y	Selects File, Close, Yes.

You are returned to the Command window. Your report should look like Figure 17.3.

Figure 17.3
Report Layout Window

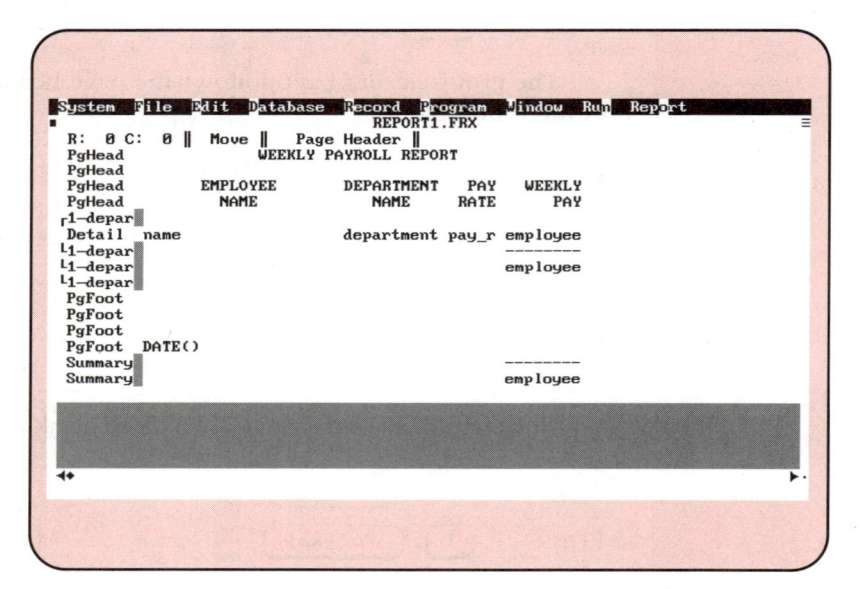

```
 System  File  Edit  Database  Record  Program  Window  Run  Report
                        REPORT1.FRX
 R:  0 C:   0 ‖  Move  ‖  Page Header ‖
 PgHead
 PgHead              WEEKLY PAYROLL REPORT
 PgHead
 PgHead         EMPLOYEE        DEPARTMENT   PAY    WEEKLY
 PgHead           NAME             NAME      RATE    PAY
 ┌1-depar
  Detail  name                  department  pay_r  employee
 └1-depar
 └1-depar
 └1-depar                                          employee
 PgFoot
 PgFoot
 PgFoot
 PgFoot  DATE()
 Summary                                           ────────
 Summary                                           employee
```

2 Print the report. You want the records to be ordered by name within department. You did have an index that you created on this combination, but you removed it. Thus you will need to re-create it. (If the index already existed, you would simply order records by this index.)

Press	ALT , F , N , I	Selects File, New, Index.
Press	SHIFT , TAB five times, ↵ ENTER	Selects OK button.
Press	TAB , ↵ ENTER	Selects EXPRESSION button.

Press	`DELETE`, `SHIFT`-`TAB`	Deletes previous expression; moves to Field Name list.
Press	`↓` three times, `ENTER`	Places DEPARTMENT in Expression window.
Press	`CTRL`-`M`, `↓`, `ENTER`	Adds + symbol to Expression window.
Press	`SHIFT`-`TAB`, `↑` twice, `ENTER`	Moves to Field Name list; adds NAME to Expression window.

This index expression indicates the combination of DEPARTMENT and NAME.

Press	`SHIFT`-`TAB` three times, `ENTER`	Selects OK button.
Press	`TAB` seven times	Moves to Tag entry.
Type	DPTNAME	
Press	`ENTER`	Gives DPTNAME as index tag.
Press	`ENTER`	Moves expression into Index On list.
Press	`TAB` four times, `ENTER`	Selects OK button.

You are returned to the Command window. Since you have just created the index ordering records by name within department, it is active. If not, you would first need to select the Database, Setup command and then select the index.

Press	`ALT`, `N`, `R`	Selects Run, Report.
Press	`↑` or `↓` as needed	Highlight REPORT2.
Press	`TAB` three times, `ENTER`	Selects RUN button.
Press	`P`	Selects To Print.
Press	`TAB`, `ENTER`	Selects RUN button; prints report.

PROCEDURE SUMMARY

GROUPING

Open the database file unless it is already active.	(your choice)
Open a report.	`ALT`, `F`, `O`
Change the file type to Report.	(arrow keys)
Select a report file.	(your choice)

Topic 17: Including Subtotals

Select the OK button.	`TAB` (as needed), `↵ ENTER`
Select Data Grouping, Add.	`ALT`, `O`, `R`, `A`
Select the GROUP button.	`G`
Select the field on which to group.	`SHIFT`-`TAB`, (your choice)
Select the OK button.	`TAB` (as needed), `↵ ENTER`
Select the OK button.	`TAB` (as needed), `↵ ENTER`
Select the OK button.	`TAB` (as needed), `↵ ENTER`

PRINTING A REPORT WITH SUBTOTALS

Open the database file. If the data in the database file is not in the correct order for the report, select an index that will order the records appropriately. If no such index exists, create one.	(your choice)
Select and copy the desired NUMERIC field for subtotals.	`SPACEBAR`, `ALT`, `E`, `C`
Deselect the field and move the cursor to the group footer band.	`SPACEBAR`, `↓` as needed
Paste the field.	`↵ ENTER`, `ALT`, `E`, `P`
Deselect the field.	`SPACEBAR`
Open the Field dialog box.	`↵ ENTER`
Select Calculate, Sum.	`C`, `S`
Indicate the desired option in the Reset popup.	`TAB` (as needed), `↵ ENTER`
Select the OK button.	`TAB` (as needed), `↵ ENTER`
Select the OK button.	`↵ ENTER`
Close the Report layout.	`ALT`, `F`, `C`, `Y`
Run the report.	`ALT`, `N`, `R`
Select To Print.	`P`
Select the RUN button.	`TAB`, `↵ ENTER`

EXERCISES

1. Modify the report format stored in CHKRPT1 so that a subtotal is taken when there is a change in Expense type.
2. Use this report format to display all the records in the CHECK database file. Be sure the records are ordered correctly.

TOPIC 18

Modifying the Structure

CONCEPTS When you initially create a database, you define its structure; that is, you indicate the names, types, and widths of all the fields. It would be nice if the structure you first defined would continue to be appropriate as long as you use the database. However, the structure of a database file might need to change for a variety of reasons. Changes in the needs of the database users might require that more fields be added. For example, if it is important to store the number of hours an employee has worked, such a field must be added to the EMPLOYEE file since it is not there already.

Characteristics of a given field might need to change. It just so happens that Mary Castleworth's name is stored incorrectly in the database. Rather than "Castleworth, Mary T.", it should be "Castleworth, Marianne K.". There is no problem changing the middle initial from "T" to "K"; there is a big problem changing the first name from "Mary" to "Marianne," however. There is not enough room in the NAME field to hold the correct name! To accommodate this change, the width of the NAME field must be increased.

It may turn out that a field that is currently in the database file is no longer necessary. If no one ever uses the DEPARTMENT field, for example, there is no point in having it in the database file. Since the field occupies space and serves no useful purpose, it would be nice to remove it from the database file.

Sometimes you discover that the structure you determined earlier has some inherent problems. Did it ever bother you, for example, that you had to type a complete department name when entering each employee? Wouldn't it be easier to simply type a code number. It would simplify the process of entering data. It would also save space in the database since storing a one- or two-character code number does not take as much space as storing a ten-character department name. Finally, it cuts down on errors during data entry. If you only have to type the number "01" rather than the name "Accounting," for example, you will be much less likely to make mistakes. Such mistakes can have serious consequences. If, for example, "Accouning" is inadvertently entered as the department for an employee, that employee will be omitted from any list of employees whose department is "Accounting." Thus you might want to store the code number rather than the department number.

What do you do, however, if you are supposed to print the department name on some crucial reports? The answer is that you create a separate database file containing department numbers and names. This would mean that rather than the single database file that you have been using (Figure 18.1), there will be two files (Figure 18.2). Notice that the first database file has no DEPARTMENT column but instead has a column for code numbers

(DEPT_NUMB). The second database file also has a DEPT_NUMB column as well as a column that contains the department name. Using these two database files still allows you to list the name of the department for each employee. To find the department name for Anthony Rapoza, for example, you would first find that he works in department 04 by looking in the DEPT_NUMB column in his row. Then you would look for the row in the second database file that contained 04 in the DEPT_NUMB column. Once you found it, you would look in the next column on the same row and see that department 04 is Shipping. Thus Anthony Rapoza works in the Shipping department.

Figure 18.1
Employee Data Stored in a Single File

EMPLOYEE NUMBER	EMPLOYEE NAME	DATE HIRED	DEPARTMENT NAME	PAY RATE	UNION MEMBER
1011	Rapoza, Anthony P.	01/10/93	Shipping	8.50	T
1013	McCormack, Nigel L.	01/15/93	Shipping	8.25	T
1016	Fong, Ronald	02/04/93	Accounting	9.75	F
1017	Ackerman, Mary R.	02/05/93	Production	6.00	T
1020	Castle, Mark C.	03/04/93	Shipping	7.50	T
1022	Dunning, Greta L.	03/12/93	Marketing	9.10	F
1025	Chaney, Joseph R.	03/23/93	Accounting	8.00	F
1026	Bender, Ginger O.	04/12/93	Production	6.75	T
1029	Anderson, Carole L.	04/18/93	Shipping	9.00	T
1030	Edwards, Kenneth J.	04/23/93	Production	8.60	T
1037	Baxter, Charles W.	05/05/93	Accounting	11.00	F
1041	Evans, John T.	05/19/93	Marketing	6.00	F
1056	Andrews, Robert M.	06/03/93	Marketing	9.00	F
1057	Hall, Sandy H.	06/10/93	Production	8.75	T
1066	Castleworth, Mary T.	07/05/93	Production	8.75	T

department name → (points to DEPARTMENT NAME column)

Figure 18.2
Employee Data Stored in Two Files

EMPLOYEE NUMBER	EMPLOYEE NAME	DATE HIRED	PAY RATE	UNION MEMBER	DEPART NUMBER
1011	Rapoza, Anthony P.	01/10/93	8.50	T	04
1013	McCormack, Nigel L.	01/15/93	8.25	T	04
1016	Fong, Ronald	02/04/93	9.75	F	01
1017	Ackerman, Mary R.	02/05/93	6.00	T	03
1020	Castle, Mark C.	03/04/93	7.50	T	04
1022	Dunning, Greta L.	03/12/93	9.10	F	02
1025	Chaney, Joseph R.	03/23/93	8.00	F	01
1026	Bender, Ginger O.	04/12/93	6.75	T	03
1029	Anderson, Carole L.	04/18/93	9.00	T	04
1030	Edwards, Kenneth J.	04/23/93	8.60	T	03
1037	Baxter, Charles W.	05/05/93	11.00	F	01
1041	Evans, John T.	05/19/93	6.00	F	02
1056	Andrews, Robert M.	06/03/93	9.00	F	02
1057	Hall, Sandy H.	06/10/93	8.75	T	03
1066	Castleworth, Mary T.	07/05/93	8.75	T	03

DEPT NUMB	DEPARTMENT NAME
01	Accounting
02	Marketing
03	Production
04	Shipping

department number → (points to DEPT NUMB column)
department name → (points to DEPARTMENT NAME column)

> **TIP** FoxPro removes the index tags of modified fields. When you change the width of a field, you should examine the reports and screens on which the field appears to see if they also need changes.

> **TIP** When you add a field, it does not automatically appear on reports or screens that you created previously. You must modify the reports or screens by including these new fields.

> **TIP** Problems occur with screens and reports that use deleted fields. Be sure to modify such screens and reports by removing the deleted fields.

You now have a database that consists of more than one database file. You need a way to relate the two database files, that is, to use information from both. This is done by using what is called a **relational query**. (You will create and use relational queries in Topics 20 and 21.)

Changing Field Characteristics

The original characteristics of a field (type and width) may no longer be appropriate. Typically, if you need to make a change, it is a width change such as increasing the width of the NAME field. Although not common, it is possible to change the type if necessary. ◄

Adding a New Field

When a new field, such as the number of hours worked, becomes necessary, you must be able to add the field to your database file. ◄

To make new entries, you can use either Change or Browse and simply proceed through each and every record. Whenever you encounter a record on which the value for DEPARTMENT is Accounting, set DEPT_NUMB to 01; if the value is Marketing, set DEPT_NUMB to 02; and so on. Does this approach seem cumbersome to you? Even with only seventeen records, it probably seems like a lot of busy work. What if there were several thousand records? It would take a long time to make these changes, with many chances to make errors. Fortunately there is an easier way. You can use the Record, Replace command.

Deleting a Field

If a field is no longer necessary, there is no point in leaving it in the database file. You are better off deleting it. ◄

TUTORIAL In this tutorial, you change the structure of the database from the one represented in Figure 18.1 to the one represented in Figure 18.2. In particular, you will:

1. Change the length of the NAME field in the EMPLOYEE database file to 24.
2. Add the DEPT_NUMB field to the EMPLOYEE file.
3. Fill in the DEPT_NUMB field with appropriate values.
4. Delete the DEPARTMENT field from the EMPLOYEE database file.

1 Change the width of the NAME field in the EMPLOYEE database file to 24.

Press   ALT , F , O   Displays File Open dialog box.

You may need to change the file type popup to Database.

Topic 18: Modifying the Structure

Select	EMPLOYEE	
Press	TAB three times, ← ENTER	Selects OPEN button.
Press	ALT, D, U, Y	Selects Database, Setup, Modify.

Your screen should now look like Figure 18.3. Note that your current structure is displayed.

Figure 18.3
Modify Structure Dialog Box

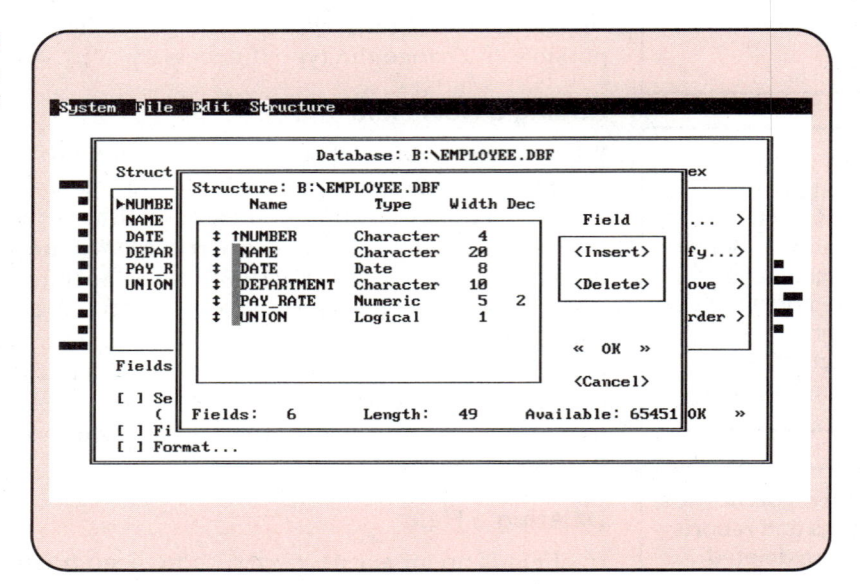

Press	TAB three times, ↓	Highlights NAME field.
Press	TAB twice	Moves to Width column.
Type	24	
Press	← ENTER	Changes width.
Press	TAB as needed, ← ENTER	Highlights and selects OK button.
Press	Y	Confirms change.
Press	TAB as needed, ← ENTER	Highlights and selects OK button.

2 **Add the DEPT_NUMB field to the EMPLOYEE database file.** It should be a CHARACTER field, have a width of 2, and be the last field in the database file.

Open	EMPLOYEE	unless already active.
Press	TAB three times, ← ENTER	Selects OK button.
Press	ALT, D, U, Y	Selects Database, Setup, Modify.
Press	TAB three times, ↓ six times	Moves to empty field name.

148   FoxPro

Type	DEPT_NUMB	
Press	⏎ ENTER	Names new field.
Press	⏎ ENTER twice	Selects Character as type.
Type	2	
Press	⏎ ENTER	Enters field width.
Press	TAB as needed, ⏎ ENTER	Selects OK button.
Press	⏎ ENTER	Confirms change.
Press	TAB as needed, ⏎ ENTER	Selects OK button.

Once the process is complete, your database looks like Figure 18.4. This window can be displayed by selecting the Database, Browse command. Note the new field, DEPT_NUMB, on the right. No entries have yet been filled in for DEPT_NUMB. Note also that the NAME field is wider than it was before.

Figure 18.4
Browse Window

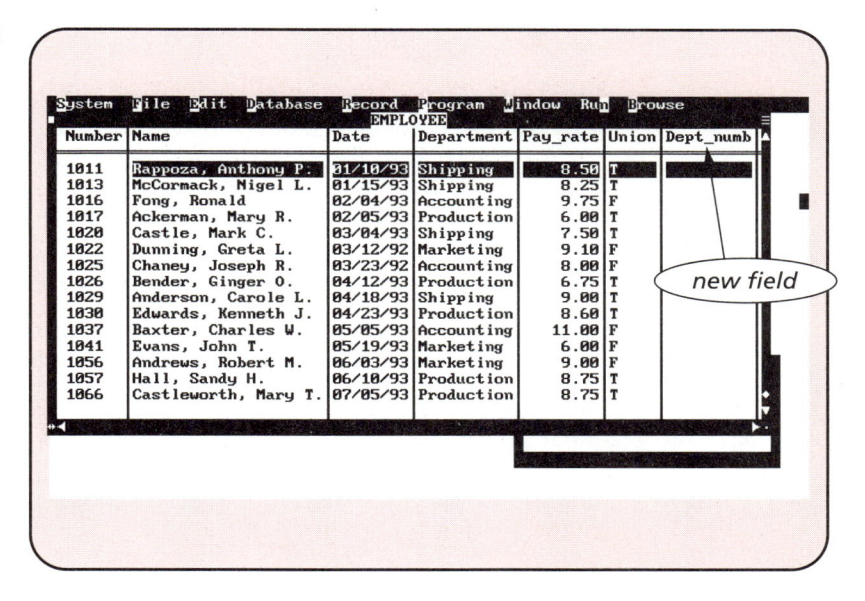

```
System  File  Edit  Database  Record  Program  Window  Run  Browse
                              EMPLOYEE
Number  Name                  Date      Department  Pay_rate  Union  Dept_numb
1011    Rappoza, Anthony P.   01/10/93  Shipping      8.50     T
1013    McCormack, Nigel L.   01/15/93  Shipping      8.25     T
1016    Fong, Ronald          02/04/93  Accounting    9.75     F
1017    Ackerman, Mary R.     02/05/93  Production    6.00     T
1020    Castle, Mark C.       03/04/93  Shipping      7.50     T
1022    Dunning, Greta L.     03/12/92  Marketing     9.10     F
1025    Chaney, Joseph R.     03/23/92  Accounting    8.00     F
1026    Bender, Ginger O.     04/12/93  Production    6.75     T
1029    Anderson, Carole L.   04/18/93  Shipping      9.00     T
1030    Edwards, Kenneth J.   04/23/93  Production    8.60     T
1037    Baxter, Charles W.    05/05/93  Accounting   11.00     F
1041    Evans, John T.        05/19/93  Marketing     6.00     F
1056    Andrews, Robert M.    06/03/93  Marketing     9.00     F
1057    Hall, Sandy H.        06/10/93  Production    8.75     T
1066    Castleworth, Mary T.  07/05/93  Production    8.75     T
```
(new field)

3 **Make the entries for the DEPT_NUMB field using the Record, Replace command.**

Open	EMPLOYEE	unless already active.
Press	ALT , R , P	Selects Record, Replace.
Press	↓ as needed	Highlights DEPT_NUMB.
Press	S , A	Selects Scope, All.
Press	SHIFT - TAB twice, ⏎ ENTER	Selects OK button.
Press	F	Selects FOR expression window.

Topic 18: Modifying the Structure **149**

Press	SHIFT - TAB	Moves to Field Name list.
Press	↓ three times, ↵ ENTER	Selects DEPARTMENT.
Press	CTRL - L	Opens logical operator popup.
Press	↓ three times, ↵ ENTER	Selects = symbol.
Type	"Accounting"	
Press	SHIFT - TAB three times, ↵ ENTER	Selects OK button.
Press	T	Selects WITH button.
Type	"01"	
Press	SHIFT - TAB three times, ↵ ENTER	Selects OK button.
Press	SHIFT - TAB three times, ↵ ENTER	Selects REPLACE button.

At this point, the update takes place and you see a message indicating that three records have been replaced.

In exactly the same way, change the value for DEPT_NUMB to 02 for all records in which DEPARTMENT is Marketing, 03 for all records in which DEPARTMENT is Production, and 04 for all records in which DEPARTMENT is Shipping. The changes are then complete and all records contain an appropriate value in the DEPT_NUMB field. You return to the Command window.

4 **Change the name on record 15 of the EMPLOYEE database file from "Castleworth, Mary T." to "Castleworth, Marianne K.".**

Open	EMPLOYEE	unless already active.
Press	ALT, R, E	Selects Record, Change.
Press	ALT, R, G, R	Selects Record, Goto, Record.
Type	15	
Press	TAB twice, ↵ ENTER	Selects GOTO button; moves to record 15.
Press	↵ ENTER	Moves to NAME field.
Press	→ as needed	to position cursor under M in Mary.
Hold down	SHIFT	continuously for selecting field information.
Press	→ as needed	Selects Mary T.
Release	SHIFT	

FoxPro

Type	Marianne K.	Changes name.
Press	ALT , F , C	Selects File, Close.

You are returned to the Command window. Your database now contains the data shown in Figure 18.5. Note that the DEPT_NUMB column contains the correct values and that Marianne K. Castleworth name is now correct.

Figure 18.5
Browse Window

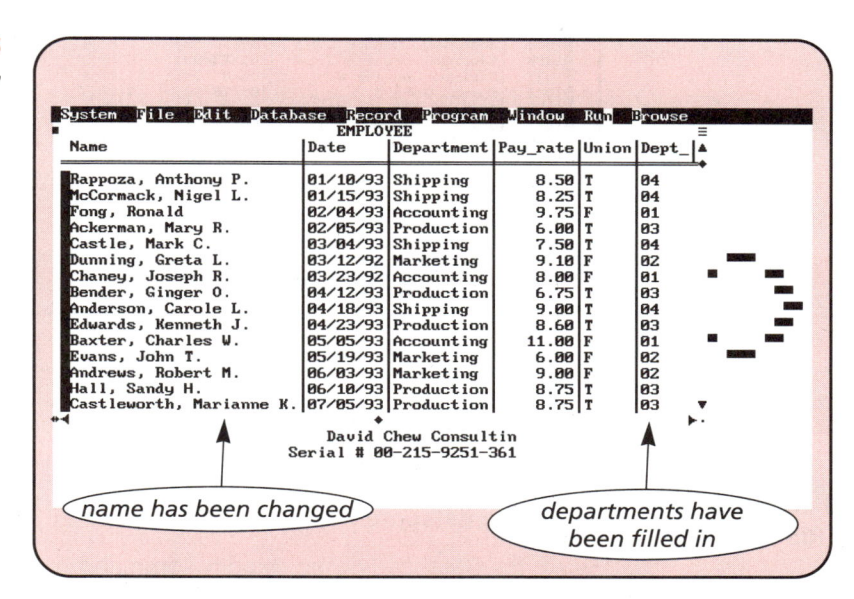

```
System File Edit Database Record Program Window Run Browse
                         EMPLOYEE
Name                     |Date    |Department |Pay_rate|Union|Dept_|
Rappoza, Anthony P.      |01/10/93|Shipping   |  8.50  |  T  | 04  |
McCormack, Nigel L.      |01/15/93|Shipping   |  8.25  |  T  | 04  |
Fong, Ronald             |02/04/93|Accounting |  9.75  |  F  | 01  |
Ackerman, Mary R.        |02/05/93|Production |  6.00  |  T  | 03  |
Castle, Mark C.          |03/04/93|Shipping   |  7.50  |  T  | 04  |
Dunning, Greta L.        |03/12/92|Marketing  |  9.10  |  F  | 02  |
Chaney, Joseph R.        |03/23/92|Accounting |  8.00  |  F  | 01  |
Bender, Ginger O.        |04/12/93|Production |  6.75  |  T  | 03  |
Anderson, Carole L.      |04/18/93|Shipping   |  9.00  |  T  | 04  |
Edwards, Kenneth J.      |04/23/93|Production |  8.60  |  T  | 03  |
Baxter, Charles W.       |05/05/93|Accounting | 11.00  |  F  | 01  |
Evans, John T.           |05/19/93|Marketing  |  6.00  |  F  | 02  |
Andrews, Robert M.       |06/03/93|Marketing  |  9.00  |  F  | 02  |
Hall, Sandy H.           |06/10/93|Production |  8.75  |  T  | 03  |
Castleworth, Marianne K. |07/05/93|Production |  8.75  |  T  | 03  |

                   David Chew Consultin
                   Serial # 00-215-9251-361
```

name has been changed — *departments have been filled in*

5 Delete the DEPARTMENT field from the EMPLOYEE database file.

Open	EMPLOYEE	unless already active.
Press	TAB three times, ← ENTER	Selects OK button.
Press	ALT , D , U , Y	Selects Database, Setup, Modify.
Press	TAB twice, ↓ three times	Moves cursor in column to left of DEPARTMENT field.
Press	DELETE	Deletes DEPARTMENT.
Press	TAB as needed, ← ENTER	Selects OK button.
Press	← ENTER	Confirms that you want to make change.
Press	TAB as needed, ← ENTER	Selects OK button.

Your database now contains the data shown in Figure 18.6. Note that there is no DEPARTMENT column.

Topic 18: Modifying the Structure **151**

Figure 18.6
Browse Window

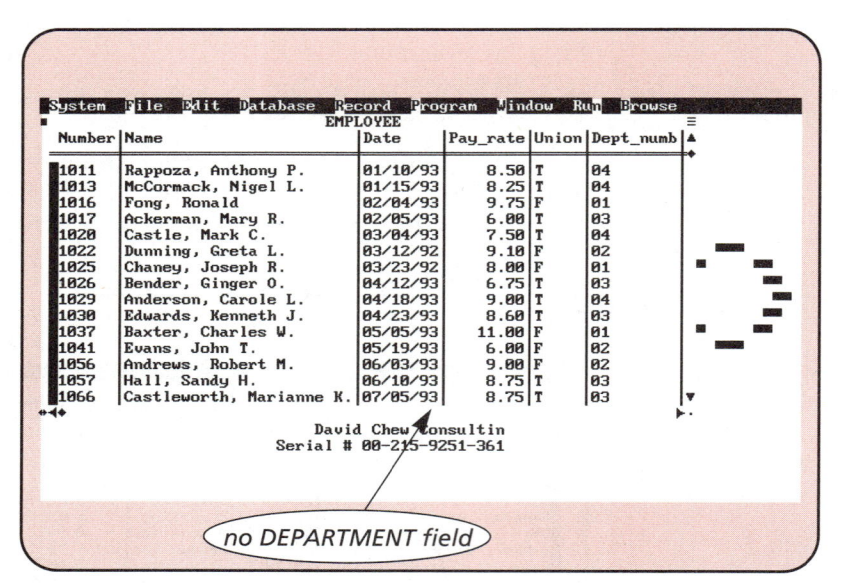

[Browse Window screenshot showing EMPLOYEE database with columns Number, Name, Date, Pay_rate, Union, Dept_numb, with callout "no DEPARTMENT field"]

PROCEDURE SUMMARY

CHANGING FIELD CHARACTERISTICS

Select the database file.	(your choice)
Select the Database, Setup, Modify command.	ALT, D, U, Y
Move to the characteristic to change.	TAB (as needed)
Make the change.	(your input)
Select the OK button.	TAB (as needed), ← ENTER
Select the OK button.	TAB (as needed), ← ENTER

ADDING A NEW FIELD

Select the database file.	(your choice)
Select the Database, Setup, Modify command.	ALT, D, U, Y
Move to the end of the field list.	TAB (as needed)
Type the field name and characteristics.	(your input)
Select the OK button.	TAB (as needed), ← ENTER
Select the OK button.	TAB (as needed), ← ENTER

DELETING A FIELD

Select the database file.	(your choice)
Select the Database, Setup, Modify command.	ALT, D, U, Y

FoxPro

Move to the column left of the field to be deleted.	TAB or ↓ (as needed)
Delete the field.	DELETE
Select the OK button.	TAB (as needed), ↵ ENTER
Select the OK button.	TAB (as needed), ↵ ENTER

EXERCISES

The structure of the CHECK database file is to be changed from:

CHECKNUM	DATE	PAYEE	AMOUNT	EXPENSE	TAXDED
109	01/19/92	Oak Apartments	750.00	Household	Y
102	01/05/92	Sav-Mor Groceries	85.00	Food	N
106	01/12/92	Performing Arts	25.00	Charity	Y
.					
.					
.					

to:

CHECKNUM	DATE	PAYEE	AMOUNT	TAXDED	EXP_CODE
109	01/19/92	Oak Apartments	750.00	Y	HH
102	01/05/92	Sav-Mor Groceries	85.00	N	FD
106	01/12/92	Performing Arts	25.00	Y	CH
.					
.					
.					

EXP_CODE	EXPENSE
HH	Household
FD	Food
CH	Charity
AU	Automobile
EN	Entertainment
PR	Personal

Topic 18: Modifying the Structure

1. Change the length of the PAYEE field in the CHECK database file to accommodate "Oakside View Apartments," which is the correct name for the PAYEE for check 109. Then make the change in the data.
2. Add the EXP_CODE field to the CHECK database.
3. Fill in the EXP_CODE field in the CHECK database with appropriate data (HH on records where EXPENSE is Household, FD on records where EXPENSE is Food, and so on).
4. Delete the EXPENSE field from the CHECK database.

TOPIC 19

Using Multiple Database Files

> **TIP:** This discussion considers only those relational queries involving two database files. The issues involving relational queries with three or more database files are similar.

CONCEPTS To access data from more than one database file in FoxPro, you use a **relational query**. A relational query is a pseudo-database file that can combine two (or more) existing database files. (Saying it is a pseudo-database file simply means it appears to the user to be a database file, even though, in fact, it might not be.) The key points of this definition are:

1. By using relational queries, you can access data from two or more database files at the same time.

2. Even though the data comes from more than one database file, it still feels as though it were a single database file. This makes working with a relational query much simpler than if you had to be concerned with all the individual database files that are involved in the relational query. ◄

To see how relational queries work, consider the two database files shown in Figure 19.1, the EMPLOYEE file and the DEPT file. The database files are related through **matching fields**. In the figure, the matching fields

Figure 19.1
Relating Database Files

EMPLOYEE NUMBER	EMPLOYEE NAME	DATE HIRED	PAY RATE	UNION MEMBER	DEPT NUMB
1011	Rapoza, Anthony P.	01/10/93	8.50	T	04
1013	McCormack, Nigel L.	01/15/93	8.25	T	04
1016	Fong, Ronald	02/04/93	9.75	F	01
1017	Ackerman, Mary R.	02/05/93	6.00	T	03
1020	Castle, Mark C.	03/04/93	7.50	T	04
1022	Dunning, Greta L.	03/12/93	9.10	F	02
1025	Chaney, Joseph R.	03/23/93	8.00	F	01
1026	Bender, Ginger O.	04/12/93	6.75	T	03
1029	Anderson, Carole L.	04/18/93	9.00	T	04
1030	Edwards, Kenneth J.	04/23/93	8.60	T	03
1037	Baxter, Charles W.	05/05/93	11.00	F	01
1041	Evans, John T.	05/19/93	6.00	F	02
1056	Andrews, Robert M.	06/03/93	9.00	F	02
1057	Hall, Sandy H.	06/10/93	8.75	T	03
1066	Castleworth, Mary T.	07/05/93	8.75	T	03

(*current active record* → 1011)

DEPT NUMB	DEPARTMENT NAME
01	Accounting
02	Marketing
03	Production
04	Shipping

(*matching department numbers*)

Topic 19: Using Multiple Database Files   155

are the DEPT_NUMB fields in both database files. A special kind of relationship, called a **one-to-many relationship**, exists between these two files. In this case, a department is associated with many employees, but each employee is associated with only one department. Looking at the values, for example, you can see that department 01 (Accounting), for example, is associated with employees 1016, 1025, 1037, and 1070. Employee 1016, on the other hand, is associated with only the Accounting department. In this relationship, you would refer to DEPT as the "one" database file and to EMPLOYEE as the "many" database file.

When two database files are related in this fashion, they can become part of a relational query. In such a case, you work with the "many" database file and FoxPro automatically keeps track of which record in the "one" file is associated with the current active record in this "many" file. For example, if record 1 (employee 1011) is the current active record, FoxPro knows that the related record in the DEPT file is record 4 (department 04) since the department numbers match (see the arrow in Figure 19.1). FoxPro allows you to use not only fields in the EMPLOYEE file, but also any fields in the DEPT file. Thus, if you list the department name for employee 1011, you will get Shipping because it is the name on the related record in the DEPT file. Suppose you make record 3 the current active record (Figure 19.2). Then the corresponding record in the DEPT file is record 1 (department 01). If you list the department name for this employee, you will get Accounting.

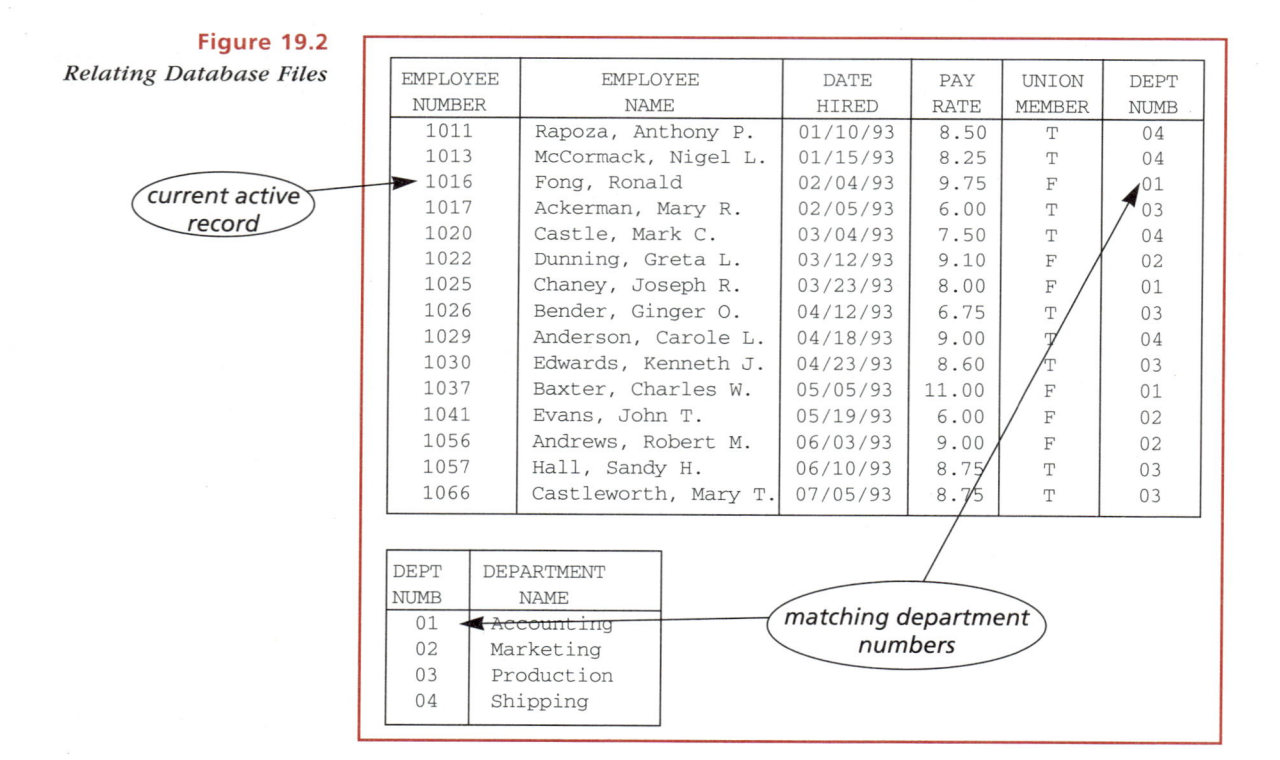

Figure 19.2
Relating Database Files

EMPLOYEE NUMBER	EMPLOYEE NAME	DATE HIRED	PAY RATE	UNION MEMBER	DEPT NUMB
1011	Rapoza, Anthony P.	01/10/93	8.50	T	04
1013	McCormack, Nigel L.	01/15/93	8.25	T	04
1016	Fong, Ronald	02/04/93	9.75	F	01
1017	Ackerman, Mary R.	02/05/93	6.00	T	03
1020	Castle, Mark C.	03/04/93	7.50	T	04
1022	Dunning, Greta L.	03/12/93	9.10	F	02
1025	Chaney, Joseph R.	03/23/93	8.00	F	01
1026	Bender, Ginger O.	04/12/93	6.75	T	03
1029	Anderson, Carole L.	04/18/93	9.00	T	04
1030	Edwards, Kenneth J.	04/23/93	8.60	T	03
1037	Baxter, Charles W.	05/05/93	11.00	F	01
1041	Evans, John T.	05/19/93	6.00	F	02
1056	Andrews, Robert M.	06/03/93	9.00	F	02
1057	Hall, Sandy H.	06/10/93	8.75	T	03
1066	Castleworth, Mary T.	07/05/93	8.75	T	03

DEPT NUMB	DEPARTMENT NAME
01	Accounting
02	Marketing
03	Production
04	Shipping

current active record

matching department numbers

> **TIP:** To make working with the relational query as efficient as possible, it is a good idea to make sure that there are indexes for the fields in the database files that are used to link the files.

When accessing such a relational query, you do not have to be aware of these details. FoxPro handles them for you automatically. You simply indicate that you want to include the department name on a display or report, and FoxPro ensures that it is the correct name.

Preparing for Relational Query Creation

Before you begin creating a relational query, you should decide exactly which database files are to be included. You should also decide how they are related; that is, which database file is the "one" and which is the "many." In addition, you need to determine the fields that will be used to link the database files. ◄

TUTORIAL In this tutorial, you determine all the information necessary to create the relational query of departments and employees. You also create the DEPT database file.

1 **Create a relational query of departments and employees called EMPDEPT.** Identify the database files involved in the relational query. Determine which one is the "one" and which one is the "many." Decide which fields will be used to relate the files; that is, determine the matching fields. Make sure indexes exist on these fields.

- The database files are EMPLOYEE and DEPT (employees and departments).
- DEPT is the "one" and EMPLOYEE is the "many." (A department is related to many employees, but an employee is related to only one department.)
- The DEPT_NUMB fields in both database files are used to relate the files. The DEPT_NUMB field in the EMPLOYEE database file is already indexed. Make sure you index the DEPT_NUMB field in the DEPT database file when you create the file.

2 **Create the DEPT database file.** The DEPT_NUMB field should be indexed.

Press	ALT, F, N, ↵ ENTER	Selects File, New; selects OK button.
Type	DEPT_NUMB	Names first field.
Press	SHIFT-TAB, SPACEBAR	Field is indexed.
Press	TAB three times	Moves to Width entry; field type remains as CHARACTER.
Type	2	
Press	↵ ENTER	Moves to second field name.
Type	DEPARTMENT	Names second field.

Topic 19: Using Multiple Database Files

Press	TAB as needed	Moves to OK button; field type and width remain default values.
Press	ENTER	Selects OK button.
Type	DEPT	Names database file.
Press	TAB as needed, ENTER	Selects SAVE button.

Then enter the data that is shown in Figure 19.3. (The first record has 01 for a department number and Accounting for a department name; the second record has 02 for a number and Marketing for a name; and so on. Make sure to enter the zeros in the department number field.)

Figure 19.3
Data for DEPT Database File

```
Record#  DEPT_NUMB  DEPARTMENT
   1       01        Accounting
   2       02        Marketing
   3       03        Production
   4       04        Shipping
```

| Press | ALT, F, C | Selects File, Close. |

You are returned to the Command window.

PROCEDURE SUMMARY

PREPARING FOR RELATIONAL QUERY CREATION

Identify the database files that will be used in the relational query.	
Determine how the files are related; that is, determine which is the "many" file and which is the "one" file.	
Decide which fields will be used to link (relate) the files.	
Be sure both database files already exist. If either one does not, create it.	(your input)
Make sure the fields used for linking the database files are both indexed.	

158 *FoxPro*

EXERCISES

1. Create the new database file (the file of expense codes and descriptions shown in the exercises in the Topic 18). Name this file EXPCATS. The EXP_CODE field should be indexed.

2. Add the indicated expense codes and descriptions to this database file.

3. Create a relational query called EXPVIEW. This relational query should contain both the EXPCATS and the CHECK database files. The EXP_CODE field in both files should be used to relate the two. Include all fields from the CHECK database and the expense description field from the EXPCATS database in this relational query. Use this information to determine the database files to be included. Determine which is the "many" database file and which is the "one" database file.

TOPIC 20

Creating Relational Queries

> **TIP**
> Although FoxPro does have a feature that allows you to strictly build a relational query and save it using the Window, View command, this feature of using the RQBE command is a much more integrated approach. Building reports, selecting records, and selecting fields can all be done under the RQBE window.

CONCEPTS In FoxPro, you use the same RQBE screen you saw earlier to create relational queries. In simplest terms, a relational query is just a saved query; that is, FoxPro considers any query you save to be a relational query. Thus all you need to do is create an appropriate query and save it. ◀

Beginning the Relational Query Process (163)

To begin the relational query creation process, you must have identified the database files and the relationship between them. Then you are ready to begin creating the relational query. The real benefits come, of course, once the relational query has been created and you can begin using it.

Relating the Database Files (164)

As part of the relational query creation process, you must indicate to FoxPro how the database files in the relational query are related; that is, you must indicate the matching fields. This is done through the **RQBE Join Relation dialog box** which appears when the second database file is added. Once you have defined this relationship, FoxPro handles it automatically for you whenever you use the relational query. You can be assured that when you use fields from more than one database file, the data will "match." For example, if you list an employee's name (from the EMPLOYEE file), department number (from the EMPLOYEE file), and also department name (from the DEPT file), you know that FoxPro will list the appropriate department name.

Selecting Fields (164)

You are not required to include all the fields from all the database files in a relational query. If you know you will not need certain fields, you can simplify the relational query by not including them. At this point, indicate which fields from the database files you want to include in the relational query.

Finishing the Relational Query Creation Process (164)

To finish the process, all you need to do is save the query. In doing so, you will give the saved query a name. You have now created your relational query.

TUTORIAL In this tutorial, you create the relational query of departments and employees. You do it by first creating an appropriate query and then saving the query as EMPDEPT (the name you will give to the relational query).

1 **Create a query containing the EMPLOYEE and DEPT database files.** This begins the creation of the EMPDEPT relational query.

Topic 20: Creating Relational Queries

Press	ALT, N, N	Selects Run, New Query.
Press	A	Selects Add button; allows you to open another file for query.

You are presented with a list of possible files.

Press	↑ or ↓ as needed, ↵ ENTER	Adds DEPT file to query.

A dialog box requesting RQBE Join Condition appears. Proceed directly to the next task.

2 Relate the database files in the query. You need to relate the files; that is, you need to indicate the fields that will be used to link them.

Press	↵ ENTER	Displays field list popup of DEPT database.
Press	↑ or ↓ as needed, ↵ ENTER	Selects DEPT.DEPT_NUMB.
Press	TAB three times, ↵ ENTER	Moves to field list popup of EMPLOYEE database.
Press	↓ as needed, ↵ ENTER	Selects EMPLOYEE.DEPT_NUMB.
Press	TAB twice, ↵ ENTER	Selects OK button.

FoxPro inserts an expression summarizing this relation. At this point, your screen should look like Figure 20.1. Do not save your work at this point. Instead proceed directly to the next task.

Figure 20.1
RQBE Window

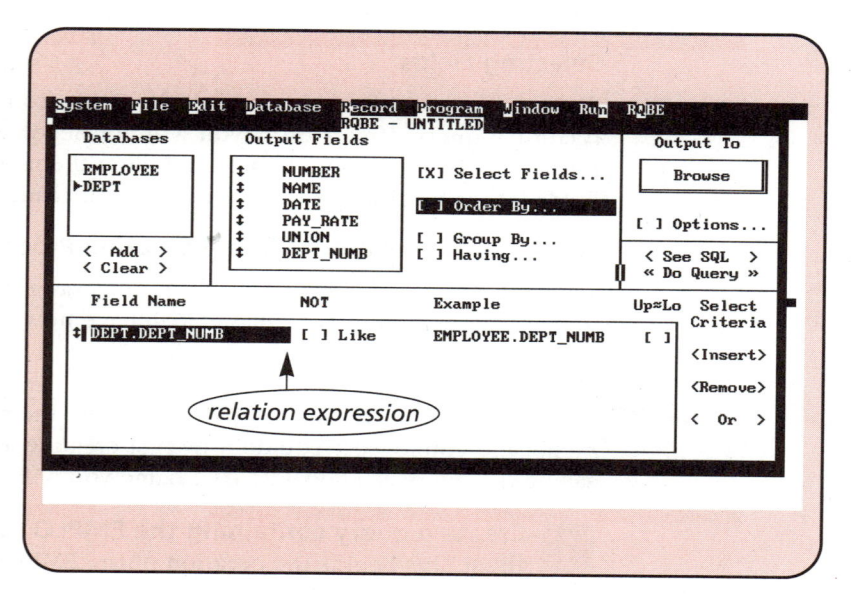

3 **Specify the fields to be included in the query.** When you are done, save the query, thus creating a **query file**. You now have included both database files, and you have linked them. The relational query has not changed, however; it still includes only fields from EMPLOYEE. You don't need to include the DEPT_NUMB field in DEPT because this field should exactly match the DEPT_NUMB field in EMPLOYEE, which is already included in the query file. You should include DEPARTMENT, however.

Press	F	Selects SELECT FIELDS button.
Press	↓ , ↵ ENTER	Selects DEPT.DEPARTMENT field.
Press	TAB as needed, ↑ as needed	Moves to EMPLOYEE.DEPT_NUMB.
Press	↵ ENTER	Removes EMPLOYEE.DEPT_NUMB from Selected Output list.
Press	TAB as needed, ↵ ENTER	Selects OK button.
Press	ALT , F , C	Selects File, Close.
Press	Y	Saves untitled query.
Type	EMPDEPT	
Press	SHIFT - TAB twice, ↵ ENTER	Saves query.

You have now saved your query as EMPDEPT. Thus you have effectively created a multiple file query and called it EMPDEPT.

PROCEDURE SUMMARY

BEGINNING THE RELATIONAL QUERY CREATION PROCESS

Run the New Query command.	ALT , N , N
Select the first database file.	↑ or ↓ (as needed), ↵ ENTER
Add the file to the query.	A
Select the other database file.	↑ or ↓ (as needed), ↵ ENTER

Topic 20: Creating Relational Queries

RELATING THE DATABASE FILES	Display the field list popup for joining database files.	`ENTER`
	Select the linking field.	`↑` or `↓` (as needed), `ENTER`
	Display the field list popup for the other database.	`TAB` three times, `ENTER`
	Select the matching field.	`↑` or `↓` (as needed), `ENTER`
	Select the OK button.	`TAB` twice, `ENTER`
SELECTING FIELDS	**To add a field to the Selected Output list:**	
	Highlight the field from the Database Fields list.	`↑` or `↓` (as needed), `ENTER`
	Add the field.	`ENTER`
	To remove a field from the Selected Output list:	
	Highlight the field you want to remove.	`TAB` or `SHIFT`-`TAB` (as needed), `↑` or `↓` (as needed)
	Remove the field.	`ENTER`
FINISHING THE RELATIONAL QUERY PROCESS	Save the query.	`ALT`, `F`, `C`
	Respond Yes if it is a new query.	`Y`
	Enter the name of the saved query.	(your input), `SHIFT`-`TAB` twice, `ENTER`

EXERCISES

1. Begin the process of creating EXPRVIEW. Create a query containing the appropriate database files.
2. Indicate to FoxPro how the database files in the query are to be related.
3. Specify the fields that are to be included in the query. Save the query as EXPVIEW.

Using Relational Queries

CONCEPTS Now that you have created your relational query, you can realize the benefits from it. Whenever you want to combine data from the various database files in the relational query, all you need to do is use the relational query. You can use it with retrieval options like "List" and "Display." You can also use it in reports and labels. In both cases, you use it just as though it were a single database file.

Using a Relational Query

Once you have created a relational query, you can begin to use it. To do so, you simply need to run it. FoxPro handles all the necessary details. The use of relational queries, however, involves some special considerations:

1. To update any of the data, update the appropriate database file. For example, to add a new employee, open the EMPLOYEE database file and use the Record, Append command. To change the name of an employee, open the EMPLOYEE database file and use the Change or Browse window. To add a new department, on the other hand, activate the DEPT database file before you use the Record, Append command.

2. The data never exists in the form represented in a relational query. Rather, FoxPro draws data from the underlying database files and assembles it in the appropriate form at the time you access the relational query. No special action is taken beforehand. The nice thing about this arrangement is that, whenever changes are made to any of the database files that are included in the relational query, you automatically see the results of these changes the next time you use the relational query. You don't need to re-create the relational query in order to access the current data.

Sorting a Relational Query

Sometimes you might want the data as defined in your relational query, but you would like it in a different order. Thus you need to be able to sort the data in your relational query. Since a relational query is just a saved query, the same techniques apply equally well to sorting the output of a query.

TUTORIAL In this tutorial, you use the relational query you have created.

1 List all the records in the EMPDEPT relational query.

Press	ALT , F , O	Selects File, Open.
Press	TAB as needed, ↵ ENTER	Selects file type popup list.
Press	↑ or ↓ as needed, ↵ ENTER	Selects Query file type.
Press	↑ or ↓ as needed	Selects EMPDEPT.
Press	TAB as needed, ↵ ENTER	Selects OPEN button.

The relational query is now active. Any subsequent options such as using the Browse window or producing a report are selected through the Output To popup list. Usually Browse is the default Output To selection. If it is not, complete the following steps.

Press	TAB as needed, ↵ ENTER	Selects Output To popup.
Press	↑ or ↓ as needed, ↵ ENTER	Selects Browse.
Press	Q	Selects DO QUERY button.

You now see the data in your relational query as in Figure 21.1. If you want to print a report of all the data, select the Report/Label choice in the Output To popup.

Figure 21.1
Relational Query Browse Window

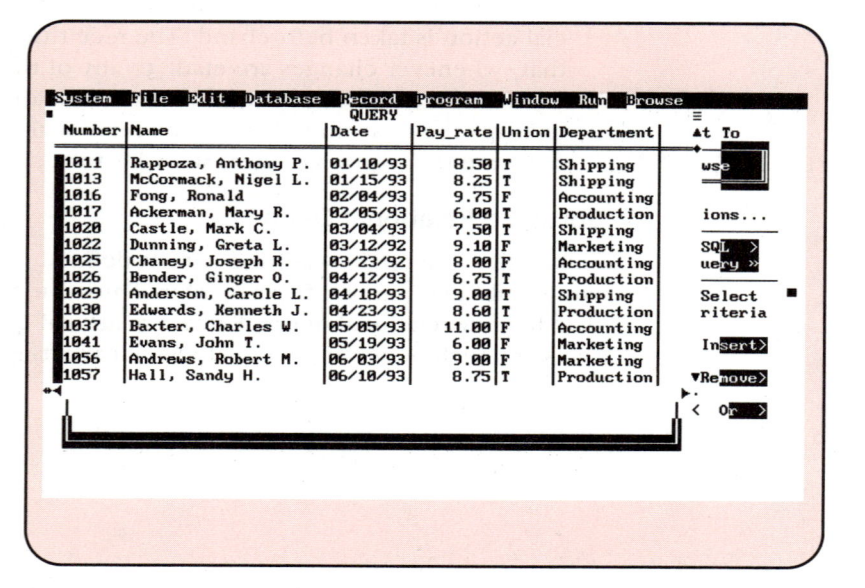

Number	Name	Date	Pay_rate	Union	Department
1011	Rappoza, Anthony P.	01/10/93	8.50	T	Shipping
1013	McCormack, Nigel L.	01/15/93	8.25	T	Shipping
1016	Fong, Ronald	02/04/93	9.75	F	Accounting
1017	Ackerman, Mary R.	02/05/93	6.00	T	Production
1020	Castle, Mark C.	03/04/93	7.50	T	Shipping
1022	Dunning, Greta L.	03/12/92	9.10	F	Marketing
1025	Chaney, Joseph R.	03/23/92	8.00	F	Accounting
1026	Bender, Ginger O.	04/12/93	6.75	T	Production
1029	Anderson, Carole L.	04/18/93	9.00	T	Shipping
1030	Edwards, Kenneth J.	04/23/93	8.60	T	Production
1037	Baxter, Charles W.	05/05/93	11.00	F	Accounting
1041	Evans, John T.	05/19/93	6.00	F	Marketing
1056	Andrews, Robert M.	06/03/93	9.00	F	Marketing
1057	Hall, Sandy H.	06/10/93	8.75	T	Production

166   FoxPro

2 Using the EMPDEPT relational query, list the number, name, and department of all employees hired after March 1, 1993.

Press	ALT, F, O	Selects File, Open.
Press	TAB as needed, ← ENTER	Selects file type popup list.
Press	↑ or ↓ as needed, ← ENTER	Selects Query file type.
Press	↑ or ↓ as needed	Selects EMPDEPT.
Press	TAB as needed, ← ENTER	Selects OPEN button.

The query you created for your relational query is displayed. You can now make appropriate changes to it and then press the DO QUERY button to see the results of your new query. You need to change your field selection to contain NUMBER and NAME from the EMPLOYEE file and DEPARTMENT from the DEPT file. The triangle pointer should be next to EMPLOYEE in the Databases file list. If it is not, select it by moving to the list using the TAB key and pressing the SPACEBAR after highlighting EMPLOYEE.

Press	F	Selects the SELECT FIELDS button.
Press	L	Removes all fields from the Selected Output list.
Press	TAB as needed	Moves to Field Names list.
Press	↑ or ↓ as needed	Moves to EMPLOYEE.NUMBER field.
Press	← ENTER	Adds NUMBER field to Selected Output list.
Press	↑ or ↓ as needed	Moves to EMPLOYEE.NAME field.
Press	← ENTER	Adds NAME field to Selected Output list.
Press	↑ or ↓ as needed	Moves to DEPT.DEPARTMENT field.
Press	← ENTER	Adds DEPARTMENT field to Selected Output list.

The Selected Output list is now correct. The final step is to enter the condition.

Press	TAB as needed, ← ENTER	Selects OK button.
Press	TAB as needed	Moves to first blank Field Name column.
Press	← ENTER	Displays Field Names list.

Topic 21: Using Relational Queries

Press	↑ or ↓ as needed, ↵ ENTER	Selects EMPLOYEE.DATE.
Press	TAB, ↵ ENTER	Moves to and opens Operator popup.
Press	↑ or ↓ as needed, ↵ ENTER	Selects More Than operator.
Type	3/01/93	
Press	↵ ENTER	Completes condition.
Press	Q	Selects DO QUERY button.

Your screen should look like Figure 21.2.

Figure 21.2
Relational Query Browse Window

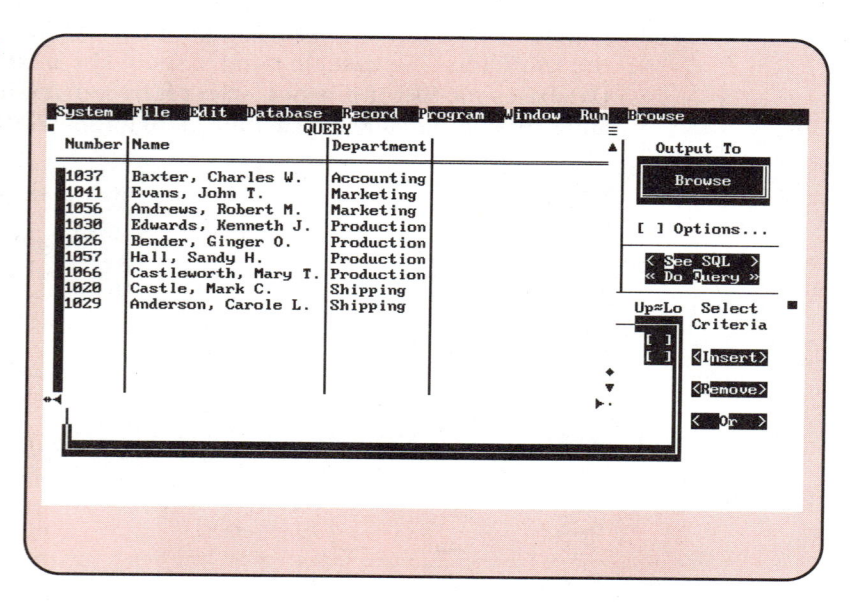

Press	ALT, F, C	Selects File, Close; closes Browse window.
Press	ALT, F, C	Selects File, Close; closes Query window.

Since you changed the definition of a query, FoxPro asks you if you want to save it. Be sure to answer No. Saving it would replace the old definition with this new one!

Press	N	Does not replace query.

168
FoxPro

3 **Display all the data in the EMPDEPT relational query.** The data is to be sorted by name.

Press	ALT, F, O	Selects File, Open.
Press	TAB as needed, ↵ ENTER	Selects file type popup list.
Press	↑ or ↓ as needed, ↵ ENTER	Selects Query file type.
Press	↑ or ↓ as needed	Selects EMPDEPT.
Press	TAB as needed, ↵ ENTER	Selects OPEN button.
Press	B	Selects Order By checkbox.

You then see the same list of possible sort types you saw when you sorted a database file.

Press	↑ or ↓, ↵ ENTER	Selects EMPLOYEE.NUMBER as ordering criteria.
Press	A	Selects Ascending order.

Your screen should look like Figure 21.3

Figure 21.3
Sort Window

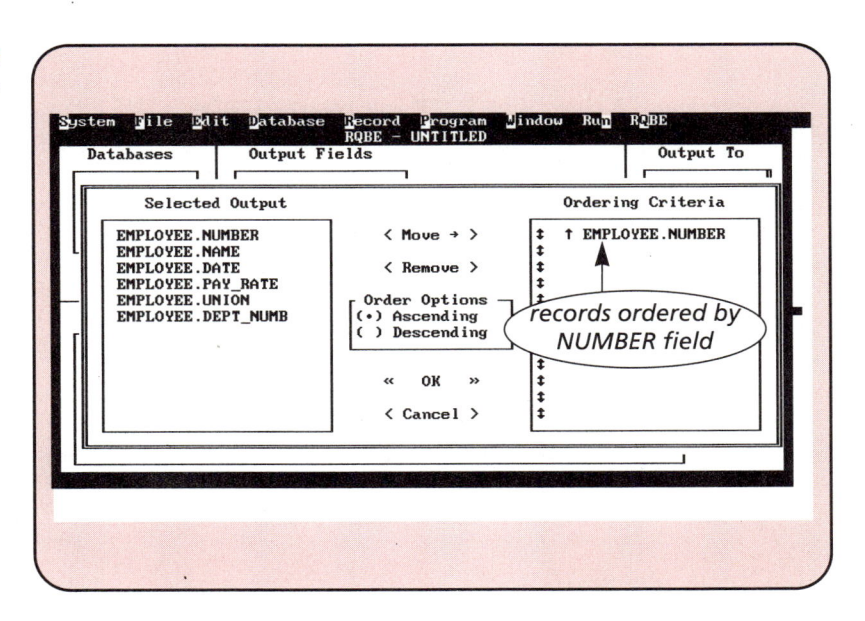

Press	TAB as needed, ↵ ENTER	Selects OK button.
Press	Q	Selects DO QUERY button.

Your data should be sorted by NAME.

Topic 21: Using Relational Queries

Press	ALT, F, C	Selects File, Close; closes Browse window.
Press	ALT, F, C	Selects File, Close; closes Query window.
Press	N	Does not replace query.

4 **Display all the data in the EMPDEPT relational query.** The data is to be sorted by name within department.

Press	ALT, F, O	Selects File, Open.
Press	TAB as needed, ←ENTER	Selects file type popup list.
Press	↑ or ↓ as needed, ←ENTER	Selects Query file type.
Press	↑ or ↓ as needed	Selects EMPDEPT.
Press	TAB as needed, ←ENTER	Selects OPEN button.
Press	B	Selects Order By checkbox.
Press	TAB and ↑ or ↓ as needed, ←ENTER	Selects DEPT.DEPARTMENT from Selected Output list; moves it to Ordering Criteria list.
Press	TAB as needed, ↑ or ↓ as needed, ←ENTER	Selects EMPLOYEE.NAME from the Selected Output list; moves it to Ordering Criteria list.
Press	A	Selects Ascending order.
Press	TAB as needed, ←ENTER	Selects OK button.
Press	Q	Selects DO QUERY button.

Your data should be sorted by NAME within DEPARTMENT.

Press	ALT, F, C	Selects File, Close; closes Browse window.
Press	ALT, F, C	Selects File, Close; closes Query window.
Press	N	Does not replace query.

Although the preceding discussion explains how to sort relational queries, this procedure also applies to single file queries. The same techniques apply to sorting a query whether or not the query will ultimately be saved.

PROCEDURE SUMMARY

USING A RELATIONAL QUERY

To use all the fields and records in the relational query:

Open the query.	`ALT`, `F`, `O`
Select the Query file type.	`TAB` (as needed), `ENTER`, `↑` or `↓` (as needed), `ENTER`
Select the query filename.	`↑` or `↓` (as needed), `ENTER`
Select the SELECT FIELDS button.	`F`
Select the ALL button.	`A`
Select the OK button.	`TAB` (as needed), `ENTER`
Be sure that no conditions exist after the first linking condition.	

To restrict the records, restrict the fields, and/or sort the data in a relational query:

Open the query.	`ALT`, `F`, `O`
Select the Query file type.	`TAB` (as needed), `ENTER`, `↑` or `↓` (as needed), `ENTER`
Select the query filename.	`↑` or `↓` (as needed), `ENTER`

Take an appropriate action from among the following options:

To restrict the records:

Move to the conditions area (first empty entry in the field names column).	`TAB` (as needed)
Enter a condition.	(your input)

To restrict the fields:

Select the SELECT FIELDS button.	`F`
Select the REMOVE ALL button.	`L`

Topic 21: Using Relational Queries

	Add the desired fields to the Selected Output list. (To add a field, move the highlight to it in the Database Field list and then press ENTER.)	TAB (as needed), ↑ or ↓ (as needed), ENTER
SORTING A RELATIONAL QUERY	Select the Order By checkbox.	B
	Move to the Ordering Criteria list and remove the sort fields.	TAB (as needed), ↑ or ↓ (as needed), ENTER
	Move to the Selected Output list and add the new sort fields.	TAB (as needed), ↑ or ↓ (as needed), ENTER
	If there are two sort keys, move the highlight to the less important sort key.	
	Move to the Selected Output list and add the new sort fields.	TAB (as needed), ↑ or ↓ (as needed), ENTER
	Select the sort type.	A or D
	Select the OK button.	TAB (as needed), ENTER

EXERCISES

1. Using the EXPVIEW relational query, display the check number, date, payee, and amount for all checks.

2. Using this relational query, display the check number, date, payee, and amount for all checks on which the description is Household.

3. Using this relational query, display the check number, date, payee, and amount for all checks on which the description is Household. Sort the data by payee.

Checkpoint 3

What You Should Know

- ✓ Before you create a report, be sure to activate the database file.
- ✓ To create a report, select the File, New, Report command.
- ✓ The various portions of a report (**page header, report title, group header, detail, group footer, page footer, and report summary**) are specified by making entries in the appropriate **bands** in the Report Layout window.
- ✓ To terminate the report creation process, select the File, Close command. You can choose not to save your work.
- ✓ To print a report, select the Run, Report command.
- ✓ To limit the records that will appear in a report, use a **query**.
- ✓ To change the layout of an existing report, select File, Open, and then choose Report from the file type popup list.
- ✓ To specify **grouping** on a report, add a **group band** using the Report, Data Grouping command.
- ✓ If you include subtotals in a report, you must make sure that the records are ordered appropriately before printing the report.
- ✓ To change the structure of a database file, select the Database, Setup command.
- ✓ To change the characteristics of a field, select the MODIFY button, highlight the data to be changed, and enter the new value.
- ✓ To add a field, highlight the beginning of the first row past all the existing fields, and then type in the name and characteristics of the new field.
- ✓ To make mass changes to the new field, use the Record, Replace command.
- ✓ To delete a field, highlight the field to be deleted on the Setup dialog box and select the REMOVE button.
- ✓ In general terms, a **relational query** is a pseudo-table (or pseudo-database file).
- ✓ A **one-to-many relationship** between two database files occurs when one record in one of the files is related to many records in the second, but each record in the second is related to only one record in the first. The first database file is called the one database file, and the second is called the many database file.
- ✓ To create a relational query, create a query that describes exactly the database files, records, and fields you want in the relational query, and then create a **relational join condition**. Then save it as a **query file**.
- ✓ The result of a relational query is in the form of a Browse window or report.
- ✓ Data may be updated in the browse output produced from the relational query. This automatically changes the information in the individual database files.

Checkpoint 3 **173**

Review Questions

1. How do you begin creating a report? How do you add a report title to a report?
2. How do you add columns to a report? How do you specify headings for the columns? How do you include a total in your report?
3. How do you print a report you have created, assuming you want all records included in the report?
4. How do you print a report you have created, assuming you only want certain records included in the report?
5. How do you include subtotals in a report? What is meant by grouping? What does it have to do with subtotals?
6. How do you print a report that includes subtotals? Are there any special issues concerning the records in the database file when you print such a report?
7. How do you change the characteristics of a field in a database file? Why might you want to do so?
8. How do you add a new field to a database file? Why might you want to do so?
9. How do you delete a field from a database file? Why might you want to do so?
10. What is a relational query? Why might you want to use one? What decisions should you make in preparation for creating a relational query?
11. How do you indicate to FoxPro which database files are to be included in a relational query? How do you order the records?
12. How do you indicate to FoxPro how the database files in a relational query are related?
13. How do you indicate to FoxPro which fields are to be included in a relational query?
14. How do you use a relational query once you have created one?

CHECKPOINT EXERCISES

1. Design a report for data in the MUSIC database file. The report is to contain page and column headings. Fields to be included on the report include the Category, Music Name, Artist Name, Type, and Cost. A final total of the Cost Amount field is to be displayed.
2. Begin the report creation process for this report. Call the report MUSRPT1. Correct the detail band.
3. Correct the report summary for MUSRPT1.
4. Correct the page header band for MUSRPT1.

5. Print a report of all records in the MUSIC database file. Use the report layout stored in MUSRPT1.

6. Print a report of those records in the MUSIC database file on which cost is less than $10.00. Use the report layout stored in MUSRPT1.

7. Modify the report format stored in MUSRPT1 so that a subtotal is taken when there is a change in category. Use this report format to display all the records in the MUSIC database file. Make sure that the records are ordered correctly.

The structure of the MUSIC database file is to be changed from:

DATE	NAME	ARTIST	TYPE	COST	CATEGORY
02/22/92	Greatest Hits	Panache, Milo	LP	8.95	Classical
02/15/92	America	Judd, Mary	CS	5.95	Vocal
01/02/92	Rio Rio	Duran, Ralph	LP	8.95	Rock

to:

DATE	NAME	ARTIST	TYPE	COST	CAT_CODE
02/22/92	Greatest Hits #1	Panache, Milo	LP	8.95	CL
02/15/92	America	Judd, Mary	CS	5.95	VO
01/02/92	Rio Rio	Duran, Ralph	LP	8.95	RK

CAT_CODE	CATEGORY
CL	Classical
CO	Country
VO	Vocal
RK	Rock

Checkpoint 3 **175**

8. Change the length of the Name field in the MUSIC database file to accommodate "Greatest Hits #1," which is the correct name for the first record. Then make the change in the data.
9. Add the CAT_CODE field to the MUSIC database.
10. Fill in the CAT_CODE field in the MUSIC database with the appropriate data (CL on records where the category is Classical, CO on records where the category is Country, and so on).
11. Delete the Category field from the MUSIC database.
12. Create the new database file. Use the name MUSCATS for this file. The CAT_CODE field should be indexed.
13. Add the indicated category codes and descriptions to this database file.
14. Create a relational query called MUSVIEW. This relational query should contain both the MUSCATS and MUSIC database files. The CAT_CODE field in both files should be used to relate the two. Include all fields from the MUSIC database and the category description field from the MUSCATS database in this relational query.
15. Using this relational query, display the date, music name, artist, and cost for all classical records.
16. Using this relational query, display the date, music name, artist, and cost for all classical records. Order the data by artist.

COMPREHENSIVE EXERCISE 1 You are to create a database file to store information about the inventory of a company that sells computer software. Fields in the database consist of the name of the software, the name of the company that sells the software, a software category, an entry T (true) or F (false) to indicate if the software is MS-DOS compatible, the quantity of software on hand, and the cost of the software. The software products in inventory are listed in the following chart.

SOFTWARE NAME	COMPANY	CATEGORY	MS_DOS	QUANTITY	COST
Databurst	Electric Software	Database	T	5	299.95
Type Ease	Edusoft Inc.	WP	F	22	29.95
Image Fonts	Graph Tech Inc.	WP	T	12	49.95
Data Filer	Anchor Software	Database	T	18	149.95
Master	Edusoft Inc.	Education	F	10	49.95
Math Tester	Learnit Software	Education	F	10	49.95
PC-Writer	Anchor Software	WP	T	30	129.95
Print File	Graph Tech Inc.	Database	T	16	99.95
Learning Calc	Edusoft Inc.	Spreadsheet	T	34	69.95
Number Crunch	Anchor Software	Spreadsheet	T	8	279.95

FIELD DESCRIPTION	FIELD NAME	FIELD TYPE	WIDTH	DECIMAL POSITIONS
SOFTWARE NAME	NAME	CHARACTER	12	
COMPANY	COMPANY	CHARACTER	18	
CATEGORY	CATEGORY	CHARACTER	12	
MS_DOS	MS_DOS	LOGICAL	1	
QUANTITY	QUANTITY	NUMERIC	4	
COST	COST	NUMERIC	6	2

Perform the following tasks:

1. Insert your data disk into drive A. Then load FoxPro.
2. Create the database file. Use the name SOFTWARE for the database file.
3. Enter the six fields in the first of the two preceding tables.
4. Enter the preceding data. When you enter the third record, enter the name as Images Font and the price as $94.95.
5. After you have entered the records, enter an additional record. You may make up whatever entries you want for the fields in this record.

Comprehensive Exercises

6. Type LIST TO PRINT in the Command window to print a list of all the data.
7. Correct the third record by changing the name to Image Fonts and the price to $49.95.
8. Delete the extra record that you added. Permanently remove the record from the database file.
9. Type LIST TO PRINT in the Command window to print a list of all the data.
10. Make backup copies of this database file and the corresponding index file. Call them SOFTBCK.DBF and SOFTBCK.CDX, respectively.
11. Activate the database file so that it can be accessed.
12. Display all the fields and all the records.
13. Display the Software Name field, the Category field, the MS-DOS field, the Quantity field, and the Cost field for all records in the database.
14. Display the Category field, the Software Name field, and the Cost field for all records in the database.
15. Display the record for the software called Image Fonts.
16. Display all software produced by the company Anchor Software.
17. Display all software with a category of Education.
18. Display all software that is MS-DOS compatible (the entry .T. in the MS-DOS field).
19. Display all records with a quantity less than 10.
20. Display all records with a quantity greater than 25.
21. Display all records in which the company name contains the word "Software."
22. Display all records in which the software name starts with "Ty."
23. Display all word processing software (WP in category field) that has a cost of less than $50.00.
24. Display all records with a category of Database or Spreadsheet.
25. Count the number of records in the database file.
26. Sum the Quantity field to determine the number of products on hand.
27. Average the Cost field to determine the average cost of the software.
28. Average the cost of the software with a category of Education.
29. Average the cost of the software with a category of Database.
30. Use the Record, Locate command to find the software named Data Filer.
31. Use the Record, Locate command to find the first record in the SOFTWARE database file that is in the WP category.
32. Use the appropriate option to locate the next record in the WP category.
33. Use the Browse window to change the cost of Math Tester to $59.95.
34. Use the Browse window to change the cost of Image Fonts to $54.95. In addition, change the category to Spreadsheet and change the quantity to 14.
35. Use Record, Replace to change the cost of Print File to $104.95.
36. Use Record, Replace to add $10.00 to the cost of all software in the Database category.

37. Use Record, Delete to mark all software in the WP category for deletion.
38. Use Record, Recall to unmark all software in the WP category.
39. Use Record, Change to mark PC-Writer for deletion.
40. Use the Browse window to mark Learning Calc for deletion.
41. Pack the marked records from the SOFTWARE database file.
42. List all the records in the SOFTWARE database file.
43. Create a screen for the SOFTWARE database file that is similar to the form you created for the EMPLOYEE database file. Call it SOFTFORM.
44. Run this screen.
45. Sort the records stored in the SOFTWARE database in alphabetical order by the name of the software. Use SORTFLE as the filename for the sorted file.
46. After the records have been sorted, print a list of all records by typing LIST TO PRINT in the Command window.
47. Sort the records in the database file in alphabetical order by software name within category. Use SORTFLE as the filename of the sorted file.
48. After the records have been sorted, print a list of all records by typing LIST TO PRINT in the Command window.
49. Create an index on the Category field in the SOFTWARE database. Use it to list the records in SOFTWARE in category order.
50. Create an index on the combination of the Category and Software Name fields in the SOFTWARE database. Use it to list the records in SOFTWARE ordered by software name within category.
51. Use an index to locate the record containing image fonts.
52. Remove the index that was created on the combination of the Category and Software Name fields.
53. Design a report for data in the SOFTWARE database file. The report is to contain column headings. Fields to be included on the report include the Software Name, Category, Company Name, Quantity, Cost, and Total Inventory Value. The total inventory value is calculated by multiplying the cost by the quantity. A final total of the total inventory value is to be displayed.
54. Begin the report creation process for this report. Call the report SOFTRPT1. Correct the detail band.
55. Correct the report summary for SOFTRPT1.
56. Correct the page header for SOFTRPT1.
57. Print a report of all records in the SOFTWARE database file. Use the report layout stored in SOFTRPT1.
58. Print a report of those records in the SOFTWARE database file on which cost is less than $100.00. Use the report layout stored in SOFTRPT1.
59. Modify the report format stored in SOFTRPT1 so that a subtotal is taken for the total inventory value when there is a change in category. Use this report format to display all the records in the SOFTWARE database file. (Hint: Be sure that the records are ordered correctly.)

The structure of the SOFTWARE database file is to be changed from:

SOFTWARE NAME	COMPANY	CATEGORY	MS_DOS	QUANTITY	COST
Databurst	Electric Software	Database	T	5	299.95
Type Ease	Edusoft Inc.	WP	F	22	29.95
Image Fonts	Graph Tech Inc.	WP	T	12	49.95
Data Filer	Anchor Software	Database	T	18	149.95
Master	Edusoft Inc.	Education	F	10	49.95

.
.
.

to:

SOFTWARE NAME	CATEGORY	MS_DOS	QUANTITY	COST	CMP_CODE
Databurst	Database	T	5	299.95	01
Type Ease	WP	F	22	29.95	05
Image Fonts	WP	T	12	49.95	04
Data File Manager	Database	T	18	149.95	02
Master	Education	F	10	49.95	05

.
.
.

CMP_CODE	COMPANY NAME
01	Electric Software
02	Anchor Software
03	Learnit Software
04	Graph Tech Inc.
05	Edusoft Inc.

60. Change the length of the Software Name field in the SOFTWARE database file to accommodate "Data File Manager."
61. Add the CMP_CODE field to the SOFTWARE database.
62. Fill in the CMP_CODE field in the SOFTWARE database with the appropriate data (01 on records where the company is Electric Software, 02 on records where the company is Anchor Software, and so on).
63. Delete the Company field from the SOFTWARE database.
64. Create the new database file. Use the name SOFTCATS for this file. The CMP_CODE field should be indexed.
65. Add the indicated company codes and names to this database file.
66. Create a relational query called SOFTVIEW. This relational query should contain both the SOFTCATS and SOFTWARE database files. The CMP_CODE field in both files should be used to relate the two. Include all fields from the SOFTWARE database and the Company field from the SOFTCATS database in the Browse output of the relational query.
67. Using this relational query, display the software name, category, and cost for all software produced by Electric Software.
68. Using this relational query, display the software name, category, and cost for all software produced by Electric Software. Sort the data by category.
69. Retrieve the SOFTVIEW relational query and use it to display software name, category, and cost for all software produced by Anchor Software.

Comprehensive Exercises

COMPREHENSIVE EXERCISE 2 You are to create a database file to store information about homes that are for sale in an area. The records contain the date the home was listed, address, city, zip code, number of bedrooms, number of bathrooms, an entry T (true) or F (false) to indicate if the home has a pool, and the selling price of the home. The homes in the database are listed in the following chart.

DATE	ADDRESS	CITY	ZIP	BDRM	BATH	POOL	PRICE
09/15/91	9661 King Pl.	Anaheim	92644	4	2	T	185000.00
09/19/91	1625 Brook St.	Fullerton	92633	3	1	F	95000.00
10/02/91	182 Oak Ave.	Fullerton	92634	4	2	T	92000.00
10/09/91	145 Oak Ave.	Garden Grove	92641	5	3	T	145000.00
10/15/91	124 Lark St.	Anaheim	92644	3	2	F	119100.00
10/22/91	926 Pine Ln.	Garden Grove	92641	3	1	F	92500.00
11/20/91	453 Adams Ave.	Costa Mesa	92688	5	3	T	185000.00
11/23/91	1456 Kern St.	Costa Mesa	92688	4	2	T	163900.00
12/10/91	862 Stanley St.	Garden Grove	92641	4	2	T	189995.00
12/13/91	1552 Weldon Pl.	Garden Grove	92641	3	2	F	169500.00

FIELD DESCRIPTION	FIELD NAME	FIELD TYPE	WIDTH	DECIMAL POSITIONS
DATE	DATE	DATE	8	
ADDRESS	ADDRESS	CHARACTER	16	
CITY	CITY	CHARACTER	12	
ZIP	ZIP	CHARACTER	5	
BDRM	BDRM	NUMERIC	2	0
BATH	BATH	NUMERIC	2	0
POOL	POOL	LOGICAL	1	
PRICE	PRICE	NUMERIC	9	2

Perform the following tasks:

1. Insert your data disk into drive A. Then load FoxPro.
2. Create the database file. Use the name HOMES for the database file.
3. Enter the eight fields in the first of the two preceding tables.
4. Enter the preceding data. When you enter the third record, enter the city as Fulerton and the price as $29000.00.

FoxPro

5. After you have entered the records, enter an additional record. You may make up whatever entries you wish for the fields in this record.
6. Type LIST TO PRINT in the Command window to print a list of all the data.
7. Correct the third record by changing the city to Fullerton and the price to $92000.00.
8. Delete the extra record that you added. Pack the database file.
9. Type LIST TO PRINT in the Command window to print a list of all the data.
10. Make backup copies of this database file and the index file. Call them HOMESBCK.DBF and HOMESBCK.CDX, respectively.
11. Open the database file so that it can be accessed.
12. Display all the fields and all the records.
13. Display the Address field, the City field, and the Price field for all records in the database.
14. Display the Price field, the Address field, the City field, and the Zip Code field for all records in the database.
15. Display the record that has 10/22/92 in the Date field.
16. Display information about the house at 145 Oak Ave.
17. Display the records for all houses listed in the city of Anaheim.
18. Display the records for all houses listed in the city of Garden Grove.
19. Display the records for all houses in the 92641 zip code area.
20. Display the records for all houses with a pool (the entry .T. in the Pool field).
21. Display the records for all houses with a price of less than $125,000.00.
22. Display the records for all houses with a price greater than $150,000.00.
23. Display the records for all houses whose address contains the word "Ave."
24. Display the records for all houses in a city that contains the word "Garden."
25. Display the records for all houses with 4 bedrooms that cost less than $100,000.00.
26. Count the number of records in the database file.
27. Find the average cost of a house in Anaheim.
28. Find the average cost of a 4-bedroom house.
29. Find the average cost of a 3-bedroom house in Garden Grove.
30. Find the average cost of houses with a price greater than $150,000.00.
31. Use the Record, Locate command to find the house whose address is 1456 Kern St.
32. Use the Record, Locate command to find the first house in the HOMES database file that is in Garden Grove.
33. Use the appropriate command to locate the next house in Garden Grove.
34. Use the Browse command to change the price of the house at 926 Pine Ln. to $95000.00.

Comprehensive Exercises

35. Use the Browse command to change the price of the house at 1456 Kern St. to $169000.00. In addition, change the number of bathrooms to 3 and the number of bedrooms to 5.
36. Use the Record, Replace command to change the price of the house at 453 Adams Ave. to $190000.00.
37. Use the Record, Replace command to add $2000.00 to the price of all houses in Garden Grove.
38. Use the Record, Replace command to mark all houses in Costa Mesa for deletion.
39. Use the Record, Replace command to unmark all houses in Costa Mesa.
40. Use the Change window to mark the house located at 1625 Brook St. for deletion.
41. Use the Browse window to mark the house located at 862 Stanley St. for deletion.
42. Pack the HOMES database file.
43. List all the records in the HOMES database file.
44. Create a screen for the HOMES database file that is similar to the form you created for the EMPLOYEE database file. Call it HMSFORM.
45. Run this screen.
46. Sort the records stored in the HOMES database file in ascending order by price. Use SORTFLE as the filename for the sorted file.
47. After the records have been sorted, print a list of all records by typing LIST TO PRINT in the Command window.
48. Sort the records in the database file by price within city. Use SORTFLE as the filename of the sorted file.
49. After the records have been sorted, print a list of all records by typing LIST TO PRINT in the Command window.
50. Create an index on the City field in the HOMES database. Use it to list the records in HOMES in city order.
51. Create an index on the combination of the City and Address fields in the HOMES database. Use it to list the records in HOMES ordered by address within city.
52. Use an index to locate the record for the house at 145 Oak Ave.
53. Remove the index that was created on the combination of the City and Address fields.
54. Design a report for data in the HOMES database file. The report is to contain page and column headings. Fields to be included on the report are the Address, City, Zip Code, and Price. A final total is to be displayed of the prices of all houses. This total lists the total value of all houses for sale in an area.
55. Begin the report creation process for this report. Call the report HMSRPT1. Correct the detail band.
56. Correct the report summary for HMSRPT1.

57. Correct the page header for HMSRPT1.

58. Print a report of all records in the HOMES database file. Use the report layout stored in HMSRPT1.

59. Print a report of those records in the HOMES database file on which the price is less than $150000.00. Use the report layout stored in HMSRPT1.

60. Modify the report format stored in HMSRPT1 so that a subtotal is taken when there is a change in city. Use this report format to display all the records in the HOMES database file. (Hint: Be sure that the records are ordered correctly.)

Max, the user of the HOMES database file, which was created in student assignment 10 of project 1, decided to make a change. Max realized that there were only a few zip codes in which the homes for sale were likely to be located. Further, since each of these zip codes uniquely identified a city, Max decided to remove the City field from the HOMES file and create a separate database file, called ZIPCODE, relating zip codes and cities. In particular, the structure is to be changed from:

DATE	ADDRESS	CITY	ZIP	BDRM	BATH	POOL	PRICE
09/15/92	9661 King Pl.	Anaheim	92644	4	2	T	185000.00
10/02/92	182 Oak Ave.	Fullerton	92634	4	2	T	92000.00
10/09/92	145 Oak Ave.	Garden Grove	92641	5	3	T	145000.00
10/15/92	124 Lark St.	Anaheim	92644	3	2	F	119000.00
10/22/92	926 Pine Ln.	Garden Grove	92641	3	1	F	92500.00

to:

DATE	ADDRESS	ZIP	BDRM	BATH	POOL	PRICE
09/15/92	9661 King Pl.	92644	4	2	T	185000.00
10/02/92	182 Oak Ave.	92634	4	2	T	92000.00
10/09/92	145 Oak Ave.	92641	5	3	T	145000.00
10/15/92	124 Lark St.	92644	3	2	F	119000.00
10/22/92	926 Pine Ln.	92641	3	1	F	92500.00

Comprehensive Exercises

ZIP	CITY
92644	Anaheim
92641	Garden Grove
92688	Costa Mesa
92633	Fullerton
92634	Fullerton

61. Delete the City field from the HOMES database.

62. Create the new database file. Use the name ZIPCODE for this file. The Zip field should be indexed.

63. Add the indicated zip codes and cities to this database file.

64. Create a relational query called ZIPVIEW. This relational query should contain both the ZIPCODE and HOMES database files. The Zip field in both files should be used to relate the two. Include all fields from the HOMES database and the City field from the ZIPCODE database in this relational query.

65. Using this relational query, display the date, address, city, zip, and price for all homes in Fullerton.

66. Using this relational query, display the date, address, city, zip, and price for all homes in Fullerton. Sort the data by address.

67. What do you think about the change that was made? Is it a good idea? What are the advantages? What are the disadvantages?

Index

< > symbols, 7
<< >> symbols, 7

A
Append window, *illus.*, 17
Average operator, 53, 56, 57

B
Backup copy, *def.*, 27. *See also* Database file, backing up.
Band(s)
  adding to deleting lines in, 122, 130
  closed, *def.*, 140
  detail, 121, 124
  group footer and header, 139, 141, 143
  open, *def.*, 140
  page footer and header, 121
  summary, 121, 127
Between operator, *def.*, 40
Boxes
  adding to screen, 84, 90, 95
  moving, 91
Browse window, *illus.*, 32, 34, *illus.*, 69
  adding records with, 70, 71
  updating records with, 69, 71
  using, 69-72

C
Case sensitivity, 40
CHARACTER field, *def.*, 12
Close box, 5
Command window, *illus.*, 5
  moving to, 6, 10
  returning to, 34, 37, 38
Comparison operators. *See* Operators, comparison.
Condition(s)
  case sensitivity in examples, 40
  combining with AND, 41, 50
  combining with OR, 41, 52
  complex, 41
  def., 39
  entering an example in, 40
  entering in RQBE window, 39, 50
  simple, 41
  using operators in, 39-40, 50
  using to change records, 73-77
  using, 39-52
Count operator, 53, 57

D
Database, *def.*, 1
  backing up, 27-29
  calculating statistics in, 53-57
  conditions in, 39-52
  loading, 17-26
  locating records in, 65-68
  querying, 31-38, 41
Database file(s), *def.*, 3
  adding records to, 17-19, 21, 22, 24
  backing up, 27-29
  changing records in, 19, 24
  closing, 27
  creating, 11-16
  defining, 12-13
  deleting records from, 19, 23, 24
  keys used when designing, 15-16
  keys used when entering data in, 18
  listing records in, 20, 23, 25
  loading, 17-26
  locating records in, 65-68
  marking records in, 19, 23, 24
  matching fields in, 155
  one-to-many relationship in, 156
  opening, 17, 20, 24
  packing, 19
  querying, 31-38, 41
  relating, *illus.*, 156
  removing, 98, 104
  restoring, 27, 28, 29
  sorting, 97-104
  unmarking records in, 19, 24
  using multiple, 155-158
  using sorted, 98, 103
Database management system (DBMS), *def.*, 2
Database structure, defining, 12-13
Databases, introduction to, 1-4
DATE field, *def.*, 12, 19
Detail lines, *def.*, 119, *illus.*, 120
Dialog box, *def.*, 17
Diamonds, 19
Do Query button, 32, 37

E
Entities, *def.*, 1
Escaping from an operation, 7, 10
Exactly Like operator, *def.*, 39
Exiting FoxPro, 7, 10
Expression dialog box, *illus.*, 56

F
Field(s), *def.*, 3
  adding new, 145, 147, 152
  changing characteristics of, 145, 147, 150, 152
  CHARACTER, *def.*, 12
  DATE, *def.*, 12, 19
  decimal places in, 12
  index for, 12, 13, 157
  LOGICAL, *def.*, 12, 19
  matching, 155
  MEMO, *def.*, 12
  moving, 84, 89, 94
  name, *def.*, 12
  NUMERIC, *def.*, 12
  removing (deleting), 34, 145, 147, 151, 152
  selecting, 34
  type, *def.*, 12, 13
  width, *def.*, 12
File. *See* Database file.
Filename extensions, 3
Footer
  group, *def.*, 120, *illus.*, 120
  page, *illus.*, 120
FoxPro 2.5, *def.*, 2
  Command window, *illus.*, 5
  exiting, 7, 10
  Help facility, *illus.*, 7, 10
  loading, 5, 9
  Logon screen for, 5
  menu bar, *illus.*, 5
  menu options, 5, 6
  menu pad, *illus.*, 6
  menu popup, *illus.*, 6
  menu system, 5, *illus.*, 6, 10
  using, 5-10

G
Grouping, 139, 143

H
Header
  group, *def.*, 120, *illus.*, 120
  page, *def.*, 119, *illus.*, 120, 128
Help facility, *illus.*, 7, 10

I
In operator, *def.*, 40
Index key, *def.*, 105
Index(es), 12
  as alternative to sorting, 106
  choosing, 13
  creating and using, 105-113
  creating on a single field, 106, 107, 112
  creating on more than one field, 106, 108, 112
  removing unwanted, 106, 111, 113
  using to find a record, 106, 110, 113
  using to order records, 106, 109, 112

K
Keys used when designing database, 15-16
Keys used when entering data, 18

L
Less Than operator, *def.*, 39
Like operator, *def.*, 39
Live copy, *def.*, 27
LOGICAL field, *def.*, 12, 19
Logon screen, 5

M
Major key, *def.*, 98
MEMO field, *def.*, 12
Menu
  bar, *illus.*, 5
  options, 5, 6, 10
  pad, 6
  popup, *illus.*,
  system, 5, *illus.*, 6, 10
Minor key, *def.*, 98
More Than operator, *def.*, 39
Mouse
  pointer, 6
  using, 6, 32, 125

N
NUMERIC field, *def.*, 12
Numlock mode, 3

O
Object-oriented screen design, 84
Objects
  highlighting, 87
  rubberbanding, 86
Operators
  comparison, 39-40. *See also* Between, Exactly Like, In, Like, More Than operators.
  summary, 53, 57. *See also* Count, Sum and Average operators.
Options, selecting, 6, 10

P
Page header, *def.*, 119
Printing. *See* Reports, printing.
Prompts, *def.*, 84
  changing, 84, 88, 94
  repositioning, 84, 94
Push buttons, 7

Q
Query. *See also* Relational query.
  applying, 32-33, 37
  creating, 31-32, 27
  displaying all fields in, 33, 38
  displaying only certain fields in, 33, 38
  feature, 31-38
  file, 163
  printing results of, 33, 37
  relational, *def.*, 155, 157, 158, 161-164

Quick Report feature, 33, 35, 37, 121
Quick Screen option, 84

R
Radio buttons, *def.*, 99
Record, *def.*, 3
  Locate dialog box, *illus.*, 67
  Locate option, 65
  Replace command, 73, 77
Records
  adding to database file, 17, 21, 22, 24
  adding with Browse window, 70, 71
  changing in database file, 19, 22, 24
  deleting from database file, 19, 22, 24, 79-82
  finding next, 66, 68
  listing, 20, 23, 25
  locating, 65-68
  marking, 19, 23, 24
  search expression for, *illus.*, 66
  unmarking, 19, 23, 24
  updating with Browse window, 69, 71
  using conditions to change, 73-77
  using conditions to mark for deletion, 80, 81
  using conditions to unmark, 80, 82
Relational query, *def.*, 155, 161
  creating, 161-164
  preparing to create, 157, 158
  relating database files in, 161, 162, 164
  saving and naming, 161, 164
  selecting fields in, 161, 163, 164
  sorting data in, 165, 169, 170, 172
  using, 165-172
Relational Query By Example (RQBE), 31, 161
Replace dialog box *illus.*, 74, 75
Replace message, *illus.*, 76
Report(s)
  adding fields to, 123, 131
  altering, 122, 129
  bands of, 121
  creating layout for, 119-132
  detail lines in, *def.*, 119, *illus.*, 120
  Field dialog box in, 122
  finishing layout of, 123, 132
  grouping records in, 139, 141, 143
  initial layout of, 121, 129
  Layout window, *illus.*, 121
  modifying layout of, 123, 132, 140
  moving fields in, 123, 130
  page footer for, *illus.*, 120
  page header for, *def.*, 119, *illus.*, 120
  printing with subtotals, 140, 144
  printing, 133-136, 142
  removing fields from, 122, 130
  resizing fields in, 123, 130
  selecting fields and text objects in, 122, 130

  selecting records for, 133, 136
  subtotals in, 139-144
  summary, *def.*, 119, *illus.*, 120, 121, 127
  title, 121
Row and column coordinates, 91
RQBE Join Relation dialog box, 161
RQBE Window, *illus.*, 31, 34, 37, 41, 161, 163
  button in, 32
  checkbox in, 32
  condition area in, 31
  File list in, 31
  Order by checkbox in, 31, 32
  Output fields list in, 31
Rubberbanding objects, 86

S
Screen
  adding blank lines to, 84, 86, 94
  adding boxes to, 84, 95
  changing the prompts in, 84, 94
  creating and using custom, 83-96
  creating initial, 84, 93
  generating screen code for, 84, 92, 95
  modifying, 86, 96
  object-oriented design of, 84
  repositioning fields and prompts in, 84, 94
  saving, 84, 92, 95
  using, 84, 96
Screen code file, 84, 92
Slide bar, *illus.*, 5, *def.*, 17
Sort keys
  major, *def.*, 98
  minor, *def.*, 98
Sorting, *def.*, 97. *See also* Database file, sorting.
  on a single field, 97, 99, 100-101, 103
  on more than one field, 98, 103
Statistics. *See also* Average, Count, and Sum operators.
  calculating, 53-57
Structure
  dialog box, *illus.*, 11, 148
  modifying, 145-153
Subtotals, including in report, 139-144
Sum dialog box, *illus.*, 55
Sum Logon screen, *illus.*, 54
Sum operator, 53, 54, 55, 57
Summary operators, *def.*, 53. *See also* Operators, summary.

V
View window, *illus.*, 33

W
Window, *def.*, 5
Work area, *def.*, 33
  returning to previous, 37, 38
Work area list, *illus.*, 33